HISTORICAL ATLAS OF OKLAHOMA

HISTORICAL ATLAS OF OKLAHOMA

Second Edition, Revised and Enlarged

by John W. Morris, Charles R. Goins,
and Edwin C. McReynolds

University of Oklahoma Press  Norman

ALSO BY JOHN W. MORRIS

Oklahoma Geography (Oklahoma City, 1952, 1962)

An Analysis of the Tourist Industry in Selected Counties of the Ozark Area (Washington, D.C., 1953)

Boreal Fringe Areas of Marsh and Swampland: A General Background Study (Washington, D.C., 1954)

World Geography (with Otis Freeman) (New York, 1958, 1965, 1972)

Historical Atlas of Oklahoma, first edition (with Edwin C. McReynolds) (Norman, 1965)

Methods of Geographic Instruction (editor and co-author) (Boston, 1968)

The Southwestern United States (New York, 1970)

ALSO BY EDWIN C. McREYNOLDS

Oklahoma: A History of the Sooner State (Norman, 1954, 1964)

The Seminoles (Norman, 1957)

Missouri: A History of the Crossroads State (Norman, 1962)

Oklahoma: A History of the State and Its People (with Alice Marriott and Estelle Faulconer) (Norman, 1961)

Historical Atlas of Oklahoma, first edition (with John W. Morris (Norman, 1965).

Library of Congress Cataloging in Publication Data

Morris, John Wesley.
    Historical atlas of Oklahoma.

    Includes bibliography and index.
    1. Oklahoma—Historical geography—Maps. 2. Oklahoma—
History. I. Goins, Charles Robert, joint author. II. McReynolds,
Edwin C., joint author. III. Title.
G1366.S1M6   1976   911'.766   75–33129
ISBN 0–8061–1322–7

                                                    Rev.

PREFACE

White men began to impose their culture upon that of the red men in what is now Oklahoma in 1541. Since that time there has been a constant procession of exploration and discovery, the development of frontier posts and forts, the removal of peoples and the formation of nations, the settlement of communities, the organization of territories, and finally the formation of the state with its increasing importance within the nation. To understand these events in the history of Oklahoma, one must know where they happened, for much of the history of the state is concerned with places.

It is the purpose of this historical atlas to present specific aspects of the history of Oklahoma in a series of maps. The first maps (1 to 9) show the location of Oklahoma within the nation, give information about the size of the state, and present some of the outstanding physical characteristics of the area. These are followed by a series of maps showing the chronological development of the history of Oklahoma. Many maps show events for the state as a whole, but others show details for a specific area or happening. The final series of maps (67 to 83) presents information dealing with present-day Oklahoma. Not all the places known to exist at a specific time can be shown on a specific map. We attempted to select those places having the greatest historical importance at the time that the map represents. On the page adjacent to each map is a brief account of the history or geography necessary to explain its importance. Although new material has been added to the text accompanying many maps, little, if any, change has been made in the historical material written for the first edition by the late Edwin C. McReynolds.

A word should be said here about spellings of names of Indian tribes, which frequently vary and so present problems to authors, who must make a choice. Thus, for example, while Pottawatomie, Potawatomi, Potowatomi, and other variants of this name are found, the first has been chosen for this book because it agrees with the spelling of the Oklahoma county of that name.

The maps in the atlas are numbered consecutively. All numbers in the index are map numbers: there are no page numbers in the maps section of the book. References for the maps and accompanying text are listed at the end of the book.

Many organizations and individuals have contributed to the revised edition of the *Historical Atlas of Oklahoma*. Special thanks are due the following: James D. Morrison, Professor of History, Southeastern Oklahoma State University, and Louise Welsh, Assistant Professor of History, University of Oklahoma, for suggestions about maps that have been added; Charles J. Mankin, Director, Oklahoma Geological Survey, for permission to use maps and textual materials from the publication *Geology and Earth Resources of Oklahoma*; Mrs. Alice Timmons, Librarian, Western History Collection, and Jack D. Haley, Assistant Curator, Western History Collection, University of Oklahoma, for assistance in locating historical and statistical materials; and librarians of the Oklahoma Historical Society for their help in checking maps and manuscript material.

It is our sincere hope that this work will be a useful aid to a correct interpretation and a better understanding of the history of Oklahoma. It has been our desire to prepare an atlas that not only will aid the professional scholar but will help secondary-school and college students gain a better understanding of the historical-geographical relationships by which the state of Oklahoma has developed.

John W. Morris
Charles R. Goins

CONTENTS

HISTORICAL ATLAS OF OKLAHOMA

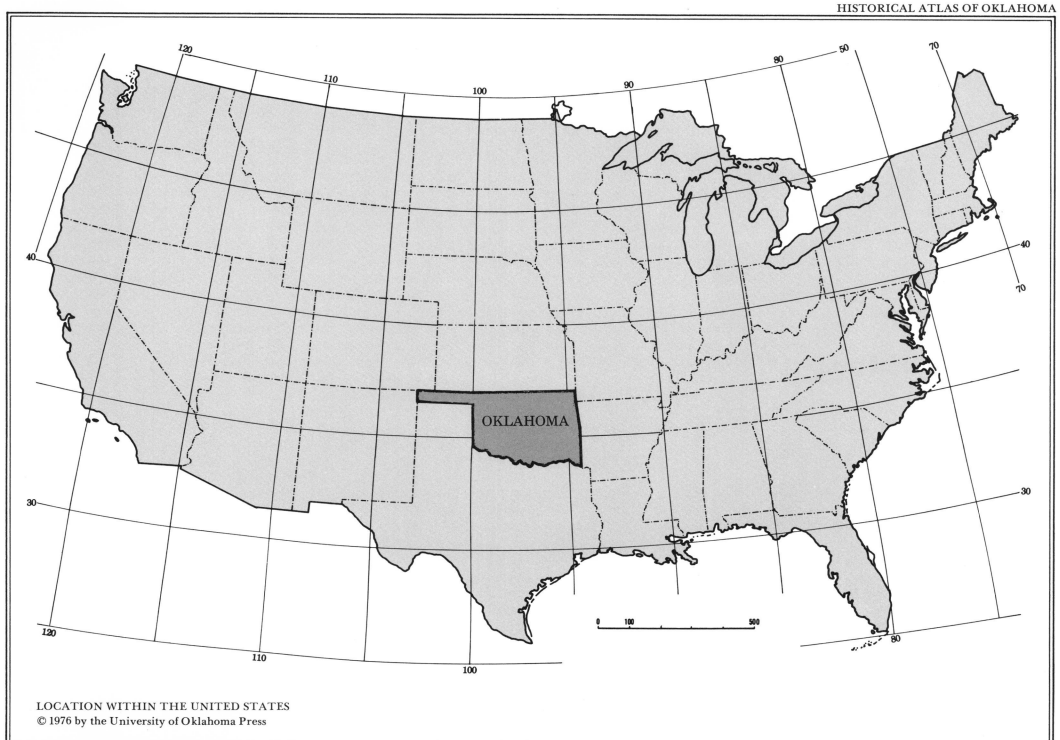

OKLAHOMA

1. LOCATION WITHIN THE UNITED STATES

Oklahoma, in the south-central part of the United States, is situated between 94°29' and 103° west longitude and 33°41' and 37° north latitude. The state has common boundaries with Colorado and Kansas on the north, Missouri and Arkansas on the east, Texas on the south, and Texas and New Mexico on the west. Some nations having about the same latitude as Oklahoma are Morocco and Algeria in North Africa, and Israel, Iran, central China, and southern Japan in Asia. The single European area having a comparable latitude is southern Spain. Only central Canada and Mexico have similar longitudes. All of South America is east of Oklahoma.

Oklahoma is the eighteenth-largest state in area in the United States, having a total area of 69,919 square miles. It is larger than any state east of it with the exception of Minnesota and, excepting the states of Washington and Hawaii, is smaller than any state north, south, or west of it. The state is approximately one-eighth the size of Alaska, but is fifty-seven times the size of Rhode Island. In fact, Oklahoma has a greater area than all six New England states combined.

Oklahoma is larger than many of the important nations of the world. None of the Central American countries has as great an area; Uruguay, in South America, is about the same size. Oklahoma is much larger than Belgium, the Netherlands, Greece, or Ireland. England is about 19,000 square miles smaller in area than Oklahoma. France, the largest European nation except the Soviet Union, is only about three times the size of Oklahoma.

The latitudinal location of Oklahoma, as well as its great size, has had a marked influence on the cultural activities of its inhabitants. Oklahoma is in the transition zone between the humid eastern and the drier western parts of the nation, between the forests of the East and the grasslands of the West, between the low elevations of the Coastal Plain and the higher elevations of the Rocky Mountain foothills, and between the long growing season of the South and the shorter growing season of the North.

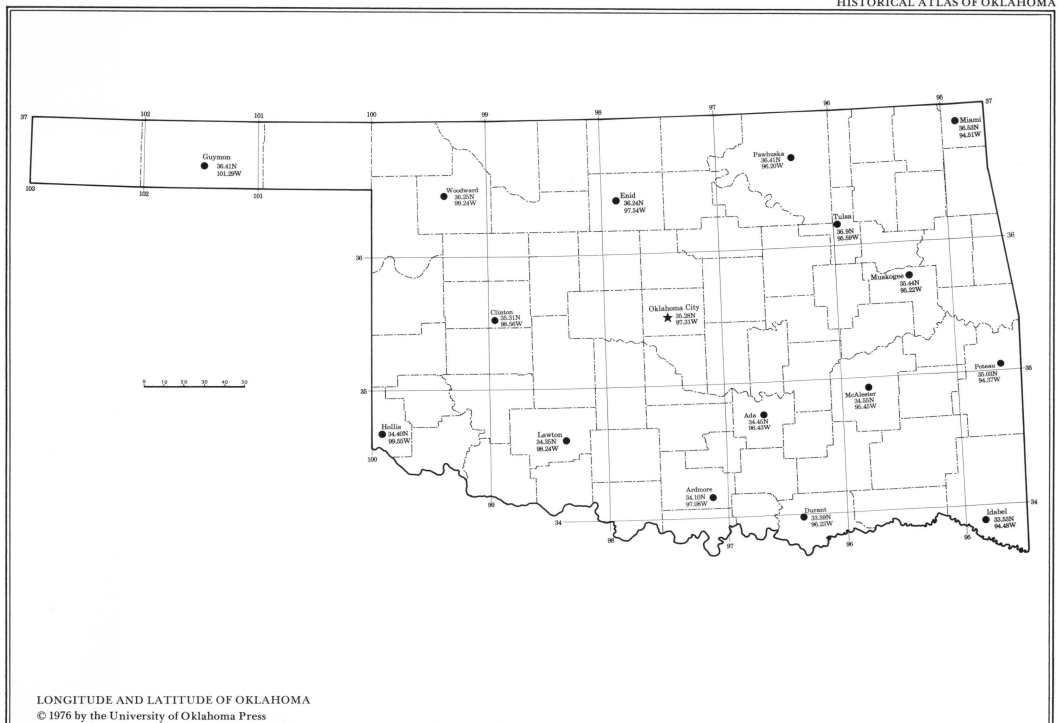

37

102   101   100   99   98   97   96   95   37

● Miami
36.53N
94.51W

Guymon
● 36.41N
101.29W

Pawhuska
36.41N ●
96.20W

103   102   101

Woodward
● 36.25N
99.24W

Enid
● 36.24N
97.54W

Tulsa
● 36.9N
95.59W

36   36

Muskogee
● 35.44N
95.22W

Clinton
● 35.31N
98.56W

Oklahoma City
★ 35.28N
97.31W

Poteau ●
35.03W
94.37W

35   35

0   10   20   30   40   50

McAlester
● 34.55N
95.45W

Ada
● 34.45N
96.43W

Hollis
● 34.40N
99.55W

Lawton
34.35N ●
98.24W

Ardmore
34.10N ●
97.08W

Idabel
33.53N
94.48W

34   34

Durant
● 33.59N
96.23W

100

99   98   97   96   95

LONGITUDE AND LATITUDE OF OKLAHOMA

© 1976 by the University of Oklahoma Press

2. LONGITUDE AND LATITUDE OF OKLAHOMA

The longest Oklahoma boundary extends eastward from 103° west longitude to 94°37′, or a distance of 463.7 miles. For the most part this northern boundary follows the 37° north latitude line, but there are some places in the Panhandle where the boundary varies as much as a quarter of a mile north or south of this parallel. The southern boundary of the Panhandle follows closely along the 36°30′ north latitude line and extends eastward from 103° to 100° west longitude, a distance of 167.1 miles. The distance from west to east across southern Oklahoma is 314.4 miles. Here the western boundary is the 100th meridian instead of the 103d. The eastern boundary with Arkansas, south of Fort Smith, is approximately 94°29′ west longitude.

The greatest north-south distance, 230.1 miles, is near the eastern boundary, where Oklahoma borders Missouri and Arkansas, or from 37° southward to 33°41′ north latitude. The distance along the 100th meridian from Red River to the 37th parallel is 166.8 miles, or approximately the same as the length of the Panhandle. The shortest distance across the state, 34.4 miles, is that across the Panhandle, for this strip of land is only one-half degree in width, 36°30′ to 37° north latitude.

In the political geography of the state longitude lines have been of greater importance than latitude lines. The 96th meridian, north from Tulsa, formed the boundary between the Cherokee Nation and the Cherokee Outlet, and the 98th meridian from Red River northward to the Canadian formed the western boundary of the Chickasaw Nation.

Oklahoma City, at 35°28′ north latitude, 97°31′ west longitude, is near the center of the state.

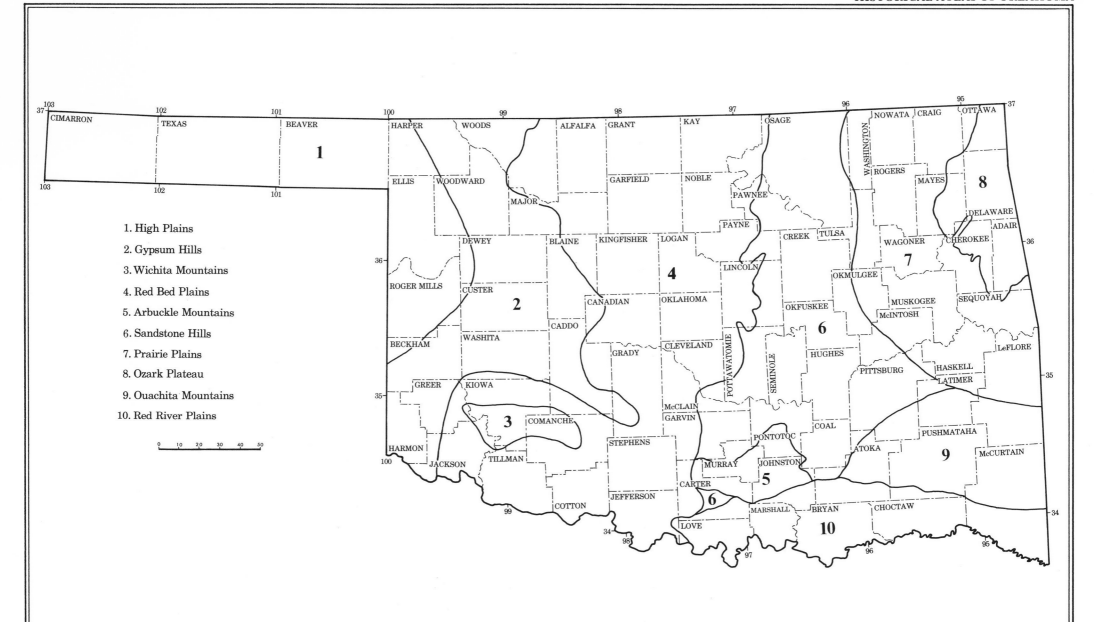

1. High Plains
2. Gypsum Hills
3. Wichita Mountains
4. Red Bed Plains
5. Arbuckle Mountains
6. Sandstone Hills
7. Prairie Plains
8. Ozark Plateau
9. Ouachita Mountains
10. Red River Plains

GEOGRAPHIC REGIONS OF OKLAHOMA
© 1976 by the University of Oklahoma Press

3. GEOGRAPHIC REGIONS OF OKLAHOMA

Three of the large physical regions of the United States extend into or across Oklahoma. These are the Interior Highlands, Coastal Plain, and Interior Plains. Oklahoma is divided into ten geographical regions, largely on a physical base. The Ozark Plateau, the Ouachita Mountains, and the intervening Arkansas River valley form a part of the Interior Highlands; the Coastal Plain extends from the Gulf of Mexico into southeastern Oklahoma; and the remainder of the geographic regions are divisions of the Interior Plains even though some parts carry the names of hills or mountains.

The Ouachita Mountains have a rougher topography than any other region in the state (Maps 4, 5). They are westward extensions of the mountains of southwestern Arkansas. There are several almost parallel ridges extending in a general east-west direction. In such a region, where the topography is rough and the soils are thin, the life of the people is strongly influenced by these physical surroundings. Farming is largely confined to the valleys, the hillsides being used for grazing and the growing of trees. The Ozark Plateau, on the other hand, has several large, fertile areas, commonly known as prairies (Map 36), on which good crops can be grown. Here, also, the more rugged land can be used for grazing and the growing of trees. All the Ouachita Mountains were in the Choctaw Nation, all of the Ozark Plateau in the Cherokee Nation.

The Coastal Plain, often called the Red River Plains in Oklahoma, extended across the southern part of the Choctaw Nation and westward from Island Bayou into the Chickasaw Nation. The region is low in elevation and the land generally level with only a few low hills. In general the soils are fertile, and it was in this area that several large plantations developed in the pre–Civil War era.

The Sandstone and Gypsum hills regions have broken lines of hills or cuestas extending in a somewhat general north-south direction. In the eastern area the hills result largely from the resistance of hard sandstones and shales to weathering and erosion. In the western region the hills are capped with layers of white gypsum fifteen to twenty feet thick. Between the hills in both regions are large areas of fertile land suitable for cropping or pasture.

The three plains areas are relatively level regions, although all have numerous topographic variations caused by wind and/or water erosion. The Prairie Plains have the greatest variety of crops, grown on smaller fields, due to climatic conditions more suitable for agricultural production (Maps 7, 8, 69). Westward, in the Red Bed Plains and on the High Plains, farm size increases and the density of population decreases; thus the High Plains region contrasts sharply with the Prairie Plains in land utilization and population density.

The Arbuckle and Wichita regions are classified as mountain areas largely because of their geologic history. The Arbuckles were formed by the faulting and folding of strata of limestone, shale, sandstone, and other materials. The layer of Arbuckle limestone is some 8,000 feet in thickness. Since being exposed the various strata have been worn down from great heights by weathering and erosion. Glass sand, granite, limestone, and asphaltic materials have been mined or quarried. The Wichita Mountains were formed when earth forces caused igneous materials to be pushed up, the land above being folded into high domes. The folded material was long ago eroded away leaving great masses of granite standing above the surrounding plains. Mt. Scott, the best-known mountain in the region, has an elevation of 2,464 feet, approximately 1,000 feet above its base.

3. GEOGRAPHIC REGIONS OF OKLAHOMA

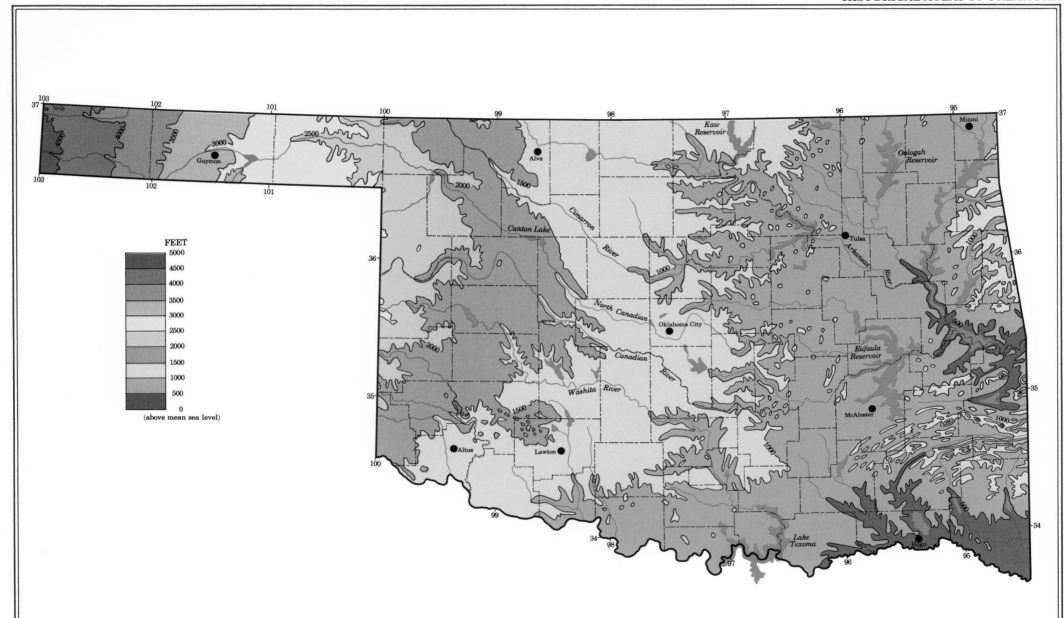

FEET
5000
4500
4000
3500
3000
2500
2000
1500
1000
500
0
(above mean sea level)

CONTOUR MAP OF OKLAHOMA
© 1976 by the University of Oklahoma Press

4. CONTOUR MAP OF OKLAHOMA

Elevations in Oklahoma extend from 287 feet, where Little River crosses the Oklahoma-Arkansas boundary in the southeastern part of the state, to 4,973 feet on Black Mesa, near the northwestern corner of the Panhandle. In general, elevations across Oklahoma increase from southeast to northwest. The chief variations to this generalization are caused by the Ouachita Mountains and the Ozark Plateau (Map 3). Local relief varies greatly in different sections of the state—from 1,500 feet in the Ouachita Mountains to as little as ten feet in extensive areas across the High Plains.

Most of the state has an elevation under 2,000 feet as that contour crosses the northwestern part of Oklahoma in Beckham, Roger Mills, Ellis, Dewey, Woodward, and Harper counties. A few small areas in southwestern Oklahoma, adjacent to the Texas border, and one area in Woods County also have elevations exceeding 2,000 feet. The only areas in eastern Oklahoma extending above this elevation are some of the higher ridges of the Ouachita Mountains, a few of which exceed 2,500 feet.

Southward from the Ouachitas elevations decrease, although the elevation of Red River is slightly higher than that of Little River. North of the Ouachitas elevations decrease to approximately 400 feet in the valley of the Arkansas River and then increase to over 1,000 feet on the Ozark Plateau. A few hills in the Sandstone Hills region exceed 1,000 feet but, in general, the 1,000 foot contour crosses the state between 96° and 97° west longitude. Long arms of this contour extend upstream along the Arkansas, Cimarron, North Canadian, Canadian, Washita, and Red rivers as well as the tributaries of these principal streams. The eastern boundary of the Gypsum Hills region is somewhat related to the 1,500 foot contour due to the southeastward extension of the gypsum capped ridges.

Elevations in the Panhandle increase more rapidly than in the rest of Oklahoma, all of the area having elevations of 2,000 feet or higher. On the average elevation increases at the rate of about 15 feet per mile from the 100th to the 103d meridians. The 2,500 foot contour crosses Beaver County and the 3,000 and 3,500 foot contours cross Texas County. Much of Cimarron County has an elevation exceeding 4,000 feet.

Elevation at the southwestern corner of Oklahoma is 1,558 feet and at the southeastern corner 305 feet; thus Red River has a fall of 1,253 feet as it flows along the southern border of the state. Eastward from the northwestern corner, where New Mexico, Colorado, and Oklahoma meet, elevation decreases from 4,438 to 1,015 feet, or 3,423 feet, at the northeastern corner, where Kansas, Missouri, and Oklahoma adjoin. The highest point in the Ouachitas is 2,660 feet on Rich Mountain, Mount Scott in the Wichitas has an elevation of 2,464 feet, and the highest point in the Arbuckles is 1,419 feet.

Elevations of Selected Oklahoma Cities

City	Elevation, feet	City	Elevation, feet
Altus	1,389	Norman	1,160
Ardmore	896	Oklahoma City	1,243
Bartlesville	694	Okmulgee	752
Boise City	4,164	Ponca City	1,003
Enid	1,246	Poteau	483
Guymon	3,125	Shawnee	1,008
Idabel	504	Stillwater	985
Lawton	1,116	Tahlequah	864
Miami	800	Tulsa	744
Muskogee	617	Woodward	1,916

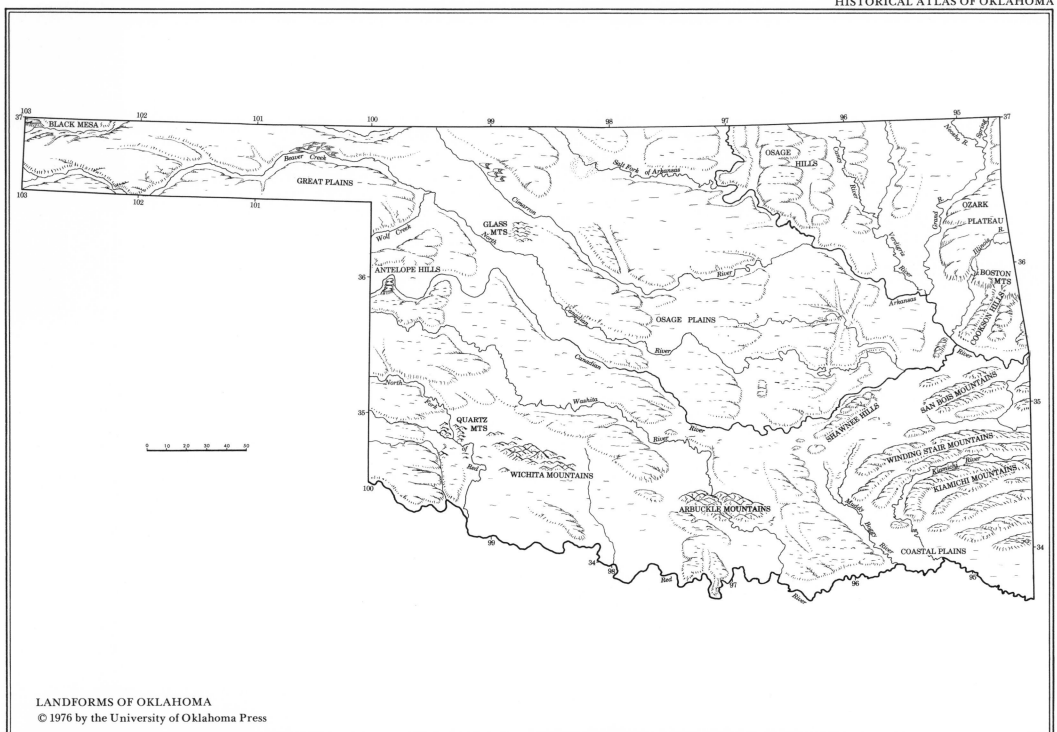

BLACK MESA

GREAT PLAINS

Beaver Creek

Cimarron

Wolf Creek

GLASS
MTS
North

ANTELOPE HILLS

Salt Fork of Arkansas

OSAGE
HILLS

Caney River

OZARK
PLATEAU

Verdigris River

Grand R.

Illinois R.

BOSTON
MTS

River

OSAGE PLAINS

Canadian

River

Canadian

Washita

North

Fork

QUARTZ
MTS

of

Red

Arkansas

COOKSON HILLS

River

River

SAN BOIS MOUNTAINS

SHAWNEE HILLS

WINDING STAIR MOUNTAINS

Kiamichi River

KIAMICHI MOUNTAINS

WICHITA MOUNTAINS

ARBUCKLE MOUNTAINS

Muddy

Boggy

River

COASTAL PLAINS

Red

River

0 10 20 30 40 50

LANDFORMS OF OKLAHOMA

© 1976 by the University of Oklahoma Press

5. LANDFORMS OF OKLAHOMA

Map 5 is a diagrammatic drawing showing the generalized variations in the local natural landscape of the geographic regions of Oklahoma as identified on Map 3. The principal rivers are also shown on the drawing, but none of the large man-made lakes are located.

The Ouachita Mountains are formed by a series of curving ridges known as the Kiamichi Mountains, Winding Stair Mountains, and other local names. The mountains form the most rugged topography in the state and the development of transportation systems within the area are therefore extremely difficult. The Kiamichi River, flowing westward in the valley north of Kiamichi Mountain, eventually flows south and southeast across the Coastal Plain into Red River. Other streams, such as Glover and Little rivers, also follow mountain valleys, but Mountain Fork River (Map 6) has cut a deep valley through some of the southern ridges. The San Bois Mountains, between the Fourche Maline and Arkansas rivers, form the northern part of the Ouachitas.

The Cookson Hills and the Boston Mountains form the rugged southern part of the Ozark Plateau, but the northern part of the Plateau has several large areas often referred to as prairies. The Illinois is the principal river flowing southwestward from the Ozarks. The western and southern boundary of the region is delimited by the Grand and Arkansas rivers.

West of the Ouachitas and Ozarks most of the remainder of Oklahoma is a vast plains area. Some local variations are: (1) the rounded hills in south-central Oklahoma known as the Arbuckle Mountains; (2) the large granite peaks of southwestern Oklahoma called the Wichita Mountains and their outlyer, the Quartz Mountains; (3) the Shawnee Hills, a sandstone cuesta area located near the Canadian River in the east-central part of the state; (4) the Antelope Hills in the most western of the large meanders of the Canadian River in Roger Mills County; (5) the gypsum-capped hills known as the Glass Mountains, located somewhat on the divide between the North Canadian and Cimarron rivers; and (6) Black Mesa, located in northwestern Cimarron County. The Osage Hills, located largely in Osage County, are a southern extension of the Flint Hills of Kansas. The elevations of the plains areas across the state increase gradually from the Coastal Plains south of the Ouachitas to the eastern edge of the Panhandle (Map 4). Once the Great Plains are reached, however, elevation increases rapidly westward across the High Plains to Black Mesa. In several places large sand dunes have formed on the left bank of the Cimarron and North Canadian rivers as well as along Beaver Creek. Much of this material is blow-sand from the rivers. Unless vegetation is able to tie the sand in place it continues to move generally eastward because of wind direction. Large salt plains are located on the Salt Fork of the Arkansas and the upper Cimarron River in Woods County.

The Arkansas, Canadian, and Red rivers, for the most part, are braided streams that meander across sand-filled beds. Several early travelers and writers noted that these rivers, as well as parts of the Cimarron, "are a mile wide but only six inches deep." Although little water may be seen flowing on the surface, much water flows through the sands below the surface. These sands are often forty to sixty feet deep. The North Canadian, formed by the confluence of Beaver and Wolf creeks, flows through a narrow drainage basin which is higher than the areas to the north or south of it. The Washita is the principal western tributary of Red River. A deep and narrow canyon has been formed where the Washita cuts through the Arbuckles. The Three Forks Area, where the Grand, Verdigris, and Arkansas rivers unite at the edge of the Ozarks, is one of the most historically important locations in Oklahoma (Map 37).

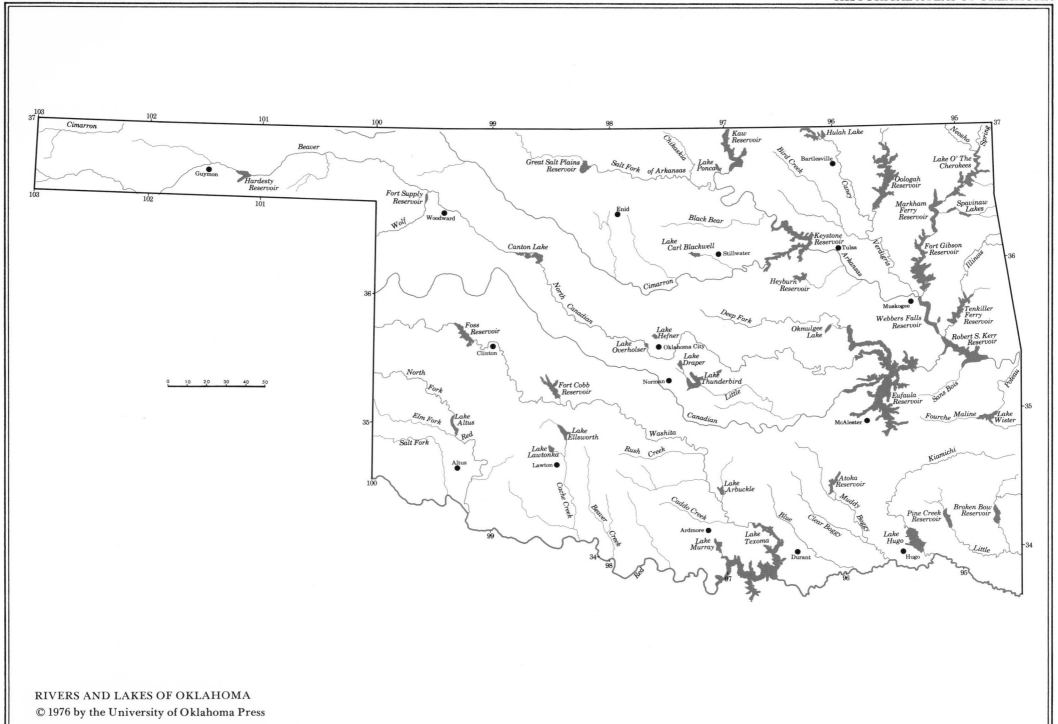

6. RIVERS AND LAKES OF OKLAHOMA

In Oklahoma there are approximately 500 named rivers and creeks, many of them short and intermittent during most of the year. There are several large streams like the Arkansas, Red, Washita, Cimarron, North Canadian, Canadian, Grand, and Verdigris, however, that carry millions of cubic feet of water through the state each year. All of northern Oklahoma and much of the central part of the state is in the drainage basin of the Arkansas River. The remainder of Oklahoma is in the drainage basin of Red River. Both are long streams, the source of the Arkansas being in the Rocky Mountains of Colorado and that of the Red on the High Plains of Texas. Parts of both rivers were used in defining the boundaries of the Adams-Onís Treaty of 1819, which set definite limits to Spanish and American territory.

Except for the rivers flowing from the Ozark Plateau or the Ouachita Mountains, the streams of Oklahoma flow in a general eastward direction. The chief tributaries of the Arkansas are the Cimarron and Canadian from the west, the Verdigris, Grand, and Illinois from the north and northeast, and the Poteau from the south. The North Canadian, one of the longest streams in the state, is the chief tributary of the Canadian. The principal tributaries of Red River are the North Fork, Washita, Blue, Boggy, and Kiamichi.

Rivers have been of primary importance in the development of Oklahoma. The Canadian, Arkansas, North Canadian, and many others formed parts of the boundaries of the Indian nations; some served as routes of travel for early trails, and others as sites for the location of pioneer settlements. A few appear in historical records under different names. The Cimarron has been known as the Red Fork of the Arkansas. Little River of Cleveland and Pottawatomie counties was called Cedar River by the Seminoles. The river now commonly called the North Canadian has been known as Río Nutrio and as the North Fork of the Canadian. The name North Canadian is often applied to Beaver Creek in the Panhandle, but the earliest maps show the North Fork of the Canadian to be formed by the confluence of Beaver and Wolf creeks. The river now commonly called the South Canadian in Oklahoma is referred to in New Mexico and Texas, as well as in most government publications, as the Canadian. Gaines Creek, in Pittsburg County—now a part of the Eufaula Reservoir—was known as the South Canadian by the early Indian settlers.

All of the large lakes in Oklahoma are man-made. They have been developed for such purposes as flood control, conservation, navigation, irrigation, recreation, power, and municipal water supply.

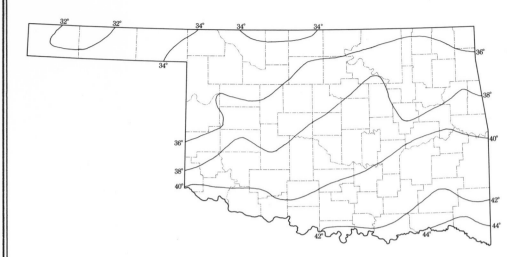

7a.   Average January Temperature

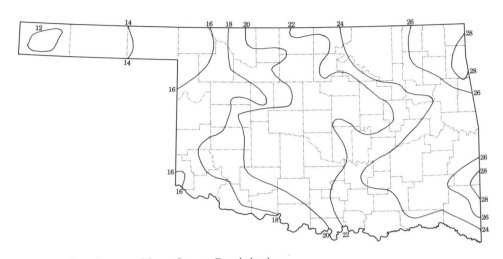

7c.   Average Warm Season Precipitation

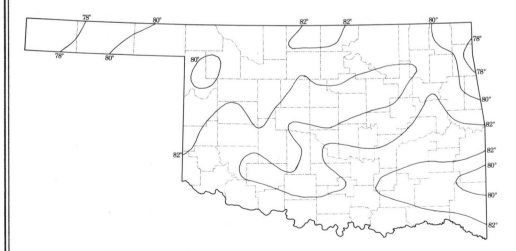

7b.   Average July Temperature

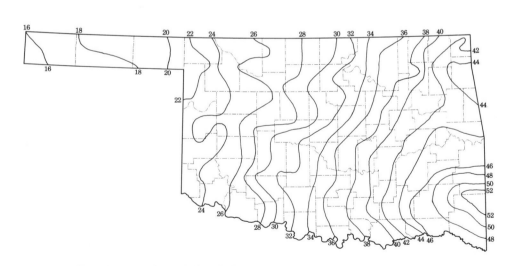

7d.   Average Annual Rainfall

TEMPERATURE AND RAINFALL MAPS OF OKLAHOMA
© 1976 by the University of Oklahoma Press

7. TEMPERATURE AND RAINFALL MAPS OF OKLAHOMA

a. Average January Temperature. During January temperatures decrease from south to north and from southeast to northwest across the state. The average January temperature in the southeastern corner of Oklahoma averages above 44° while that in the western part of the Panhandle is less than 32° F. (The average January temperature at Boise City is 33.5°, while that of Idabel is 44° F.) The 38° isotherm almost divides the state, zigzagging across central Oklahoma from Harmon County to Adair County. January has a colder average annual temperature than any other month. Temperature extremes in Oklahoma during any given month are not uncommon. On January 18, 1930, a temperature of −27° was recorded at Watts, but a temperature of 92° F. has also been recorded during January. During the third week of January, 1957, over twelve inches of snow caused drifts of six to nine feet in the Panhandle, but at the same time the Coastal Plain part of the state recorded temperatures of 70°.

b. Average July Temperature. Temperature variation across Oklahoma during July is not as great as that for January. In general, however, the average temperature is lower in the Panhandle than in the southeastern and southern parts of the state. Average temperatures in the Ozark Plateau and the Ouachita Mountains are lower than those in the adjacent plains. July and August are the two hottest months. During July a maximum daily temperature of 120° has been recorded in both Altus and Alva. The lowest temperature recorded during July is 41° F. The average high temperature during July for Oklahoma City, near the center of the state, is 80.6° F.

c. Average Warm-Season Precipitation. The warm season in Oklahoma includes the months of April through September. Rainfall during this period is critical to crop growing, forestry, availability of water for urban and industrial uses, and cooling effects on temperature. Over 75 percent of the rainfall in that part of the state west of the 96th meridian falls during the warm season. The Ozark Plateau also receives more than half of its total annual rainfall during this period. Only the Ouachita Mountains get less than half their rainfall during the warm season. Rainfall during this period, however, varies greatly from year to year. During some decades, especially that of 1930 and 1950, less than half the amount shown as average fell. It was necessary for all activities to adjust accordingly.

d. Average Annual Rainfall. During most years the total rainfall in Oklahoma will vary from over 50 inches in the Ouachita Mountains to less than 15 inches in the western part of the Panhandle. The maximum rainfall recorded by the Weather Bureau was 84.47 inches at Kiamichi Tower in the Ouachita Mountains in 1957. In 1949, when records were being kept by the Oklahoma Forestry Service, the same tower recorded 119 inches of rainfall. Minimum annual precipitation recorded in Cimarron County lists 8.6 inches reported at Boise City in 1934 and 6.63 inches at Regnier in 1956. This great difference in rainfall between the eastern and western parts of the state is due in part to location with respect to the source of moisture, the Gulf of Mexico, and in part to local topography, the Ouachita Mountains in the southeast and the High Plains in the northwest. Much of Oklahoma receives between 26 and 40 inches of rainfall annually, an amount sufficient for most agricultural production. It is not, however, evenly distributed throughout the year. For the state as a whole, spring is the wettest season, winter the driest. There are many variations for local areas, such as the Ouachita Mountains, where summer is the driest season.

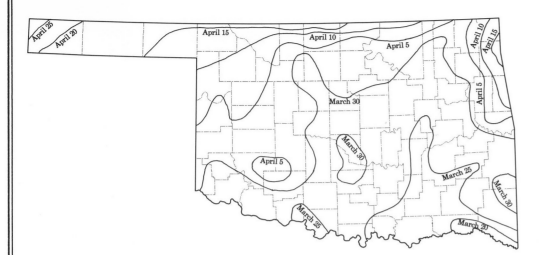

8a.   Last Killing Frost in Spring

8b.   First Killing Frost in Fall

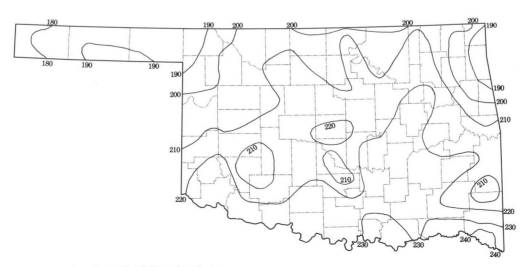

8c.   Length of Growing Season

FROST DATES AND GROWING-SEASON MAPS OF OKLAHOMA

© 1976 by the University of Oklahoma Press

8. FROST DATES AND GROWING-SEASON MAPS OF OKLAHOMA

a. Last Killing Frost in Spring. In the southern parts of Mc-Curtain and Choctaw counties there will probably be no killing frosts after March 20. The people of Cimarron County, however, may expect to have killing frosts for at least a month longer, or until April 20. The March 30 frost line, which winds back and forth across the state, somewhat divides Oklahoma, indicating that much of the area south of 36° north latitude has less than a 50 percent chance of having a killing frost after that date. The course followed by the various frost lines is closely related to elevations (Map 4) and local relief. The Ozark Plateau, Ouachita Mountains, and High Plains are good examples.

b. First Killing Frost in Fall. Frost comes earlier in the Panhandle than in any other part of Oklahoma. The southeastern part of the state, especially Marshall and Bryan counties, will be the last to have a killing frost. Again elevations, topography, and variations in local relief greatly influence frost formation. The October 30 frost line practically divides the state so that all of Oklahoma south of the October 30 lines, except for the Ouachita Mountains, can reasonably be expected not to have a killing frost until after that date. The first killing frost in the fall on the High Plains will usually occur 20 to 25 days earlier than on the Coastal Plain.

c. Length of Growing Season. The growing season is that period of time between the last killing frost in the spring and the first killing frost in the fall. South-central McCurtain County has an average growing season of more than 240 days, northwestern Cimarron County averages less than 180 days, or a difference of approximately two months. Most of Oklahoma has a growing season of 200 days or longer—a long enough period for the chief cereal crops of wheat and corn and the principal fiber crop of cotton to mature. Oklahoma City, near the center of the state, has a growing season in excess of 220 days.

Maps 7a, b, c, d and Maps 8a, b, c should be studied in conjunction with Map 4, which shows contours and elevations, and Map 5, showing landforms. There is also a close relationship between these maps and Maps 9 and 69.

The length of the frost-free period, the amount of rainfall, and temperatures greatly influenced the activities of the Indians, early explorers, and pioneer settlers. Technology has diminished the influence of these seasonal changes on the lives of present-day Oklahomans.

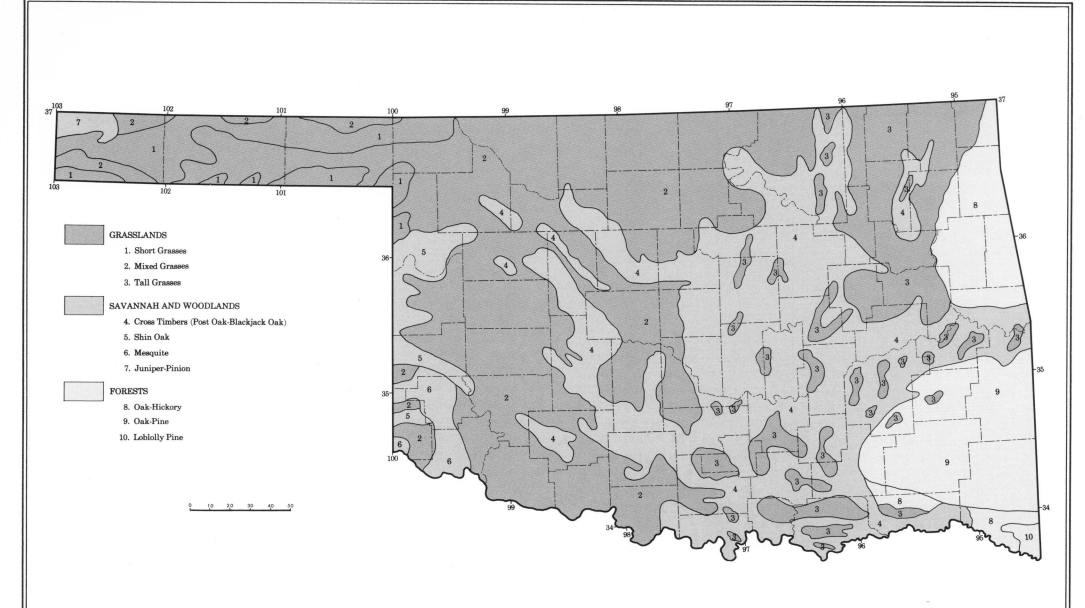

GRASSLANDS
1. Short Grasses
2. Mixed Grasses
3. Tall Grasses

SAVANNAH AND WOODLANDS
4. Cross Timbers (Post Oak-Blackjack Oak)
5. Shin Oak
6. Mesquite
7. Juniper-Pinion

FORESTS
8. Oak-Hickory
9. Oak-Pine
10. Loblolly Pine

0 10 20 30 40 50

GENERALIZED NATURAL-VEGETATION MAP OF OKLAHOMA
© 1976 by the University of Oklahoma Press

9. GENERALIZED NATURAL-VEGETATION MAP OF OKLAHOMA

The natural vegetation of Oklahoma can be divided into three large categories—grasslands, savannah and woodlands, and forests. These three divisions are closely related to the physical elements of climate, soils, topography, and elevation.

Grasses of various kinds are found in all parts of the state, but they are the dominant natural vegetation in the drier and more elevated western regions. Most of the short grasses and xerophytes are found in the Panhandle. They grow well in areas having ten to twenty inches of rainfall annually and can withstand the hot, dry summer winds. Most short grasses make good grazing land for cattle. Near the streams in the Panhandle and in the western part of Oklahoma, where the annual precipitation increases to 25 to 30 inches a year, short grasses give way to an area of mixed grasses. Here the grasses are more luxuriant and of greater variety than farther west. Many thousands of acres once covered by mixed grasses have been plowed and planted to wheat, cotton, and other crops. Tall grasses dominate the natural vegetation of the Prairie Plains and also occupy numerous valleys and cleared areas in the Sandstone Hills, Arbuckle Mountains, and Red River Plains. In several areas the tall grasses compete with the cross timbers for land occupancy.

The savannah and woodland types of vegetation are found in all parts of the state with the exceptions of the Ouachita Mountains and the Ozark Plateau. The cross timbers form the largest natural vegetation area in Oklahoma. Post oak and blackjack oak are the dominant vegetation covering large parts of central Oklahoma. These trees grow so close together that the first travelers and settlers in the region had much difficulty in getting through them; Washington Irving in *A Tour of the Prairies* discusses the problem at length. Getting cattle through the cross timbers also created many complications for the cattle drives along the Chisholm, Texas, and Shawnee trails. Shin oak and mesquite are found largely on the rougher, drier lands near the 100th meridian. They cover much of the territory around the Antelope Hills and the eroded land of northern Harmon and Greer counties. Although such areas are used for grazing, they leave much to be desired for it takes many acres to feed one cow. The juniper-pinion type of vegetation is found only in the more elevated northwestern corner of the Panhandle. This area is an eastward extension from the Rocky Mountains of Colorado and New Mexico.

Large forest areas are located in eastern Oklahoma where rainfall is sufficient for good tree growth and the local topography is too rough for agricultural use other than grazing. Oak and hickory are the dominant natural vegetation of the Ozark Plateau. Much land in this region has been cut over and the more level areas have been cleared for farming. During recent years, however, second growth has reclaimed a considerable amount of land formerly used for crops. The Ouachita Mountains are the most densely forested section of Oklahoma. Most of the region is too rough and rugged for uses other than tree farming and grazing. Pines dominate the higher elevations with oaks at lower elevations although there is some mixing at all levels. Cyprus grows in the swampy areas adjacent to Little River at the south edge of the mountains. Lumbering is the dominant commercial activity in the Ouachitas. Much of the land is leased by a large lumber and pulp company or is included in the Ouachita National Forest. Two oak-hickory areas are to be found on the more level land just south of the Ouachitas. Loblolly pine grows extensively in the southeastern part of McCurtain County.

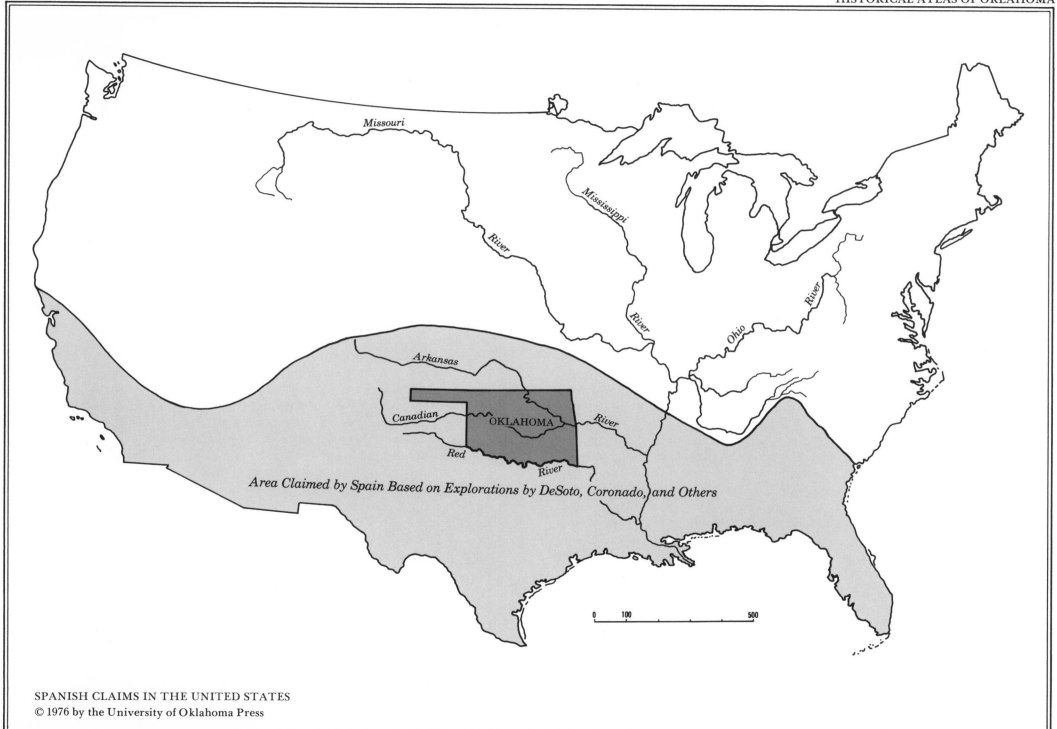

Missouri

Mississippi

River

River

Ohio

River

Arkansas

Canadian

OKLAHOMA

River

Red

River

Area Claimed by Spain Based on Explorations by DeSoto, Coronado, and Others

0   100   500

SPANISH CLAIMS IN THE UNITED STATES

10. SPANISH CLAIMS IN THE UNITED STATES

For more than two hundred years after the voyages of Christopher Columbus to America, Spain was engaged in the conquest of new lands and the consolidation of her claims. With the rise of English sea power and the growth of privateering during the second half of the sixteenth century, Spain's profits in the New World were threatened. French colonial enterprise early in the seventeenth century established another rival for Spain, particularly in the Mississippi Valley and on the northern coast of the Gulf of Mexico.

Great military expeditions under Francisco Vásquez de Coronado, Hernando De Soto, Juan de Oñate, and other Spanish conquerors led to claims upon vast areas north of Mexico and the Gulf of Mexico. In a large portion of the North American continent the claims of Spain, France, and England overlapped. Spain at various times asserted a strong claim to the western coast all the way north to Alaska, to the Mississippi Basin, and to the entire Gulf Coast. She held Florida against all rivals until 1819—with the exception of twenty years—and in the treaties of 1763 was recognized by France and England as the owner of Louisiana, west of the Mississippi.

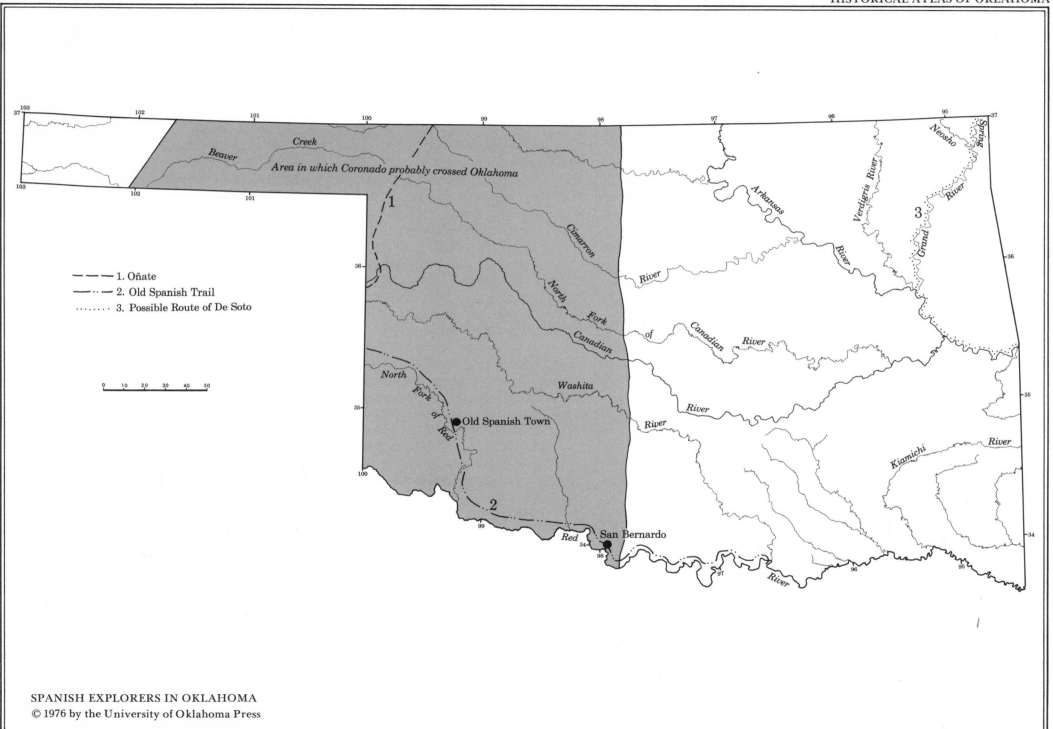

Beaver Creek

Area in which Coronado probably crossed Oklahoma

1

— — — 1. Oñate
— · — · 2. Old Spanish Trail
· · · · · · 3. Possible Route of De Soto

Cimarron

North Fork

Canadian

Arkansas

River

Verdigris River

Neosho

Spring

3

Grand River

River

0 10 20 30 40 50

North Fork of Red

Washita

Old Spanish Town

River

River

of

Canadian

River

River

2

Red

San Bernardo

River

Kiamichi

River

River

SPANISH EXPLORERS IN OKLAHOMA
© 1976 by the University of Oklahoma Press

11. SPANISH EXPLORERS IN OKLAHOMA

On February 23, 1540, Francisco Vásquez de Coronado began an expedition that resulted in the earliest European acquaintance with Oklahoma. He marched his army northward from the Mexican town, Compostela, to search for gold. His force consisted of about thirteen hundred men; but at Culiacán he selected eighty horsemen and twenty-five foot soldiers for the march across the rough, arid district to the north. With Friar Marcos as guide, the party reached Cíbola in seventy-three days. The Spaniards captured the first of the fabled "Seven Golden Cities of Cíbola" on July 7, 1540. Cíbola was six hundred miles west of the site where Oklahoma City now stands, and nearly four hundred miles southwest of Black Mesa.

The Spanish invaders found no gold, silver, or precious stones at Cíbola. On the basis of rumors current among the Indians, Coronado pushed on to a point in the Brazos Valley, possibly near the 98th meridian. With a new Indian guide and thirty men he then turned northward. This party crossed Oklahoma and reached Quivira, on the Arkansas River, after a march of forty-two days. (Historians do not agree about the location of the trail blazed by Coronado. Some believe that he crossed only the Panhandle area of present-day Oklahoma, probably in Beaver County, both going to and returning from Quivira.)

The Quivira Indians were ancestors of the Caddoans of the present time. The conical grass houses and cultivated gardens of the Quiviras were similar to those of the Wichitas and Pawnees in 1790 and 1890. Many examples of Caddoan culture are to be seen now at Indian City, near Anadarko, Oklahoma.

Possibly Hernando De Soto or some of his men traveled across northeastern Oklahoma during his three-year expedition in North America (1539–42). The exact route of De Soto, like that of Coronado, is a subject of wide disagreement.

Juan de Oñate led a colony to the upper Río Grande in 1598 and from his headquarters in New Mexico explored widely. In 1601 he crossed the Canadian in Oklahoma and marched his party northeast to Quivira, on the Arkansas River—a place identified by H. E. Bolton as the site of Wichita, Kansas.

The "Great Spanish Road to Red River" extended from Santa Fe to the mouth of the Washita. The road crossed the Texas Panhandle, entered Oklahoma on the 100th meridian near the North Fork of Red River, crossed that branch twice, and followed the main stream along the left bank to the Washita. Beyond that point the route extended along the right bank of the Red. After Americans settled the area, Edwards' Post at the mouth of Little River on the Canadian received buffalo robes, lariats, rawhide, and blankets from traders on the Spanish Road at the site of San Bernardo. Sometimes Apache captives from Texas were taken to the post on Little River for ransom.

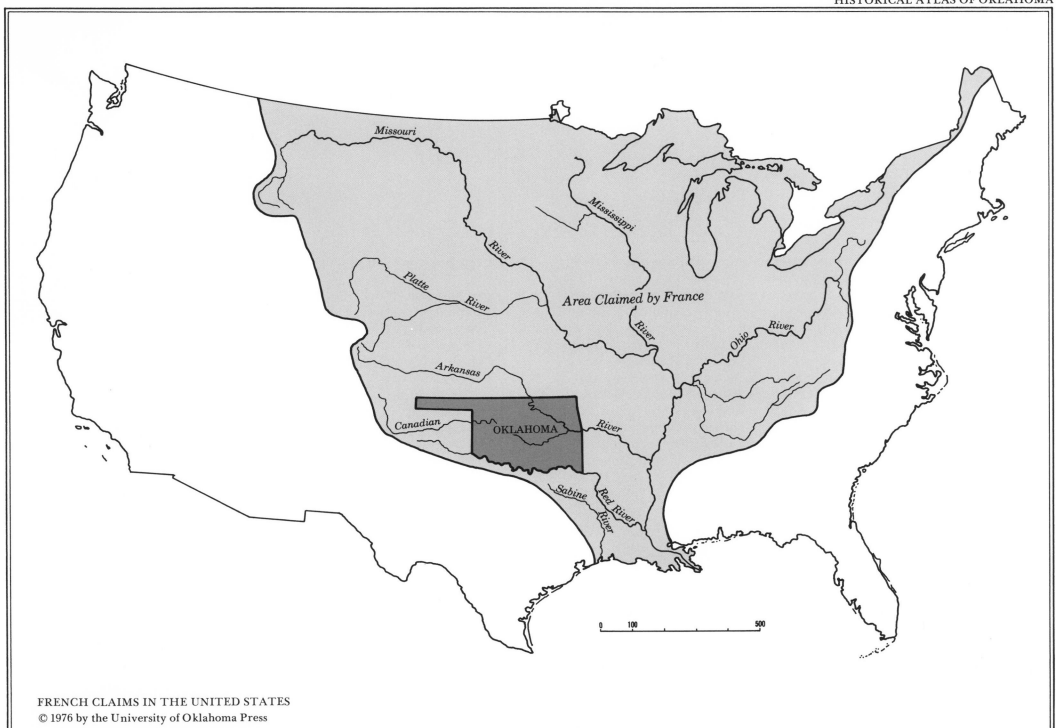

Missouri

Mississippi

Platte

River

Area Claimed by France

River

Ohio River

Arkansas

Canadian

OKLAHOMA

River

Sabine

Red River

River

0   100   500

FRENCH CLAIMS IN THE UNITED STATES
© 1976 by the University of Oklahoma Press

12. FRENCH CLAIMS IN THE UNITED STATES

France, like England, started late in the exploration of the new lands of the Western Hemisphere. The first permanent French settlement in North America (Quebec, 1608) was contemporary with English beginnings in Virginia (1607–19). A remarkable group of explorers sent out by Henry IV, Louis XIII, and Louis XIV elevated colonial France to a position of rivalry with the British. In the great armed conflicts over possession of America north of the Gulf of Mexico and the Río Grande, the basic struggle was between France and England. Between 1689 and 1763, colonial wars recessed only for recovery of strength and regrouping of allies.

England's claims, based chiefly upon exploration of the Atlantic coast and rising national confidence in sea power, were set down in charters to commercial companies. Vast stretches of unexplored territory all the way from the Atlantic to the Pacific were covered by these charters.

French claims were based upon the great explorations and settlements of such pioneers as Samuel de Champlain and Sieur de Monts, founders of Quebec, and their successors. Jean Nicolet explored in the St. Lawrence and Great Lakes basin. Father Jacques Marquette, intent upon his work as a missionary to the Indians, and Louis Joliet, primarily interested in expansion of French trade, reached the Mississippi River on June 17, 1673. Robert Cavelier, Sieur de la Salle, explored the Mississippi from the Illinois to the Gulf of Mexico in 1682 and became the chief advocate of a vast inland empire for France in North America.

Between the activities of La Salle, who claimed for France all of the territory drained by the Mississippi, and the final colonial struggles of the Seven Years' War, the region that is now Oklahoma was claimed by Spain, France, and England. In the treaties of 1762–63, it was awarded to Spain as a part of Louisiana Territory.

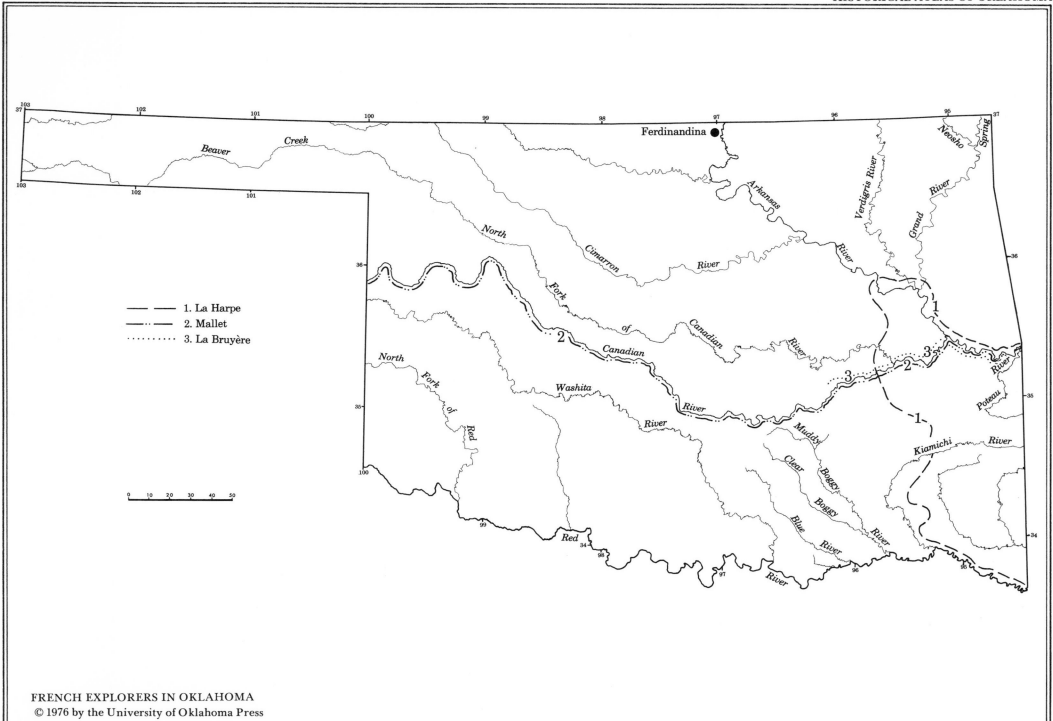

Ferdinandina

Beaver Creek

North

Cimarron River

North Fork

Canadian

of

Canadian

Washita River

River

North Fork of Red River

Red

River

Muddy

Clear Boggy

Boggy

Blue River

River

Kiamichi

River

Arkansas River

Verdigris River

Grand River

Neosho

Spring

Poteau

River

1. La Harpe
2. Mallet
3. La Bruyère

0 10 20 30 40 50

FRENCH EXPLORERS IN OKLAHOMA
© 1976 by the University of Oklahoma Press

13. FRENCH EXPLORERS IN OKLAHOMA

Hundreds of French *coureurs de bois* came upstream to Oklahoma in search of peltries. Many of these men were illiterate, and meager records of sales are the chief historical accounts of their activities. They brought few French wives into the wilderness, and their marriages to Indian mates generally followed native customs. Second-generation woods-rangers were likely to regard themselves as Indians rather than Frenchmen and to make use of the tribal language of their mothers. French names for streams, mountains, and villages came into use, however, as a natural result of the trade in French goods. By 1759 many Indians along Red River were well equipped with French guns and ammunition. The French governor of Louisiana, Kerléric, regarded the Caddoan and other tribes of the area as subjects of France.

Gradually records emerged and were assembled. It is known that French traders had some acquaintance with the Caddoans before 1700, that a lively trade was begun with the Wichita villages through La Harpe's efforts in 1719, and that the "Twin Villages" on Red River were given the names San Bernardo and San Teodoro by Athanase de Mézières in 1778 (Map 11).

This Louisiana Frenchman, whom Professor Bolton regarded the "foremost Indian agent and diplomat of the Louisiana-Texas frontier," became a subject of Spain with the transfer of Louisiana Territory to that nation.

Ferdinandina was a trading post west of the Arkansas River in what is now Kay County, Oklahoma, near the site of the Chilocco Indian School. This place was regarded by Joseph Thoburn as the "first white settlement in Oklahoma"—though he attached little significance to the term, probably because he understood thoroughly the mixed character of the population in trading posts frequented by the *coureurs de bois*.

Bernard de la Harpe received a grant of land above Natchitoches on Red River in 1718 for the purpose of opening trade with Indian tribes of the region north and northwest. He traveled through eastern Oklahoma and western Arkansas, making careful observations on the valleys of the Red, Ouachita, Arkansas, Grand, and Canadian rivers. In his journal La Harpe mentioned a visit to lead mines north of the Arkansas River and gave an account of Indian trade in metals with the Spaniards of New Mexico.

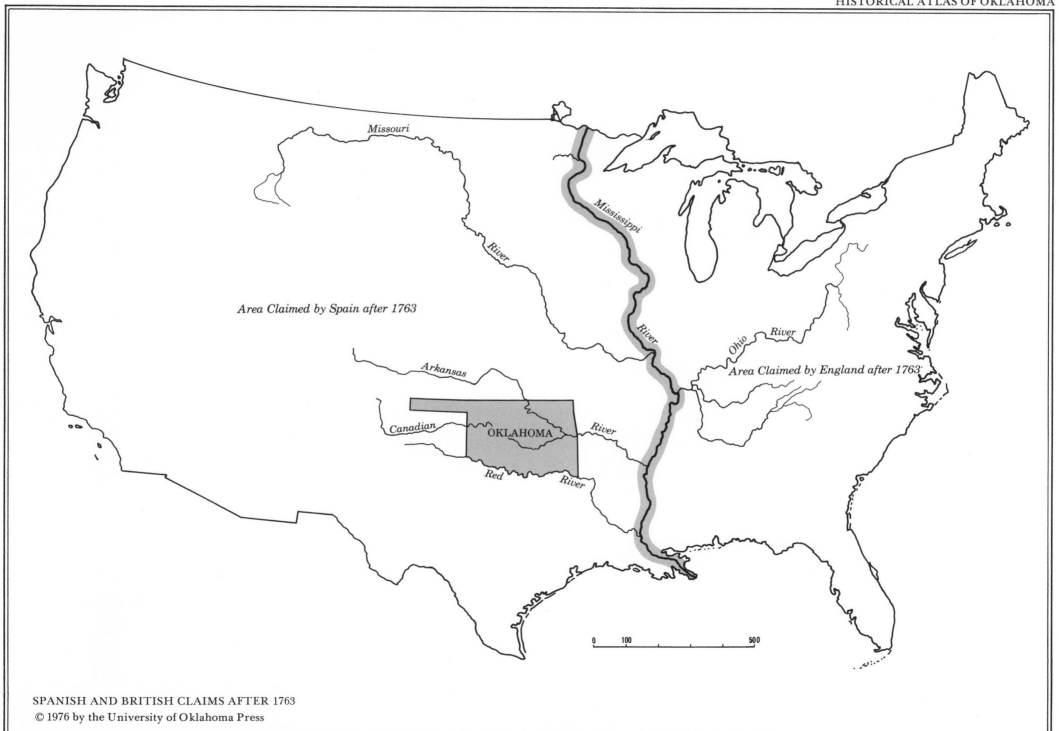

Missouri

River

Mississippi

River

Area Claimed by Spain after 1763

Ohio   River

Area Claimed by England after 1763

Arkansas

River

Canadian

OKLAHOMA

Red   River

0   100   500

SPANISH AND BRITISH CLAIMS AFTER 1763

© 1976 by the University of Oklahoma Press

14. SPANISH AND BRITISH CLAIMS AFTER 1763

France lost her claims to territory in North America as a result of the Seven Years' War, 1756–63. British naval units had seized the Philippine Islands and Cuba from Spain—France's ally—but these possessions were returned to Spanish control by the treaties of 1763. England obtained East and West Florida and all other territory east of the Mississippi, with the exception of the Isle of Orleans.

In the Treaty of Fontainebleau, 1762, Louisiana west of the Mississippi and the Isle of Orleans, east of the river, had been ceded to Spain. The Rivers Iberville and Amité, together with Lakes Maurepas, Pontchartrain, and Borgne, formed the northern boundary of the Isle of Orleans.

British possession of the Floridas continued until the end of the American Revolution in 1783. By the terms of the Treaty of Paris in that year Spain recovered Florida and retained possession of Louisiana west of the Mississippi, along with the Isle of Orleans east of it.

Spanish colonial policy was changed to a marked degree by the acquisition of undisputed title to Louisiana in 1762. Previously the Spanish frontier had been at the Red and the Sabine rivers, but the withdrawal of France from the area moved the frontier to the Mississippi and brought Spain into direct contact with England.

St. Louis and other Spanish posts adjacent to the British were strengthened. Upon the outbreak of the American Revolution, Spain immediately disclosed sympathy for the colonists against England and eventually a willingness to join France in an alliance to promote American independence.

The establishment of the United States of America, 1776–83, as an independent federal republic again transformed the situation of Spain in Louisiana Territory. American investors and frontiersmen were eager to settle the West and their insistence upon expansion was the most potent factor in determining a national policy that was to move the American boundaries to the Pacific.

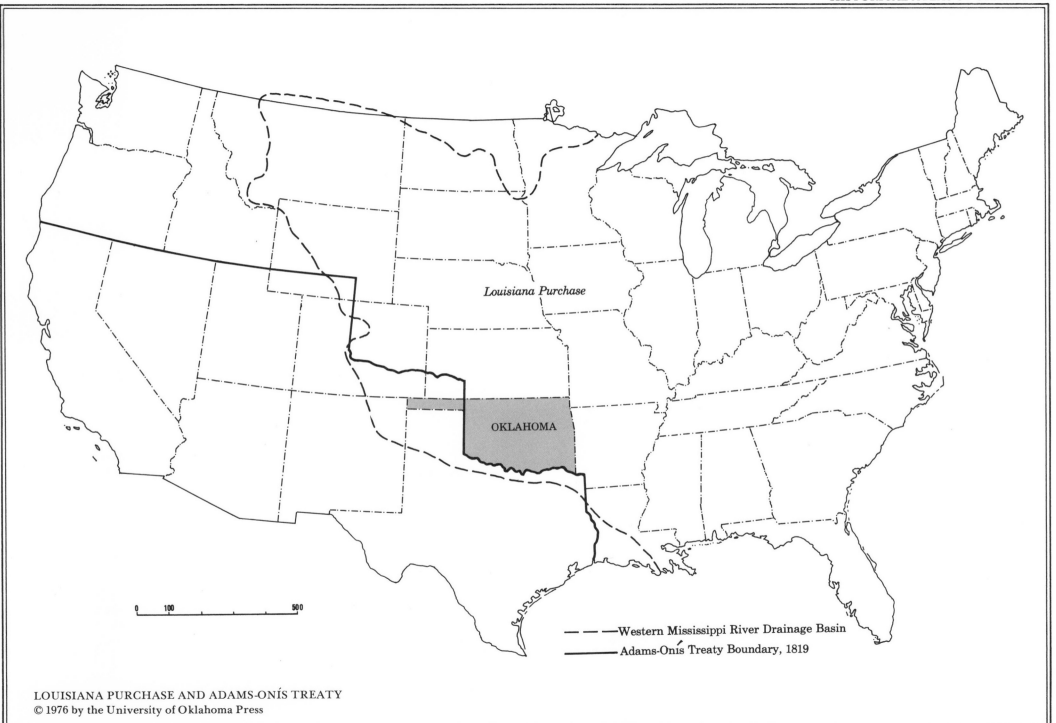

Louisiana Purchase

OKLAHOMA

0   100   500

———— Western Mississippi River Drainage Basin
———— Adams-Onís Treaty Boundary, 1819

LOUISIANA PURCHASE AND ADAMS-ONÍS TREATY
© 1976 by the University of Oklahoma Press

15. LOUISIANA PURCHASE AND ADAMS-ONÍS TREATY

The expansion of American population to the West brought an acute need for control of the Mississippi River as a commercial outlet. That need was brought into focus by the Treaty of San Ildefonso in 1800, which included the transfer of Louisiana's title to Napoleonic France. The French consul made it clear at once that his presence as a neighbor on the western border of the United States carried many unpleasant, dangerous possibilities.

It was rare good fortune for the young American republic that President Jefferson's offer to purchase the Isle of Orleans was coincident with Napoleon's need for a substantial sum of money and his recognition of the difficulties inherent in revival of the French empire in America. The failure of French operations in Haiti turned the scale in favor of Napoleon's sudden shift in plans.

When Jefferson's agent, Robert R. Livingston, suggested to Bishop Talleyrand that the United States would be willing to pay a good price for the left bank of the Mississippi below Lake Pontchartrain, the French diplomat suddenly offered to sell the entire province of Louisiana. After some bargaining—marked on both sides by nervous haste to close the deal—Livingston and Talleyrand agreed upon terms.

The United States Senate ratified the treaty, Congress voted the necessary sum—a total of $15,000,000 including claims against France—and November 3, 1803, was set as the date for transfer of Louisiana to the United States.

The purchase of this great area west of the Mississippi was perhaps the most notable achievement of a great administration. At a single stroke President Jefferson acquired for the United States control of the Mississippi River as a commercial artery, got rid of Napoleon Bonaparte as a neighbor, and practically doubled the nation's area.

By the terms of the treaty Louisiana was to include the same land as that acquired by France in 1800, that is, the "same extent" that it had "in the hands of Spain." The boundaries with Spanish territory to the southwest remained indefinite until John Quincy Adams and Luis Onís agreed upon the terms of the Florida Purchase Treaty in 1819.

The right bank of the Sabine, the right bank of the Red, the right bank of the Arkansas, the 100th meridian, and the 42d parallel were the principal segments of the Spanish boundary. A year earlier, 1818, a convention with the British had resulted in agreement upon the 49th parallel as the northern boundary of Louisiana from the Lake of the Woods to the Continental Divide in the Great Stony (Rocky) Mountains.

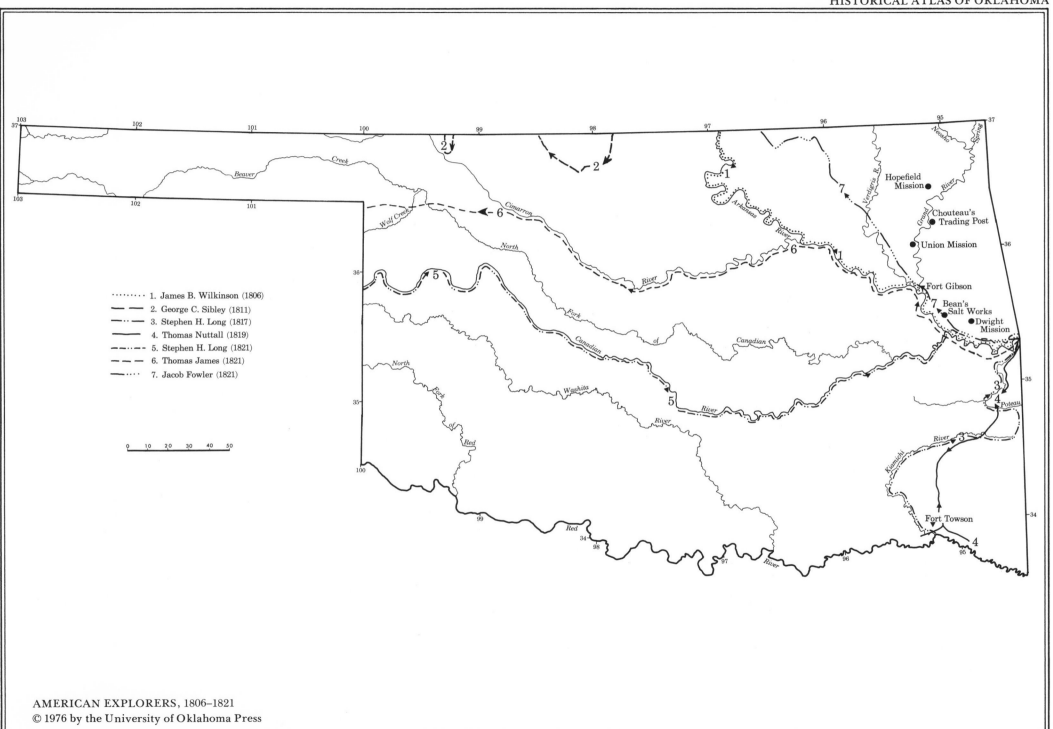

1. James B. Wilkinson (1806)
2. George C. Sibley (1811)
3. Stephen H. Long (1817)
4. Thomas Nuttall (1819)
5. Stephen H. Long (1821)
6. Thomas James (1821)
7. Jacob Fowler (1821)

AMERICAN EXPLORERS, 1806–1821
© 1976 by the University of Oklahoma Press

16. AMERICAN EXPLORERS, 1806–1821

Earliest of the major explorers in Oklahoma under the authority of the United States was Lieutenant James B. Wilkinson in 1806. The party left St. Louis under the command of Lieutenant Zebulon Pike, traveling up the Missouri and Osage rivers and northwest into Kansas. From Pawnee Village they turned west to the Great Bend of the Arkansas.

Lieutenant Wilkinson began the descent of that stream in October with five soldiers. By making side trips, he visited the sites of Pawhuska and Claremore but each time returned to the Arkansas and on December 29 reached the site of Webbers Falls. Lieutenant Wilkinson completed the descent of the Arkansas and continued to New Orleans with the journal of his expedition.

In 1811, Colonel George Sibley, Indian agent in Missouri, returned a party of Osages to the Platte River and headed south, crossing the Arkansas in Kansas. He explored the upper Chikaskia and followed the Salt Fork of the Arkansas River southward to the region in northern Oklahoma that became known as the Great Salt Plains.

Major Stephen H. Long, in his search for a suitable place for a fort on the Arkansas River in 1817, explored the Kiamichi Valley. His route from Arkopolis (site of Little Rock) extended through the site of Hot Springs, across upper Mountain Fork, and to the mouth of the Kiamichi. From that point on Red River he followed the Kiamichi and Poteau rivers to Belle Point on the Arkansas, which became the location of Fort Smith. Major Long named the place for his commander, General Thomas A. Smith.

The Thomas Nuttall expedition reached Oklahoma by way of the Arkansas River in April, 1819. Nuttall, a botanist, traveled south with Major William Bradford and a party of soldiers from Fort Smith. His journal describes the streams and mountains of southeastern Oklahoma. After his return to Fort Smith, Nuttall explored along the Arkansas, Grand, Verdigris, Canadian, North Canadian, Deep Fork, and Cimarron rivers. His record, filled with details of river travel and descriptions of the Indian bands, has unique value for students of history and geography.

The great Long-Bell expedition to the Rocky Mountains started at Pittsburgh under Major Stephen H. Long on May 5, 1819. Their route took them down the Ohio, north to the Missouri and up that stream to the Platte, westward to the Rocky Mountains, and southward toward Pikes Peak. Captain Bell returned along the Arkansas, but Major Long continued south to the headwaters of the Canadian—which he supposed to be the Red River.

The botanist Edwin James left a detailed report of the expedition down the Canadian, through the Texas Panhandle and Oklahoma. Major Long realized that he was not on Red River when he reached the Arkansas on September 10, 1820. Captain Bell's party rejoined Major Long at Fort Smith.

In May, 1821, Thomas James traveled up the Arkansas River with John McKnight on a journey to New Mexico. After leaving the Cimarron, the party crossed the North Canadian in western Oklahoma and reached Santa Fe in December, 1821.

The Hugh Glenn-Jacob Fowler expedition of 1821 was a trading enterprise. The party of twenty men left Fort Smith on September 6, made brief stops at Bean and Saunders' salt works on the Illinois River, Colonel Glenn's trading post on the Verdigris, and Chief Clermont's Osage Village. West of the Arkansas River the traders began to exchange goods with Kiowa, Cheyenne, and Arapaho Indians. At Taos, with trade goods exhausted and pack animals loaded with pelts and furs, the party turned back.

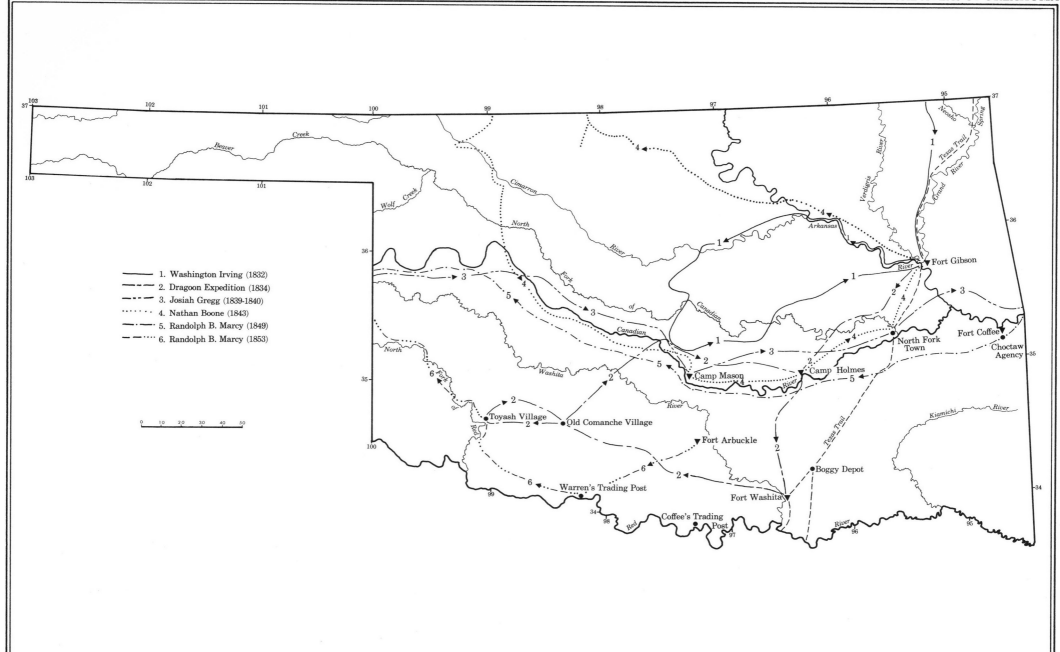

1. Washington Irving (1832)
2. Dragoon Expedition (1834)
3. Josiah Gregg (1839-1840)
4. Nathan Boone (1843)
5. Randolph B. Marcy (1849)
6. Randolph B. Marcy (1853)

AMERICAN EXPLORERS, 1832–1853
© 1976 by the University of Oklahoma Press

17. AMERICAN EXPLORERS, 1832–1853

The Washington Irving Expedition through Oklahoma in 1832 included Henry Ellsworth of the Stokes Commission and Charles J. Latrobe, author of *The Rambler in North America*. Accompanied by Captain Bean's Rangers, the party covered parts of the Arkansas, Cimarron, and North Canadian valleys, all of which had been traversed previously. No person, however, had described the region and its inhabitants in such detail and with such lively, charming narrative as Irving did.

The Dragoon Expedition of 1834 under General Henry Leavenworth was a major effort to establish peace on the Southern Plains. Five hundred dragoons under Colonel Henry Dodge, with additional Indian scouts and interpreters and two infantry companies from Fort Towson, made up the party. George Catlin, the distinguished painter of Indian life, was permitted to ride along with them.

The dragoons marched towards Edwards' Post on June 15, established Camp Holmes, crossed the Canadian River, and reached the lower Washita on July 4. Beyond the Washita, General Leavenworth died in a hospital camp. Colonel Dodge marched the dragoons west to Old Comanche Village and to Toyash Village on the North Fork of the Red. From that point he returned to Fort Gibson, reaching the post on August 15.

Josiah Gregg, one of the great Santa Fe traders, began his expedition of 1839 at Van Buren, Arkansas. Goods for New Mexico were carried in fourteen wagons. Gregg traveled on the north side of the Canadian beyond Camp Mason, crossed that stream between the sites of Bridgeport and Taloga, and continued west to Santa Fe and south to Chihuahua. He returned in 1840 with twenty-eight wagons, two hundred mules, and a large flock of sheep and goats.

Captain Nathan Boone of Missouri led an expedition from Fort Gibson to the Great Salt Plains in 1843. The route was along the Arkansas River to the site of Osage, northwest to Salt Fork, and north of the 37th parallel. Returning, Boone crossed the Cimarron, marched south to the Canadian, and followed that stream to North Fork Town.

In 1849 a band of California emigrants was escorted through Oklahoma by Captain R. B. Marcy. Four years later Marcy explored a part of southwestern Oklahoma in his search for the headwaters of Red River.

Nez Percé

Modoc

Chippewa

Ottawa
Wyandotte

Mohawk
Stockbridge

Piankashaw

Seneca
Cayuga

Sac and Fox

Pottawatomie

Munsee
Delaware

Cheyenne

Iowa

Erie

Kickapoo

Conestoga

Arapaho

Ponca

Michigamea

Miami

Skidi

Moingwena

Kaskaskia

Wea

Shawnee

Oto and Missouri

Illinois

Peoria

Eel River

Pawnee

Tamaroa

Kaw

Cahokia

Osage

Tuscarora

Kiowa

Quapaw

Kiowa-Apache

OKLAHOMA

Cherokee

Catawba

Apache

Tuskegee

Yuchi

Chickasaw

Koasati

Creek

Comanche

Wichita

Kichai

Alabama

Caddo

Choctaw

Tawakoni
Waco
Tonkawa
Anadarko
Hainai

Natchez

Hitchiti
Apalachicola

Lipan

Seminole

0   100   400

HOMELANDS OF OKLAHOMA INDIANS
© 1976 by the University of Oklahoma Press

18. HOMELANDS OF OKLAHOMA INDIANS

Oklahoma became the residence of many Indian tribes by the process of removal, a policy of the United States government. The mobility of Indians—particularly after they became acquainted with Spanish horses—and the absence of specific boundaries among the native tribes, made definitive location of tribes impossible. However, Indian groups—not in every case united primarily by the fact of common linguistic stock—did regard certain regions as their respective homes. Acquaintance with those areas in connection with the tribes which claimed them is useful in the study of historic migrations and settlements.

Authorities have presented a variety of views in regard to the "homeland" of Indian tribes. A considerable part of the controversy involved in ascribing locations to the tribes is due to the fact that Indians were mobile even before the horse became known among them. For example, the Cherokees were relatives of the other Iroquoian Indians of New York, and we find evidence of their presence in Virginia, North Carolina, and Tennessee before a major part of the tribe moved to Georgia. The Chickasaws (Muskhogean) lived in Kentucky and Tennessee before the period of their removal from northern Mississippi to Oklahoma.

Most useful for the study of the tribes that came to Oklahoma is Muriel H. Wright's *A Guide to the Indian Tribes of Oklahoma*. Miss Wright lists alphabetically and discusses sixty-five tribes. The *Handbook of American Indians North of Mexico* (2 vols., 1907–10), edited by F. W. Hodge, has the advantages of wide coverage and scholarly expertise.

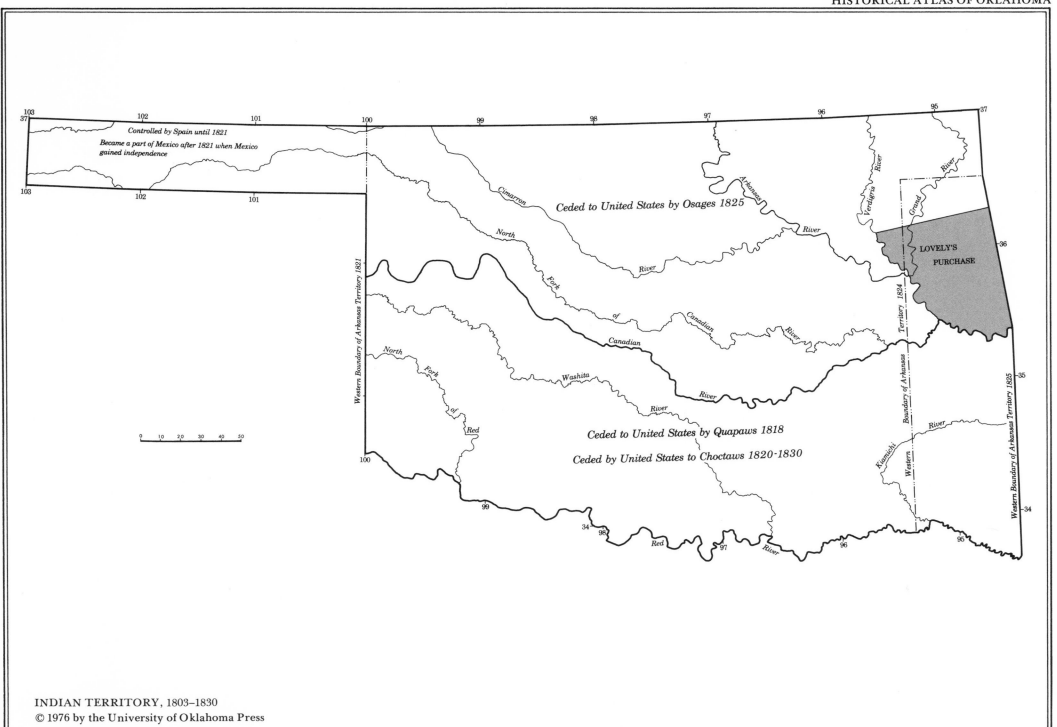

Controlled by Spain until 1821

Became a part of Mexico after 1821 when Mexico gained independence

Ceded to United States by Osages 1825

LOVELY'S PURCHASE

Western Boundary of Arkansas Territory 1821

Boundary of Arkansas Territory 1824

Western Boundary of Arkansas Territory 1825

Cimarron River

North Fork

Arkansas River

Verdigris River

Grand River

Canadian River

Canadian

North Fork of Red

Washita River

Red River

Kiamichi River

Western

Ceded to United States by Quapaws 1818

Ceded by United States to Choctaws 1820-1830

INDIAN TERRITORY, 1803–1830

© 1976 by the University of Oklahoma Press

19. INDIAN TERRITORY, 1803–1830

When Congress created Arkansas Territory (March 2, 1819), the region that is now Oklahoma, west to the 100th meridian, was included within its boundaries. Removal of the Choctaws created friction between white settlers and the Indians and led eventually to the establishment of a permanent western boundary for Arkansas.

Removal of the Choctaws from Arkansas by the terms of the Treaty of 1825 was followed by a Cherokee removal treaty in 1828. The Choctaw boundary line was defined as follows: "A line beginning on the Arkansas, one hundred paces east of Fort Smith and running thence due south to the Red River." The Cherokee line, from the 37th parallel to 36°30', was the western border of Missouri. From the southwest corner of Missouri the boundary was to be a straight line to the intersection of the Choctaw boundary with the Arkansas River.

Spain had title to the land west of the 100th meridian and south of the Red River by the terms of the Adams-Onís treaty of 1819. Within two years, however, the Mexican revolution had given the new Mexican government a permanent hold upon former Spanish territory southwest of the United States.

"Lovely's Purchase" was the result of a conference between the Osages and Cherokees, convened at the mouth of the Verdigris in 1816. Major William Lovely, Cherokee agent in the West, obtained an agreement whereby the Osages ceded to the United States the land defined as follows: "Beginning at the Arkansaw River at . . . Frog Bayou; then up the Arkansaw and Verdigris to the falls of the Verdigris River; thence eastwardly, to the said Osage boundary line, at a point twenty leagues north from the Arkansaw River; and, with that line, to the point of beginning."

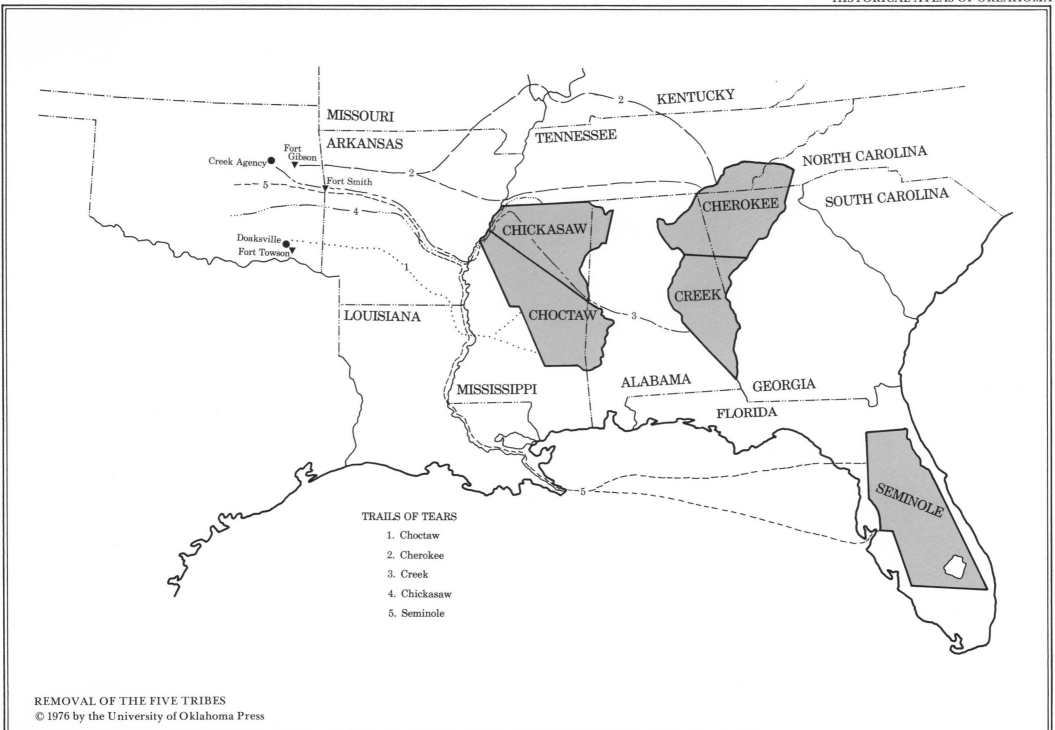

MISSOURI

ARKANSAS

Creek Agency ● ▼ Fort Gibson

5

▼ Fort Smith

4

Doaksville ● ▼ Fort Towson

1

LOUISIANA

KENTUCKY

2

TENNESSEE

2

NORTH CAROLINA

CHEROKEE

SOUTH CAROLINA

CHICKASAW

CHOCTAW

3

CREEK

MISSISSIPPI

ALABAMA

GEORGIA

FLORIDA

5

SEMINOLE

TRAILS OF TEARS

1. Choctaw

2. Cherokee

3. Creek

4. Chickasaw

5. Seminole

REMOVAL OF THE FIVE TRIBES

© 1976 by the University of Oklahoma Press

20. REMOVAL OF THE FIVE TRIBES

Removal of the Five Civilized Tribes to Oklahoma was a process which lasted more than twenty years, beginning with the Choctaw treaties of 1816, 1820, and 1825 and the Cherokee treaties of 1817 and 1828. The movement ended with the efforts to comb the Seminoles out of the Florida swamps in the 1840's. Some small bands of southeastern Indians went west before the removal treaties, and many Indian hunters regularly crossed the Arkansas country to reach the buffalo plains.

In exchange for their land in Mississippi and Alabama the Choctaws were to receive a large tract south of the Arkansas and Canadian rivers. The Treaty of Doak's Stand, 1820, provided an eastern boundary for the Choctaw settlements on a line extending north from the mouth of Little River to the Arkansas. Because of white squatters in the area, however, a new treaty in 1825 moved the boundary west approximately to the present border of Arkansas from the Red River to the Arkansas River.

In a series of removals the Choctaws traveled west by various routes, in some instances using riverboats for a part of the journey. Although they endured great hardships on the road west, their travail was, perhaps, less painful than the suffering of tribes that moved a longer distance.

Most of the Chickasaws traveled across Arkansas by wagon, at least for part of the way. Riverboats on the Mississippi, St. Francis, and Arkansas rivers provided a part of the removal facilities.

Cherokee removal parties usually crossed western Kentucky to Golconda on the Ohio, and moved across southern Illinois to the Cape Girardeau ferry on the Mississippi. The "Trail of Tears" was the overland passage across Missouri and Arkansas. Many of the people, especially infants and the elderly, died and were buried along one or another of the trails. One of the fourteen wagon trains went west across central Arkansas from Chickasaw Bluff (Memphis), and a few bands moved west from Cape Girardeau to southwestern Missouri before turning south to the Cherokee lands in the Indian territory.

Creek migration was complicated by warfare, since some bands resisted the process of removal. Like the Cherokees, the Creeks suffered because of bitter controversy within the tribe over removal.

Perhaps Seminole removal was the most costly of all. For seven years this least "civilized" of the five tribes fought against the government's order to leave Florida. Most bands traveled by boat from the Florida coast to New Orleans and by river steamers to Little Rock or farther upstream. The final stage was accomplished by wagon. The tribe was reduced by one-third as a result of the war and the hardships of the long journey.

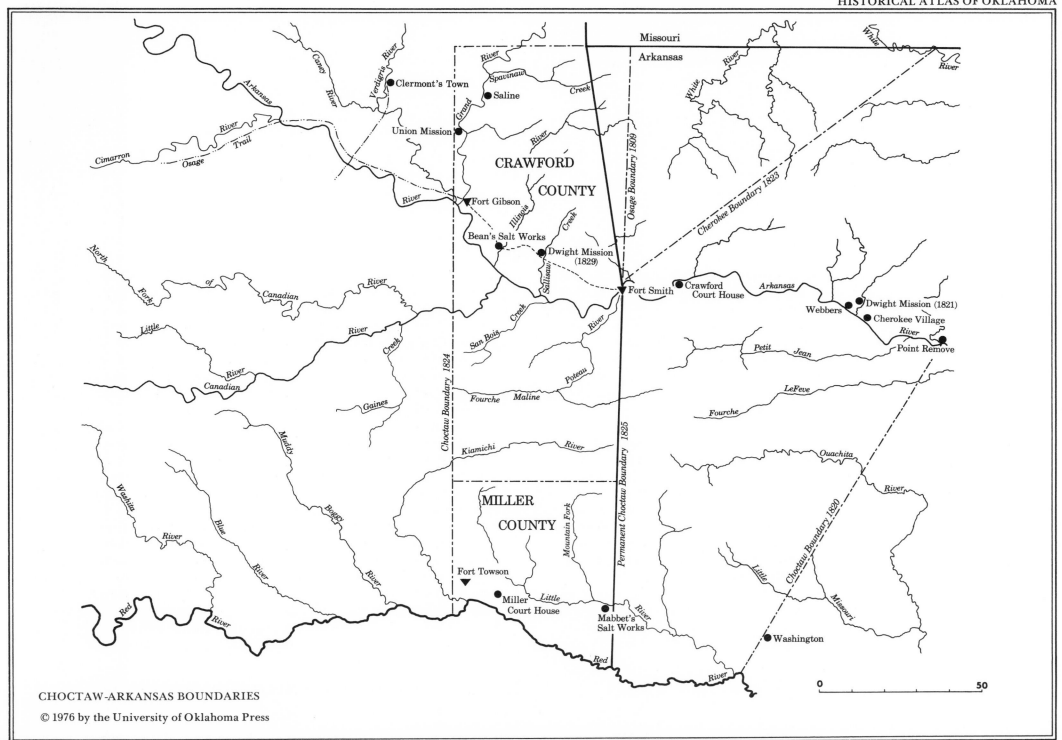

Missouri

Arkansas

Clermont's Town

Saline

Spavinaw Creek

Union Mission

CRAWFORD
COUNTY

White River

Osage Boundary 1809

Cherokee Boundary 1823

Fort Gibson

Illinois

Bean's Salt Works

Dwight Mission
(1829)

Fort Smith

Crawford
Court House

Arkansas

Webbers

Dwight Mission (1821)

Cherokee Village

Point Remove

San Bois Creek

Poteau River

Petit Jean

LeFeve

Fourche Maline

Fourche

Choctaw Boundary 1824

Kiamichi River

Permanent Choctaw Boundary 1825

Ouachita River

MILLER
COUNTY

Mountain Fork

Choctaw Boundary 1820

Little River

Missouri

Fort Towson

Miller
Court House

Little River

Mabbet's
Salt Works

Washington

Red River

CHOCTAW-ARKANSAS BOUNDARIES

© 1976 by the University of Oklahoma Press

0   50

21. CHOCTAW-ARKANSAS BOUNDARIES

In 1824 an act of Congress fixed the western boundary of Arkansas Territory on a line forty miles west of the southwest corner of Missouri. As surveyed by John C. Brown, the new Arkansas boundary cut through the lower Kiamichi near the stream's mouth and crossed west of the Three Forks area. The act was a clear violation of the Treaty of Doak's Stand.

By the Treaty of Washington, 1825, the Choctaw Nation ceded to the United States all of its western land "lying east of a line beginning on the Arkansas, one hundred paces east of Fort Smith, and running thence due south to the Red River." The United States agreed to pay an annual sum of $6,000 to the Choctaw Nation "forever," to remove all white citizens from the newly defined Choctaw Nation, and to prevent future settlement of United States citizens on Choctaw lands.

The Arkansas delegate to Congress, Henry W. Conway, protested the treaty line, declaring in a letter to Secretary of War John C. Calhoun that such a boundary would cut off a large number of Arkansas citizens. Calhoun pointed out, however, that Arkansas had obtained a substantial addition from the earlier Choctaw grant. President John Quincy Adams appointed James S. Conway to survey the new line, and on November 2, 1825, the work was begun at Fort Smith. It was completed on December 7.

The Conway line was inaccurate, as later surveys proved conclusively. After a long diplomatic struggle, Peter P. Pitchlynn of the Choctaw Nation obtained passage of an act of Congress authorizing a new survey.

Henry E. McKee, United States surveyor, ran the line "due south" in April and May, 1877, not for the purpose of recovering land for the Choctaws, but as a basis for payment of damages. According to McKee's survey, the boundary established in 1825 crossed Red River west of the treaty line by four miles and sixteen chains and deprived the Choctaws of 136,204.02 acres.

The tribe was paid $68,102.00 for the land given to Arkansas by error. Of the sum awarded to the Choctaws, however, 30 percent was taken for attorney fees and 20 percent to pay the expenses of the Pitchlynn delegation.

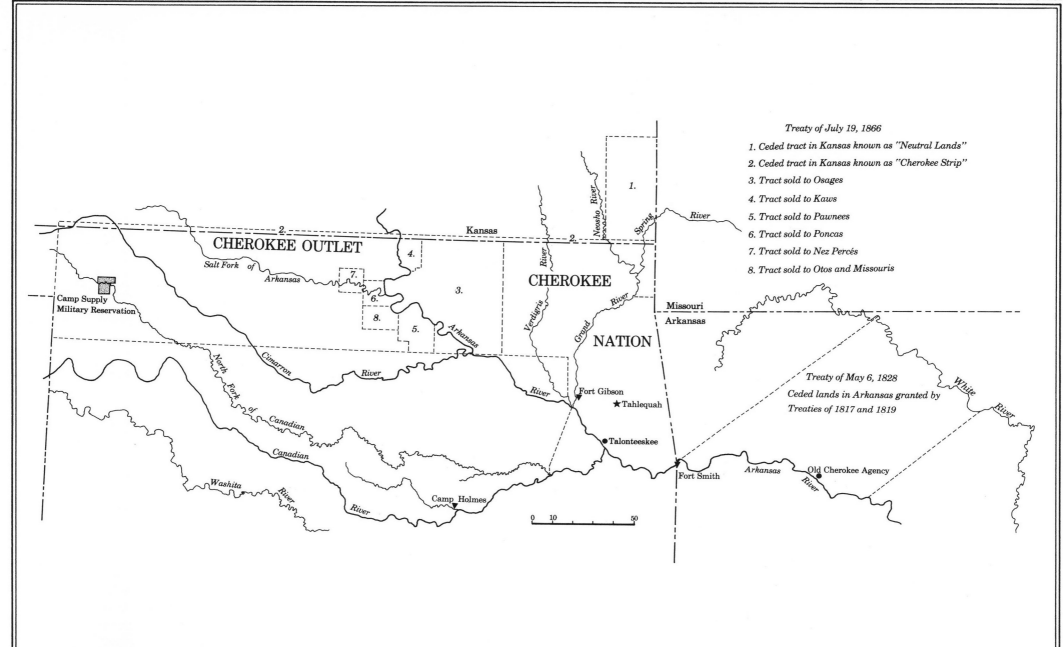

Treaty of July 19, 1866

1. *Ceded tract in Kansas known as "Neutral Lands"*
2. *Ceded tract in Kansas known as "Cherokee Strip"*
3. *Tract sold to Osages*
4. *Tract sold to Kaws*
5. *Tract sold to Pawnees*
6. *Tract sold to Poncas*
7. *Tract sold to Nez Percés*
8. *Tract sold to Otos and Missouris*

Treaty of May 6, 1828
Ceded lands in Arkansas granted by
Treaties of 1817 and 1819

CHEROKEE LANDS IN THE WEST
© 1976 by the University of Oklahoma Press

22. CHEROKEE LANDS IN THE WEST

The first Cherokee removal to Arkansas lands occurred in 1817. Removal was on a voluntary basis, and the tribe ceded about one-third of the Cherokee lands in the East in exchange for equal acreage between the White and Arkansas rivers. Enforcement of the treaty terms, which guaranteed the Cherokees freedom from the encroachment of white settlers, was impossible, and the Western Cherokees were persuaded to move farther west in 1828. Seven million acres of land in the Verdigris, Grand, and Arkansas valleys were exchanged for the holdings of the Cherokees in the Territory of Arkansas.

On December 29, 1835, an agreement was reached at New Echota, Georgia, between commissioners of the United States and leaders who purported to speak for the Eastern Cherokees. The Treaty of New Echota provided for removal of all the remaining members of the tribe to the land west of Arkansas and Missouri that had been assigned to the Western Cherokees. An additional tract of land in Kansas was conveyed to the Cherokees in consideration of the payment of $500,000 to the United States. This area, twenty-five miles wide and extending fifty miles along the western border of Missouri—800,000 acres—was known as the "Neutral Lands."

The Cherokee Outlet, as provided in Article 2 of the New Echota Treaty, was assurance to the Cherokee Nation of a "perpetual outlet west, and a free and unmolested use of all the country west of . . . said seven million acres."

By the terms of Article 17 of the Treaty of Washington in 1866, the United States held the "Neutral Lands" in trust to be sold for the benefit of the Cherokee Nation. The "Cherokee Strip," about two and one-half miles wide and lying along the 37th parallel within the state of Kansas, was also held in trust for the benefit of the Cherokee Nation.

By the terms of Article 15 and Article 16, friendly tribes were to be settled on surplus Cherokee lands. The Osage (3) and Kaw (also called Kansa or Kansas) (4) tribes were settled in the portion of the Cherokee Outlet lying between the Arkansas River and the 96th meridian. Other tribes settled on Cherokee lands were the Pawnee (5), Ponca (6), Nez Percé (7), and the Oto-Missouri (8). In 1885 the Nez Percés moved back to their earlier home in Idaho, and their lands were occupied by a remnant of the Tonkawas from Texas.

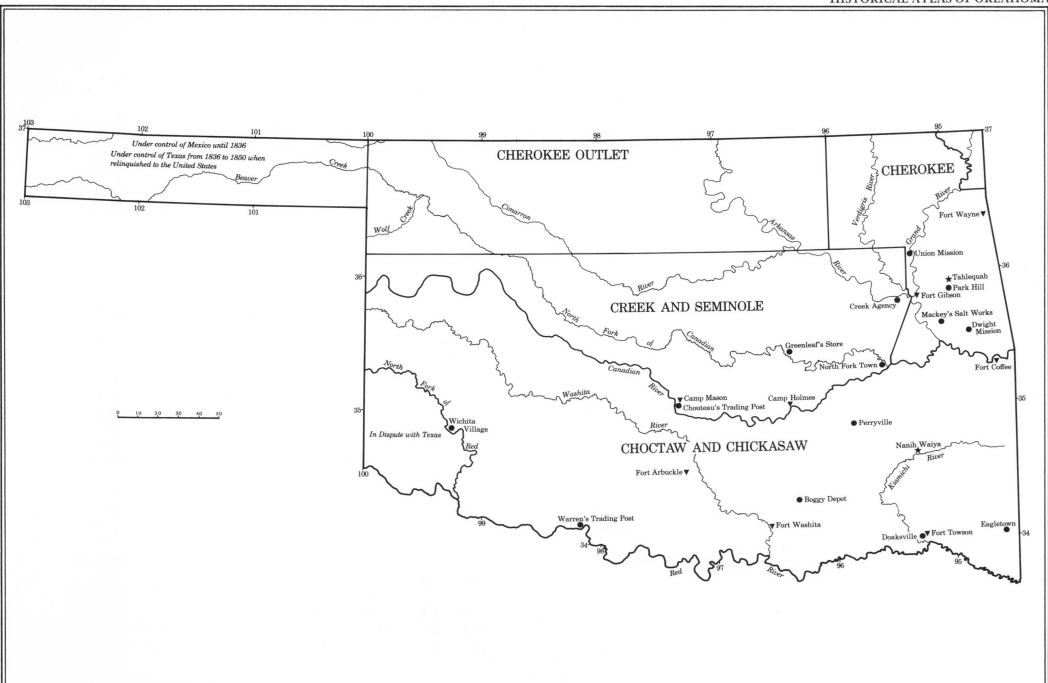

Under control of Mexico until 1836
Under control of Texas from 1836 to 1850 when
relinquished to the United States

Beaver *Creek*

CHEROKEE OUTLET

Wolf *Creek*

Cimarron

Arkansas

CHEROKEE

Verdigris River

Grand

River

Fort Wayne ▼

Union Mission ●

★ Tahlequah
● Park Hill

River

CREEK AND SEMINOLE

North *Fork* *of* *Canadian*

Creek Agency ● ▼ Fort Gibson

Mackey's Salt Works ●

Dwight
Mission ●

Greenleaf's Store ●

Canadian *River*

North Fork Town ●

Fort Coffee ▼

North *Fork* *of*

Washita

▼ Camp Mason
● Chouteau's Trading Post

Camp Holmes ▼

Red

● Wichita
Village

River

● Perryville

In Dispute with Texas

CHOCTAW AND CHICKASAW

Nanih Waiya ★

Kiamichi

River

Fort Arbuckle ▼

● Boggy Depot

Warren's Trading Post ●

▼ Fort Washita

Eagletown ●

Doaksville ● ▼ Fort Towson

Red *River*

0 10 20 30 40 50

INDIAN TERRITORY, 1830–1855
© 1976 by the University of Oklahoma Press

By the Treaty of Dancing Rabbit Creek in 1830, the Choctaws ceded all their land east of the Mississippi to the United States. In exchange they received the land between the western border of Arkansas and the 100th meridian, with the Red River as the southern boundary and the Canadian-Arkansas rivers as their northern limit.

The Choctaws agreed to arrange for moving as many members of the tribe as possible "during the falls of 1831 and 1832," and the rest during the fall of 1833. After three years, about 7,000 Choctaws remained in Mississippi. In January, 1837, Chickasaw and Choctaw commissioners met at Doaksville on the lower Kiamichi and agreed upon terms of Chickasaw removal.

The Treaty of Doaksville provided that the Chickasaws should move into a district west of the Choctaw settlements. The two governments were to be combined, and members of both tribes were to have the right to settle in any part of the Choctaw Nation. Separate tribal annuities were to be continued, but all other privileges were equal.

By the end of 1840 most of the Chickasaws had moved into their district. The Kiowas and some other western tribes resented the presence of Chickasaws on land which the Plains Indians regarded as their own. Raids by Kiowas and Comanches were frequent, and the Chickasaws were forced to maintain a constant guard over their livestock and other property. Also, they could not obtain an equal voice in united tribal affairs.

Fort Washita, established in 1842 about fifteen miles from the Texas border, provided protection against raids; and a new treaty in 1855 gave the Chickasaws relief from the frustration of representative government in which their votes had little weight.

Creek removal was marked by war within the tribe and terrible suffering during migration. Chief William McIntosh was executed in 1825 for ceding land without tribal consent. The Treaty of Washington in 1832 provided for the cession of all Creek land east of the Mississippi and settlement of the tribe west of Arkansas. Another treaty in 1833 defined the boundaries of Creek lands.

The northern line, which was also a Cherokee boundary, began at a distance of twenty-five miles from the Arkansas River and extended west to the 100th meridian. The western line lay along the Mexican boundary, and the southern limit was the Canadian River. The eastern line was the result of compromise with the Cherokees, negotiated by the Stokes Commission in 1833.

James Gadsden reached an agreement with a party of Seminoles at Payne's Landing, Florida, in 1832. The "treaty" provided that the Seminoles should send an exploring party to the Creek lands in the West, and if the explorers should be satisfied with the country and "the favorable disposition of the Creeks to reunite with the Seminoles as one people," the removal agreement should be binding.

At Fort Gibson reluctant consent of the Seminole explorers was incorporated in a brief "treaty" which purported to be a completion of the Payne's Landing agreement. In Florida, Seminole tribal leaders objected strongly to migration, and the attempt to remove them by force resulted in a costly war. Most of the Seminoles were moved west between 1836 and 1842.

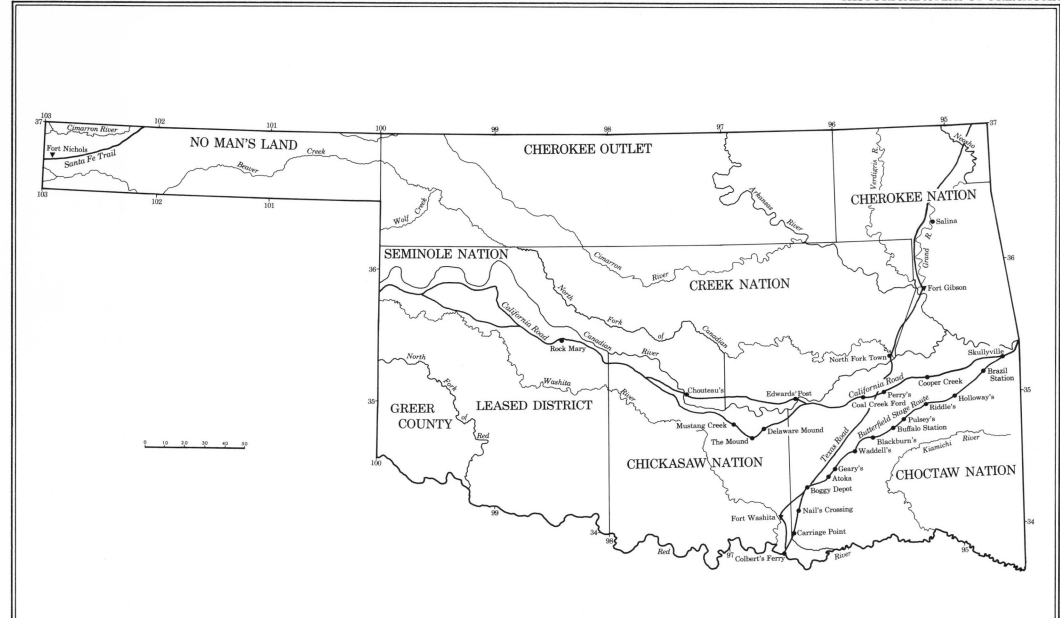

NO MAN'S LAND

Fort Nichols

Cimarron River

Santa Fe Trail

Beaver Creek

CHEROKEE OUTLET

CHEROKEE NATION

Verdigris R.

Neosho

Salina

Grand R.

Wolf Creek

Arkansas River

SEMINOLE NATION

Cimarron River

CREEK NATION

Fort Gibson

California Road

North Fork of Canadian River

Canadian

North Fork Town

Skullyville

Rock Mary

Chouteau's

Edwards' Post

California Road

Cooper Creek

Brazil Station

North Fork of Red

Washita River

GREER COUNTY

LEASED DISTRICT

CHICKASAW NATION

Mustang Creek

The Mound

Delaware Mound

Perry's

Coal Creek Ford

Butterfield Stage Route

Riddle's

Holloway's

Buffalo Station

Pulsey's

Texas Road

Blackburn's

Waddell's

Kiamichi River

CHOCTAW NATION

Geary's

Atoka

Boggy Depot

Nail's Crossing

Fort Washita

Carriage Point

Colbert's Ferry

Red River

0 10 20 30 40 50

IMPORTANT ROUTES AND TRAILS
© 1976 by the University of Oklahoma Press

24. IMPORTANT ROUTES AND TRAILS

Most important of the trails to Santa Fe, the route from the great bend of the Arkansas to New Mexico had one great branch which crossed the Cimarron and cut across the Oklahoma Panhandle. This trail, more famous than Gregg's route from Van Buren, Arkansas, affected exchange of goods in the Indian Territory less directly than the road followed by Gregg's livestock traders. Some adventurers from the Indian nations entered the service of freighters on the great trail from Independence, Missouri, in the capacity of teamsters or drovers.

The Texas Road developed as a natural result of travel from the north and east into the Indian country and later from the demand for a route to the Mexican province of Texas. The flood of travelers along this route made it the most important artery of commerce between the settlements of Missouri and Kansas, at one end, and the Red River, at the other. Immigrants who came in from Arkansas reached the Texas Road at Three Forks or farther south.

Salina, North Fork Town, Boggy Depot, and many other towns felt the impact of trade incidental to the Texas migration and the return of many settlers to their homes in Missouri, Arkansas, or Tennessee.

The California Road through Indian Territory was a route which became common to emigrants from southern states during the gold rush. Like the Texas Road, this frontier passageway stimulated the business of trading posts and introduced thousands of visitors to the land which is now Oklahoma. Fort Smith, connected with the East both by riverboats and the means of overland travel, was the gathering point for a wide range of gold-seekers, not only from the South, but from the upper Mississippi and the eastern seaboard.

Edwards' Post (Store), on the north side of the Canadian, increased its volume of trade sharply because many emigrants regarded it the last chance east of New Mexico to supplement their supplies. Usually the wagon trains crossed to the south bank before they traveled as far west as Rock Mary, which became one of the principal landmarks on the trail.

One of the most romantic adventures in the history of common carriers began with the first run of the Butterfield Stage Line in the fall of 1858. The route through Indian Territory— 192 miles from Fort Smith to Colbert's Ferry—had twelve stage stations. Not all of them grew into towns, but all were famous in their day. As examples, Holloway's, Boggy Depot, and Nail's Crossing of the Blue were all distinct in the minds of Indian Territory travelers and the subjects of frequent reference in letters and trip reports.

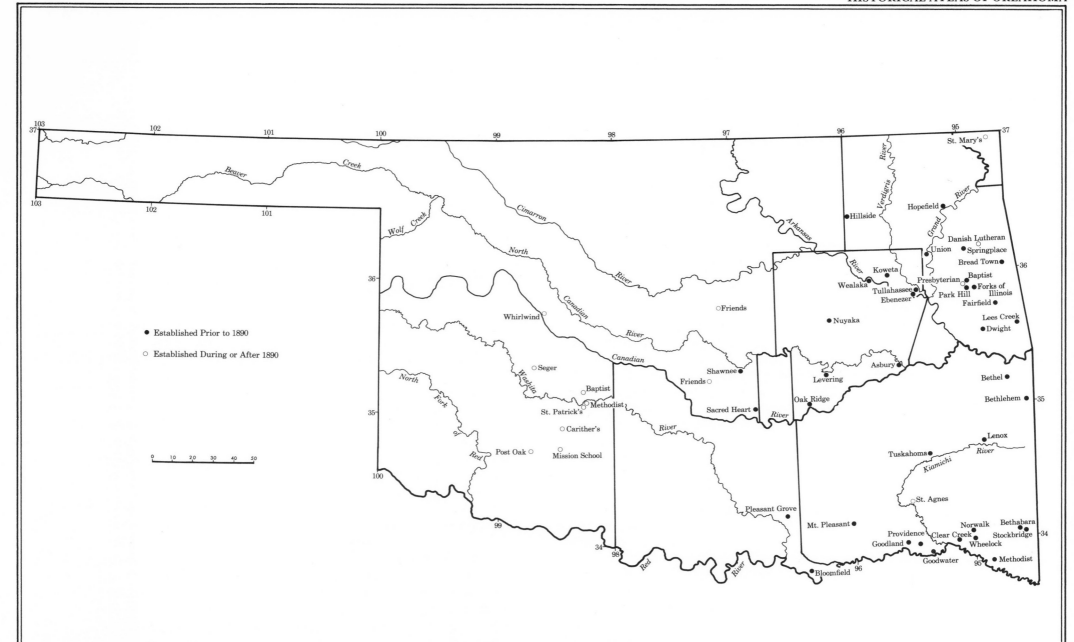

103 37 102 101 100 99 98 97 96 95 37

Beaver   Creek

Cimarron

Wolf Creek

North   River

○ St. Mary's

● Hillside

Hopefield ●

Grand River

○ Danish Lutheran
● Union ● Springplace
● Bread Town ● 36
● Koweta
Wealaka ● Baptist
● Tullahassee Presbyterian ● Forks of
Ebenezer ● Park Hill ○ Illinois
Fairfield ●
Lees Creek ●
Dwight ●

103 102 101

36

Canadian   River

Arkansas

Verdigris River

Whirlwind ○

○ Friends

● Nuyaka

● Established Prior to 1890

○ Established During or After 1890

Canadian

○ Seger

Washita

North

Fork

Baptist ○

Methodist ○
St. Patrick's ○

○ Carither's

Post Oak ○

Red

○ Mission School

Shawnee ●
Friends ○

Levering ●

Asbury ●

Oak Ridge ○

Sacred Heart ● River

Bethel ●

Bethlehem ● 35

Lenox ●

Tuskahoma ● River

Kiamichi

St. Agnes ○

Pleasant Grove ○

Mt. Pleasant ●

Norwalk ● Bethabara ●
Providence ● Clear Creek ● Stockbridge ● 34
Goodland ● Wheelock ●
Goodwater ● Methodist ●
Bloomfield ● 96 95

0 10 20 30 40 50

35

100

34 98

Red   River

99

25. MISSIONS IN OKLAHOMA

The most powerful factor in the transformation of Indian culture—prior to individual allotments of land and the extensive mingling of native Americans with people of European descent in schools, churches, and business—were the missions. The process of helping Indians adjust to the demands of citizenship in an alien state was necessarily slow. Usually the missions were active in general education, and many of the notable school men were ministers of the gospel. Some of the best academies and elementary schools were established and maintained, wholly or in part, by religious organizations.

The missions brought men and women of superior character and intellectual attainment to the Indians. Isaac McCoy, Alfred Wright, Cyrus Kingsbury, Ebenezer Hotchkin, John H. Carr, and Samuel Austin Worcester are but a few of the great missionaries who gained the respect of the Indians and helped them to make difficult adjustments. The mission schools introduced the study of music and chromatic art, in both of which the Indians displayed great natural talent. A high standard of instruction in a wide range of subjects came to the Indian Territory from New England with the great teachers brought in by the missions.

Quite naturally, Indian missionaries were very effective when working among their own people. One of the greatest of the Seminoles in the Indian Territory was John Bemo, who devoted his life to the instruction of his people. Chief John Jumper resigned his office as chief executive of the Seminole tribe in 1877 to devote his full attention to his work as a preacher. John McIntosh, son of the Creek leader Chilly McIntosh, was welcomed as an Indian missionary among the tribes of the Southwest in the 1870's.

The missions were useful as inns for travelers in the Indian Territory. Many persons who came to the region of the Five Civilized Tribes, on business or as frontier tourists, were glad to find safety and comfort at Bloomfield, Asbury, Tuskahoma, or Sacred Heart. To a considerable extent the location of the missions determined the routes of roads and the movement of freight and persons.

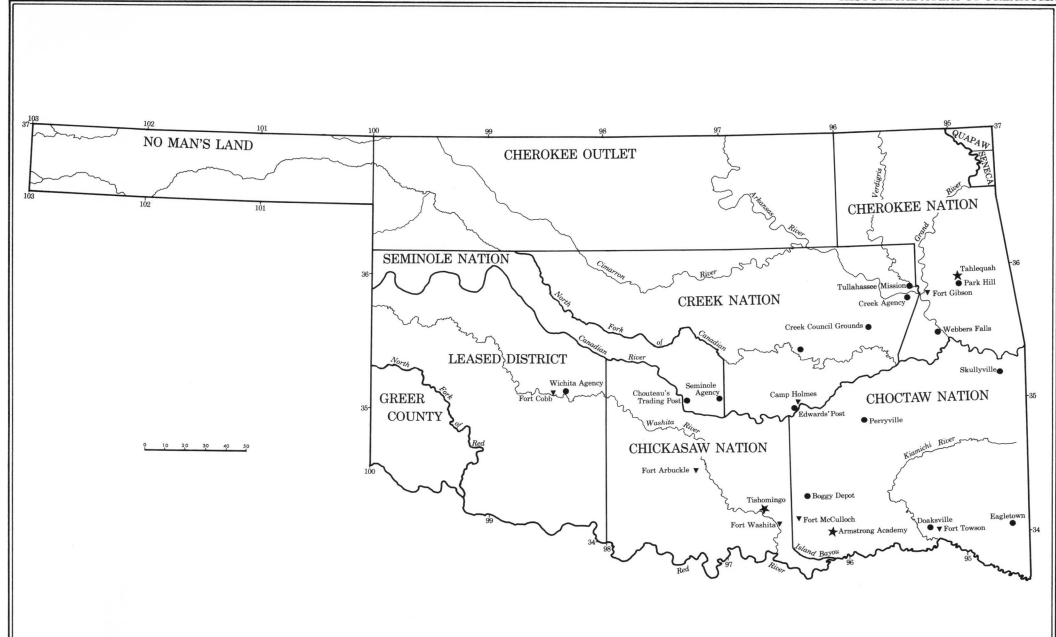

NO MAN'S LAND

CHEROKEE OUTLET

QUAPAW

SENECA

Verdigris

River

CHEROKEE NATION

Arkansas River

SEMINOLE NATION

Cimarron River

Grand

Tahlequah ★
● Park Hill

CREEK NATION

Tullahassee Mission ●
▼ Fort Gibson
Creek Agency ●

North

Fork

Creek Council Grounds ●

of

Canadian

Canadian River

●

● Webbers Falls

LEASED DISTRICT

North

Skullyville ●

Wichita Agency ●
Fort Cobb ▼

Chouteau's
Trading Post ●

Seminole
Agency ●

Camp Holmes ●
▼

CHOCTAW NATION

GREER
COUNTY

Fork

of

Red

Washita

River

Edwards' Post ●

● Perryville

CHICKASAW NATION

Kiamichi River

Fort Arbuckle ▼

● Boggy Depot

Tishomingo ★

Fort Washita ▼

▼ Fort McCulloch

★ Armstrong Academy

Doaksville ●
▼ Fort Towson

● Eagletown

Island Bayou

Red

River

0 10 20 30 40 50

INDIAN TERRITORY, 1855–1866

© 1976 by the University of Oklahoma Press

Major changes in the condition of the Chickasaws and Seminoles resulted from new treaties with the United States in 1855 and 1856. Secretary of the Interior Robert McClelland and Commissioner of Indian Affairs George W. Manypenny recognized the principle of self-government in dealing with the two smaller tribes.

By the terms of the Choctaw-Chickasaw agreement in June, 1855, Choctaw land west of the 98th meridian was leased to the United States to provide a home for the Wichitas and "such other tribes of Indians as the Government may desire to locate therein." For the lease, the United States agreed to pay $600,000 to the Choctaws and $200,000 to the Chickasaws.

In consideration of the establishment of a separate Chickasaw Nation, the tribe agreed to pay the Choctaws $150,000. The Chickasaw western boundary was the 98th meridian from the Canadian to the Red; and the eastern boundary followed Island Bayou from its mouth to the source of its eastern branch, thence due north to the Canadian River.

Each tribe was "secured in the unrestricted right of self-government, and full jurisdiction over persons and property within their respective limits," with the proviso that the Constitution of the United States should be recognized as the final authority.

The Seminole-Creek agreement in 1856 to maintain separate tribal organizations was a parallel movement toward self-government. The Seminole lands began with a line extending due north from the mouth of Pond Creek (Ock-hi-appo) on the Canadian to the North Fork of the Canadian; thence up that stream to the southern line of the Cherokee Outlet and west along that line to the 100th meridian; thence down the Canadian to the point of beginning.

Of great importance to the Seminoles was the provision for separate tribal government, which relieved them from the domination of the Creek majority. The United States agreed to construct an agency building for the Seminoles and to pay the tribe $90,000 to cover the losses involved in moving to the new location. The contract for the new agency building and council house was awarded to Henry Pope of Arkansas, and the buildings were constructed "one mile west of the eastern boundary of the Seminole country, and about two miles north of the road recently laid out by Lieutenant Beale."

The rectangle between the 100th meridian and the 103d meridian, from 36°30′ north latitude to the 37th parallel, was not claimed by any of the adjacent states or territories. The Texas Panhandle extended north to 36°30′; the state of Kansas had the 37th parallel as its southern boundary; the Cherokee Outlet extended west to the 100th meridian; and the eastern boundary of New Mexico was along the 103d meridian. Therefore, the rectangle that became the seventh county of the original Oklahoma Territory was frequently called "No Man's Land."

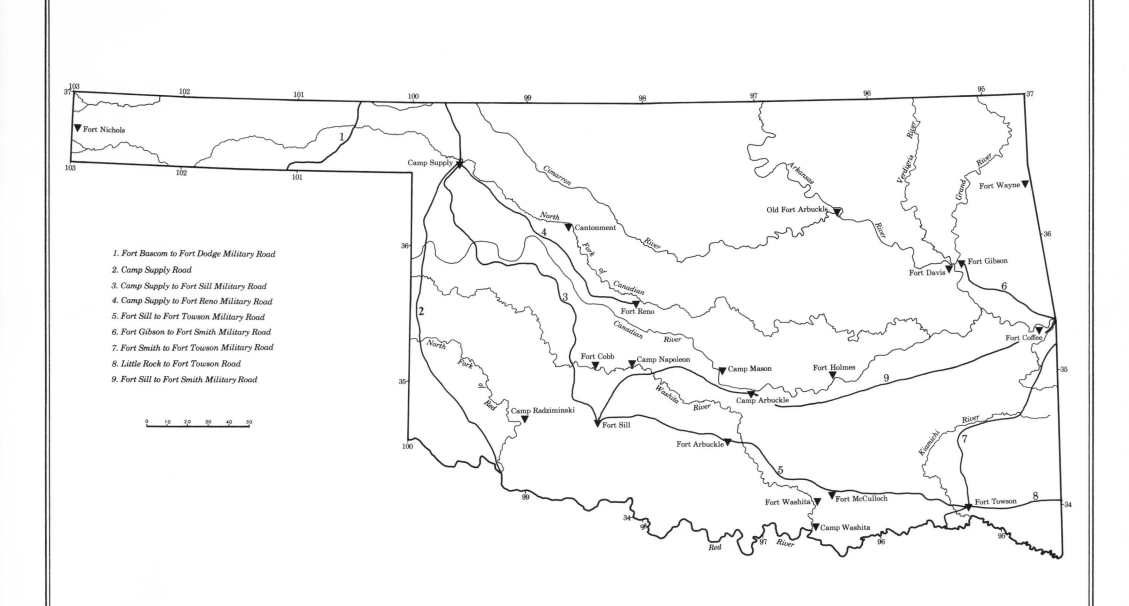

Fort Nichols

1. *Fort Bascom to Fort Dodge Military Road*

2. *Camp Supply Road*

3. *Camp Supply to Fort Sill Military Road*

4. *Camp Supply to Fort Reno Military Road*

5. *Fort Sill to Fort Towson Military Road*

6. *Fort Gibson to Fort Smith Military Road*

7. *Fort Smith to Fort Towson Military Road*

8. *Little Rock to Fort Towson Road*

9. *Fort Sill to Fort Smith Military Road*

0 10 20 30 40 50

Camp Supply

Cimarron

Cantonment

North Fork of Canadian River

Fort Reno

Canadian River

Fort Cobb

Camp Napoleon

Camp Mason

Fort Holmes

Washita River

Camp Arbuckle

Camp Radziminski

North Fork of Red

Fort Sill

Fort Arbuckle

Fort Washita

Fort McCulloch

Camp Washita

Red River

Old Fort Arbuckle

Arkansas River

Verdigris River

Grand River

Fort Wayne

Fort Davis

Fort Gibson

Fort Coffee

Kiamichi River

Fort Towson

FORTS, CAMPS, AND MILITARY ROADS, 1817–1876

© 1976 by the University of Oklahoma Press

27. FORTS, CAMPS, AND MILITARY ROADS, 1817–1876

Fort Smith, which was established at Belle Point near the Choctaw border in 1817, was one of the most important centers of defense and Indian administration of the entire frontier area. The Choctaw eastern boundary, by the terms of the Treaty of Washington in 1825, began on the Arkansas River "one hundred paces east of Fort Smith" and extended "due south" to the Red River. This imperfectly surveyed line between Arkansas and the Choctaw Nation has continued as a boundary to the present day, except for the "Choctaw Strip," which was purchased from the Choctaws and added to Arkansas, 1905–1909 (Map 61). The area thus annexed to the town of Fort Smith, Arkansas, approximately 130 acres in extent, contained the old fort.

Fort Gibson and Fort Towson were established in 1824 by Colonel Matthew Arbuckle. The first surveyed road in Oklahoma was the military route from Fort Smith to Fort Gibson, marked off in 1825. The road from Fort Smith to Fort Towson began as a blazed trail, marked by Robert Bean and Jesse Chisholm in 1832. During the previous year, the log structures at Fort Towson had been replaced by new stone buildings.

In 1834, Captain John Stuart established Fort Coffee on the right bank of the Arkansas, about ten miles above Belle Point. Captain Stuart, with a small cannon trained on the river, hoped to control the importation of whisky into the Indian country. His efforts were not entirely successful, however, since illegal shipments across the border by wagon could make deliveries to "whisky boats" farther upstream.

Fort Holmes on the Canadian near the mouth of Little River was established by Colonel Henry Dodge's dragoons as a hospital camp in 1834. Located near Edwards' trading post, it was sometimes called Fort Edwards. Camp Mason, a mile from the site of present-day Lexington, was the location of a great conference of Plains Indians, called together by Major R. B. Mason in 1835.

Fort Wayne (1838), Fort Washita (1842), Fort Arbuckle (1850–51), Camp Radziminski (1858), and Fort Cobb (1859) were other important military posts before the Civil War.

The most important Confederate forts during the Civil War in the Indian Territory were Fort Davis, on the south bank of the Arkansas opposite Three Forks, and Fort McCulloch, established by Albert Pike in 1862. Fort Davis was destroyed by Federal troops under Colonel W. A. Phillips on December 28, 1862. Albert Pike built Fort McCulloch so far south that it was practically out of the danger zone in the struggle for Indian Territory.

The establishment of military camps and permanent posts in the Indian Territory made roads a necessity and thus gave an impulse to opening the area to travelers and eventually to white settlement. Camp Supply was established by General Alfred Sully in 1868 at the mouth of Wolf Creek on the North Fork of the Canadian. A road to the Texas border and later roads to Fort Sill (1869) and Fort Reno (1874) gave Fort Supply a degree of permanence, in spite of flimsy barracks hastily constructed during a winter of stormy weather.

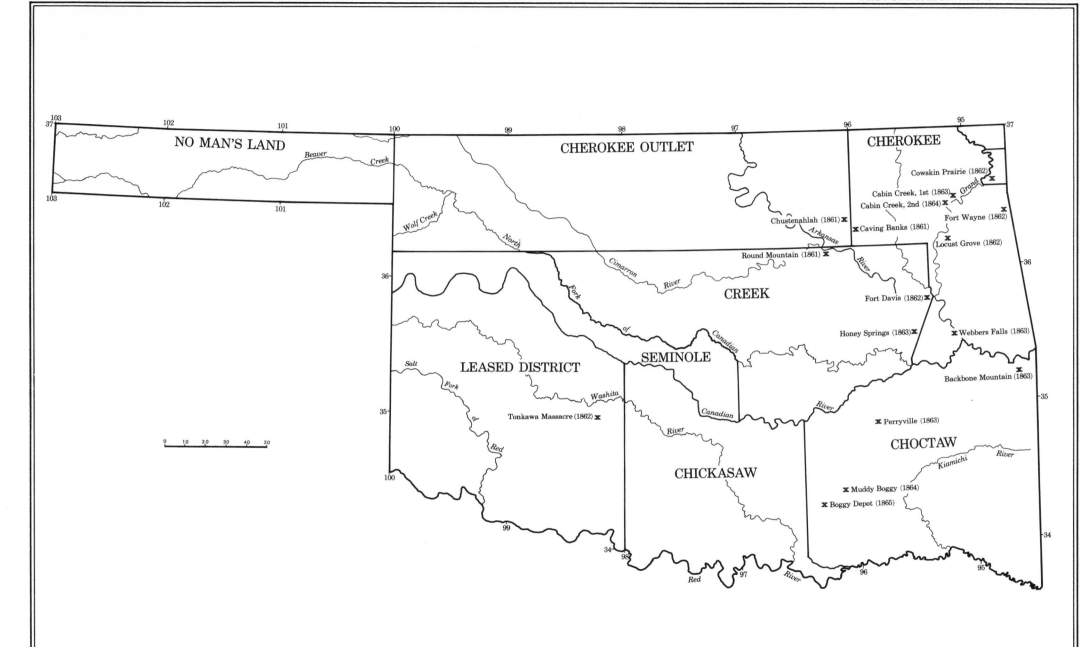

NO MAN'S LAND

Beaver *Creek*

CHEROKEE OUTLET

CHEROKEE

Cowskin Prairie (1862) ✖

Cabin Creek, 1st (1863) ✖
Cabin Creek, 2nd (1864) ✖
Fort Wayne (1862) ✖

Chustenahlah (1861) ✖
✖ Caving Banks (1861)

Locust Grove (1862) ✖

Round Mountain (1861) ✖

Wolf Creek

North

Cimarron *River*

Arkansas *River*

Grand

CREEK

Fort Davis (1862) ✖

Honey Springs (1863) ✖

✖ Webbers Falls (1863)

Fork

of

Canadian

LEASED DISTRICT

SEMINOLE

Salt

Fork

Washita

Canadian

River

Canadian

Tonkawa Massacre (1862) ✖

Backbone Mountain (1863) ✖

✖ Perryville (1863)

CHOCTAW

Red

River

River

CHICKASAW

Kiamichi *River*

✖ Muddy Boggy (1864)

✖ Boggy Depot (1865)

Red

River

0 10 20 30 40 50

CIVIL WAR BATTLE SITES

© 1976 by the University of Oklahoma Press

28. CIVIL WAR BATTLE SITES

The Civil War in the Indian Territory found citizens of the Five Civilized Tribes sharply divided on the question of support for the Confederacy. In the final analysis, it was geographical position that determined the attitude of each tribe. The Choctaws, wedged between Texas and Arkansas, had little choice, and the larger tribe on Red River tipped the balance for the Chickasaws, also, in favor of the Confederacy.

Partisan conflict dating back to the dispute over westward removal pushed the Cherokees and Creeks toward internal conflict. When John Ross of the Cherokees took a strong stand for neutrality, the Ridge-Boudinot faction of the tribe found alliance with the Confederacy more attractive. Inclination of the McIntosh family toward giving Creek support to the South stiffened the determination of Opothle Yahola in the direction of loyalty to the Union.

The Seminole tribe, which had been united in opposition to westward removal, became divided through the influence of Creek partisans and the vigor of Confederate diplomacy.

Nearly all Choctaws and Chickasaws supported the Confederacy until its final destruction. The Cherokees, Creeks, and Seminoles, after an early movement toward cooperation with the Confederacy, divided into hostile parties. Eventually the Creeks enlisted 1,575 men in the Confederate armies and 1,675 men in the Union forces. Union Cherokee soldiers numbered 2,220 and Confederate Cherokees about 1,400. Colonel John Jumper's Confederate Seminoles were probably outnumbered by Seminole recruits who fought for the Union under John Chupco and Halleck Tustenuggee.

There were no great battles in the Indian Territory to compare, in numbers of soldiers engaged, with the decisive battles in the East, or even with Wilson's Creek, Pea Ridge, and Westport in the West. There was hard fighting, however, at Round Mountain and Chustenahlah, Locust Grove and Fort Wayne, Cabin Creek and Honey Springs.

Most destructive was the irregular fighting of partisan groups—raids, the flight and pursuit of civilian bands, the burning of homes and schools, and the readjustments to refugee camps. No people in the United States suffered heavier losses than the Cherokee, Creek, and Seminole tribes, where the bitterness of internal strife was added to the destruction of large-scale war.

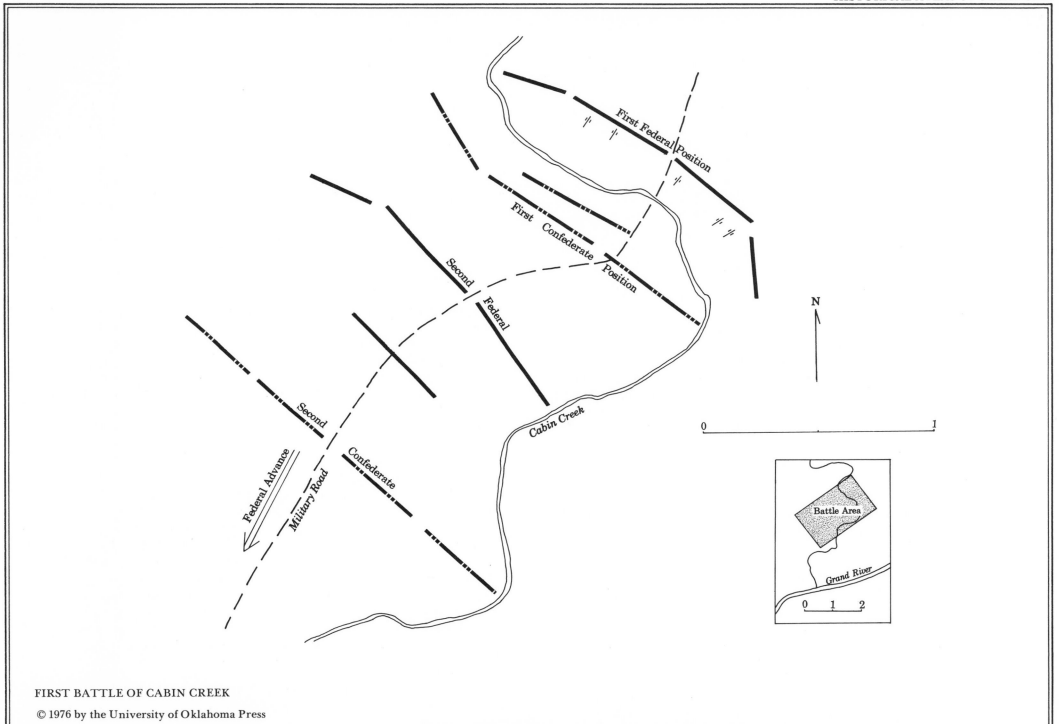

First Federal Position

First Confederate Position

Second Federal

Second Confederate

Federal Advance

Military Road

Cabin Creek

N

0   1

Battle Area

Grand River

0   1   2

FIRST BATTLE OF CABIN CREEK

© 1976 by the University of Oklahoma Press

29. FIRST BATTLE OF CABIN CREEK

The campaign which included the fight at Cabin Creek on July 2 and the battle at Honey Springs on July 17, 1863, gave the Union forces strategic command of the Indian Territory and led directly to the capture of Fort Smith on the border of Arkansas. The clash at Cabin Creek was primarily for possession of General Blunt's supply train.

Both of the Indian Territory commanders, General Douglas H. Cooper, Confederate, and Major General James G. Blunt, Union, understood fully the importance of the Federal supply train from Kansas. To protect the 218 mule-wagons and 40 ox-wagons, laden with provisions and military goods that were an absolute necessity for the campaign, the Union commander ordered an escort of 1,000 soldiers. Before the wagon train moved south from Baxter Springs, Major John A. Foreman was sent out from Fort Gibson—with 600 mounted men and one howitzer—to serve as reinforcements for the escort.

Stand Watie, the boldest and most resourceful of the Confederate Indian leaders, took a position at the Cabin Creek crossing on the military road. Prisoners captured by Major Foreman's party reported Watie's force at 1,600 men, but the estimate was high—probably his total was nearer 1,400. General William C. Cabell had come over from Fort Smith, however, with 1,500 men, infantry and cavalry. If Cabell's force could cross Grand River (swollen by heavy rains) to join Stand Watie, their combined strength would make capture of the wagon train almost certain.

Colonel J. M. Williams, in charge of the Union supplies, was compelled by high water to camp for one night before attempting the Cabin Creek ford. On the morning of July 2, after taking soundings in the ford, Williams opened fire with three artillery units and shelled the Confederate position for forty minutes. Foreman then advanced with the Third Indian Regiment to cross the creek. When this party had almost reached the south bank, a line of Confederate Indians suddenly opened fire from a trench concealed under low-hanging willow boughs. Major Foreman was wounded and his men were thrown into confusion.

The second Federal line, composed of Kansas black infantry, moved forward rapidly and broke through the Confederate battle line. Stand Watie's troops rallied and formed a second line, but Colonel Williams came up with his reserve units, and Lieutenant R. C. Philbrick charged the new Confederate position. Stand Watie's army scattered in all directions—to minimize capture—and their leader rode south with two companions to report the failure to General Douglas Cooper at Honey Springs.

Cabell's Confederate party on the left bank of Grand River had not been able to cross. The Federal wagon train completed the crossing of Cabin Creek and moved on to Fort Gibson with the precious supplies.

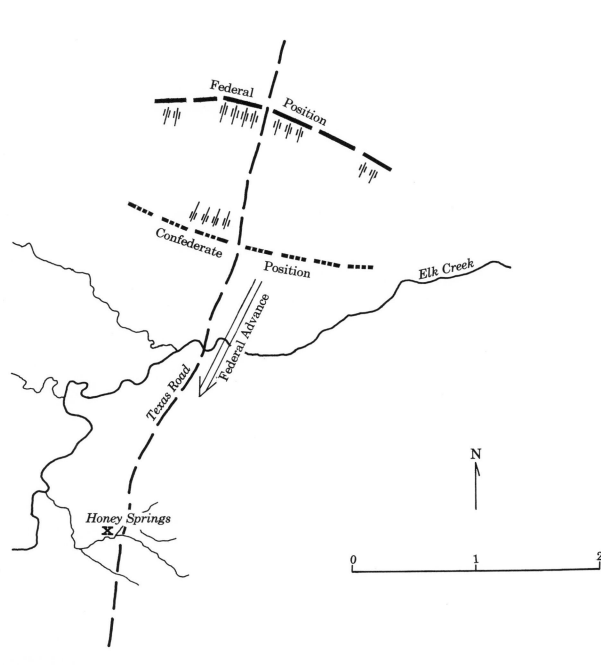

Federal Position

Confederate Position

Elk Creek

Texas Road

Federal Advance

N

Honey Springs
X

0   1   2

BATTLE OF HONEY SPRINGS
© 1976 by the University of Oklahoma Press

30. BATTLE OF HONEY SPRINGS

General Blunt came south to Fort Gibson after his supply train arrived there. He knew that General Douglas Cooper was less than one day's march from the Arkansas River with the principal Confederate force of the area, and that General Cabell could join him from Fort Smith with a force of 1,500 men at short notice. From Kansas, Blunt brought two additional twelve-pound howitzers and a party of 600 men under Colonel William R. Judson. In his introduction of Blunt to the officers at Fort Gibson, Colonel Phillips reviewed his military record: victories over the Confederates at Newtonia, Missouri; Cane Hill and Prairie Grove, Arkansas; and Fort Wayne in the Indian Territory. He had suffered no defeats.

General Blunt moved rapidly to prevent combination of the two Confederate forces. With four pieces of light artillery he crossed the Arkansas River, thirteen miles above the mouth of the Grand, and drove Cooper's advance guard back to Honey Springs. On July 16 he crossed his entire army to the south bank. At 10:00 P.M. he was ready to march south, and at daybreak he made contact with the Confederate outpost about five miles from Elk Creek and drove the small force back to Cooper's battle line.

Blunt's command included three regiments of Indian Home Guards—Seminoles, Creeks, and others; the Second Colorado Infantry; the First Kansas Infantry (colored); the Sixth Kansas Cavalry; the Third Wisconsin Cavalry; the Second Kansas Battery; and the Hopkins Kansas Battery. The Confederate force is summarized in Cooper's orders of July 14, in which he assigned Colonel Stand Watie to command of the brigade's right wing—the First and Second Cherokee Regiments; Colonel D. N. McIntosh to the left wing—First and Second Creek Regiments; and Colonel Thomas C. Bass to the center—Twenty-ninth Texas Cavalry, Twentieth Texas (dismounted cavalry), Fifth Texas Partisan Rangers, and Lee's Light Battery.

Each of the commanders overestimated the numerical strength of the enemy in the official report. To Douglas Cooper, the scant 3,000 men in Blunt's army became "at least six thousand." In fact, the Confederate force had the larger number, but the Union Army had better artillery and more dependable ammunition. General Cooper believed that he lost the battle on account of "worthless" ammunition. Both armies provided many examples of cool, steady valor and of reckless, raw courage.

The Confederate line held for a time at Elk Creek. In the words of General Blunt's report, "Fighting was unremitting and terrific" for two hours during that phase of the battle. Then General Cooper's center began to fall back, and soon the withdrawal became a rout. With the Confederates in full retreat and the pursuit slackening because of exhausted cavalry horses, Blunt ordered his men to stop and prepare a meal. They ate supper on the battlefield, making use of captured provisions— flour, bacon, and beef.

Late in the afternoon General Cabell arrived with 1,500 mounted men and four pieces of artillery, after a hard march from Fort Smith. His force was in no condition to attack Blunt's victorious troops, however, and the campaign was practically ended.

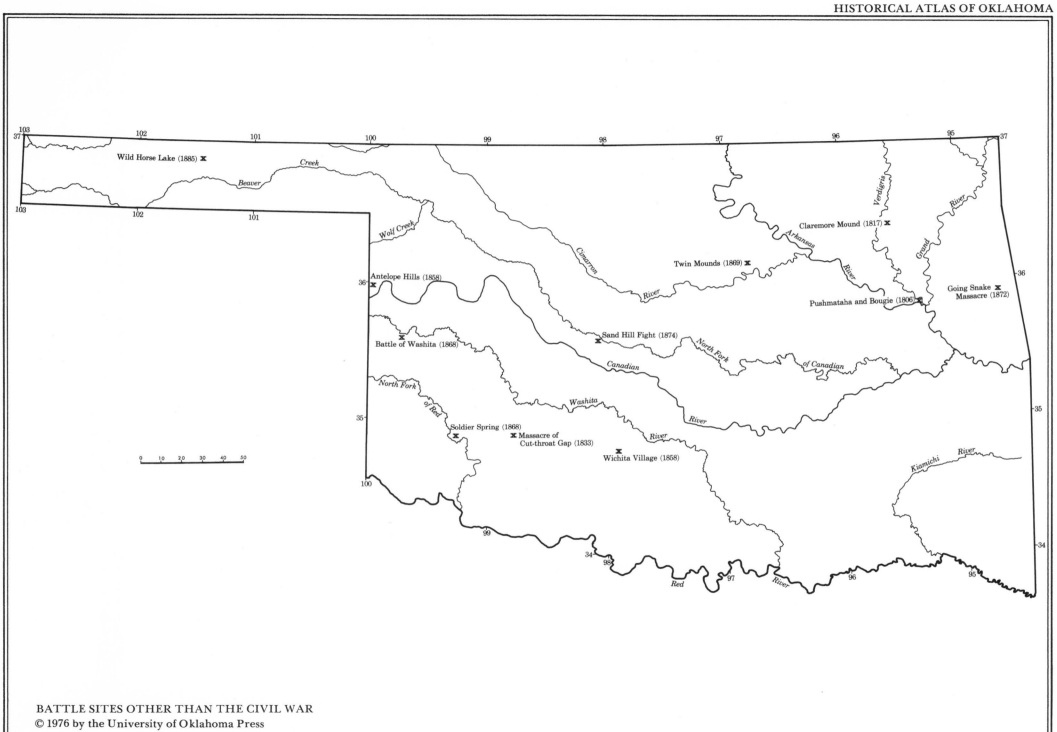

BATTLE SITES OTHER THAN THE CIVIL WAR
© 1976 by the University of Oklahoma Press

31. BATTLE SITES OTHER THAN THE CIVIL WAR

Early Oklahoma, in common with all Indian frontiers in America, saw occasional armed conflict between the United States and tribal war parties. In some instances there were hostilities between tribes, or between traders and Indian raiders.

Joseph Bogy (or Bougie), a French trader at Arkansas Post, came up to Three Forks in 1806 with goods valued at $10,000 for trade with the Osages. Chief Pushmataha of the Choctaws, regarding the enterprise an Osage project since warriors of the hostile tribe accompanied the trader, attacked Bogy's party above the Verdigris landing, scattered the escort, and seized the trade goods.

At Claremore Mound in 1817 a party of Cherokees routed Osage defenders and killed all who did not escape by flight. After the raid, the Osages returned to bury their dead, one of whom was Chief Clermont.

On September 15, 1858, Captain Earl Van Dorn marched north from Texas with one infantry and four cavalry companies. The Comanches were in camp near Wichita Village, which was situated about five miles southeast of present-day Rush Springs. Captain Van Dorn attacked the camp at dawn on October 11 and dispersed the Comanches with heavy losses.

Among the armed clashes at Twin Mounds in eastern Payne County was a fight in 1869 between Texas Rangers and a party of cattle thieves. Material remains of the "battle" and others in the vicinity have been the source of confusion in recent studies of the battle sites. Rumors of buried treasure are common, and some scholars have placed the first major clash of the Civil War in the Indian Territory at the Twin Mounds. The theory on which this error is based ignores the slowness with which Opothle Yahola was compelled to move—retarded by the presence of women and children in his camp—and overlooks also the specific language of the official reports.

The Battle of the Washita (Map 32) was one of the major clashes between United States troops and Indian warriors on the Southern Plains. Chief Black Kettle (Moke-ta-ra-to) of the Cheyennes, after trying without success to obtain a promise of safety for his band, had informed General Hazen at Fort Cobb that his people were going into winter camp on the Washita near the site of Cheyenne. Black Kettle's camp was made up of 180 lodges; but down along the river, within ten or twelve miles, were more than 400 additional lodges, in which Kiowas, Comanches, Apaches, and Arapahoes had settled for the winter. In all, there were no fewer than 600 warriors and several thousand Indians, including women and children.

General Philip Sheridan ordered General George A. Custer to ride south from Fort Supply to attack Black Kettle's band. The surprise attack came at dawn on the cold morning of November 27, 1868. The 800 mounted soldiers in Custer's party, with 40 sharpshooters held in reserve at a carefully chosen spot, charged through the Cheyenne camp. The Indians had taken no steps toward uniting into a defensive unit the separate bands encamped along the Washita. Custer prudently withdrew his force when the rout of the Cheyennes was complete, and he lived to fight again, eight years later, on the Little Big Horn in Montana.

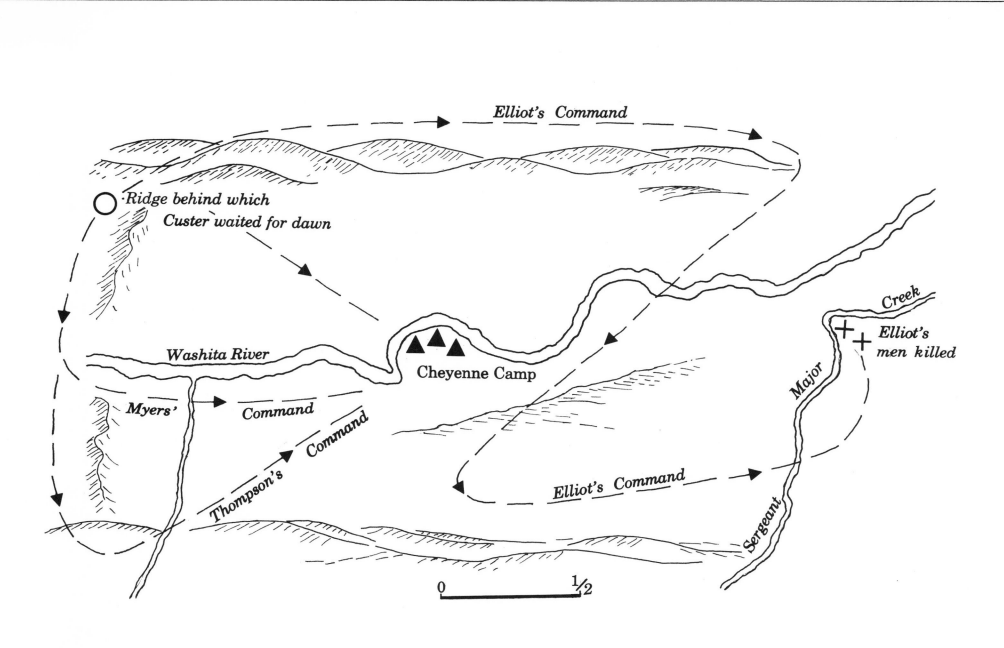

Elliot's Command

Ridge behind which
Custer waited for dawn

Washita River

Cheyenne Camp

Myers' *Command*

Thompson's Command

Creek

Elliot's
men killed

Major

Sergeant

Elliot's Command

0 ½

BATTLE·OF THE WASHITA
© 1976 by the University of Oklahoma Press

32. BATTLE OF THE WASHITA

Indians on the Great Plains regularly avoided military campaigns during winter months. Lacking grain for their horses, the most active raiders preferred the comfort of the lodge to matching their ponies, subsisting on meager winter pasturage, against the grain-fed mounts of the United States Cavalry. Furthermore, young warriors sometimes sought refuge in the winter camp of a peaceful friend. United States Army commanders were provoked to desperation by the elusive tactics of hostile Indian leaders.

The Battle of the Washita was the result of Black Kettle's (Moke-ta-ra-to's) loyalty to Indian friends who were wanted by United States officers, together with determined winter campaigning by General George A. Custer and the difficulty of communication between the two races. In effect, it was a surprise assault of United States troops upon a camp whose leader was well disposed toward the authority of the United States. Black Kettle had shown interest in the Peace Commission of 1867 and a strong tendency toward cooperation with N. G. Taylor, the Indian commissioner.

However, Custer had orders from General Philip Sheridan to conduct a cold-weather campaign. The blizzard that descended upon the Southwest in November, 1868, offered the earliest opportunity for trial of the new policy, and Custer was the man chosen to attack the Cheyennes.

With Custer twelve troops of the Seventh Cavalry, a party of about 800 men, rode south. Ben Clark, California Joe, Hard Rope the Osage, and Jimmy Morrison—all first-rate scouts—accompanied the soldiers. Custer knew the extent of the Cheyenne camp before he attacked. Two young Cheyenne raiders,

Crow Neck and Black Shield, had recently come back from Kansas with fresh scalps as trophies. The young men were confident that white troops would not venture an attack on the camp during cold weather, but Black Kettle was in doubt and thought it best to post a sentry.

Approaching from the north, Custer waited for dawn behind a low hill. He divided his command into four bands of about 200 men each. Major Joel Elliot was sent downstream nearly three miles to approach the camp from the east. Captain William Thompson cut south across the Washita to come in from the southwest. The soldiers under Colonel Edward Myers advanced on the right, crossing the stream to approach the Cheyenne camp on the south bank as Custer's band moved in directly from the northwest. With Custer rode forty sharpshooters under Lieutenant W. W. Cook.

The savage barking of dogs aroused Double Wolf, the sentinel, who had slipped inside a lodge to warm himself; but the Cheyenne warriors did not get warning soon enough to catch their ponies and mount. A rear guard was outnumbered four to one. Black Kettle did manage to get on his pony and help his wife to mount behind him, but a volley from Cook's sharpshooters killed them both.

Custer learned from a captive, Black Kettle's sister, that there were one thousand Indian lodges farther down the Washita. He determined to pull out without pursuing the fugitives farther. His report showed that he had killed 103 warriors, 16 women, and "a few" children. The United States force lost highly valued officers and men, including Major Elliot, Sergeant-Major Walter Kennedy, and Captain Louis Hamilton.

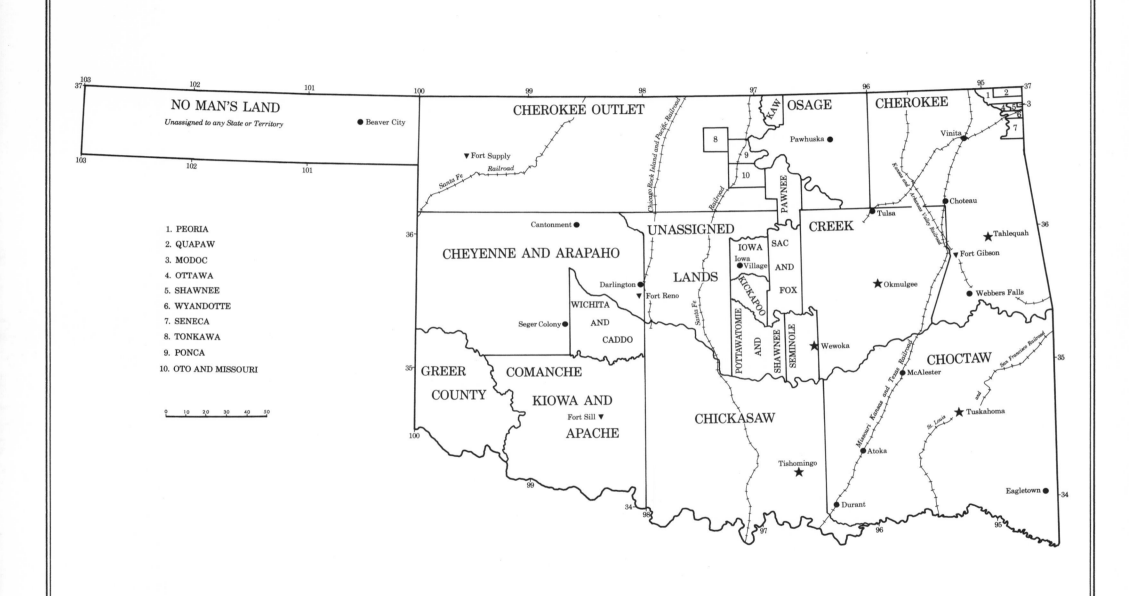

NO MAN'S LAND

Unassigned to any State or Territory ● Beaver City

CHEROKEE OUTLET

▼ Fort Supply

Santa Fe Railroad

1. PEORIA
2. QUAPAW
3. MODOC
4. OTTAWA
5. SHAWNEE
6. WYANDOTTE
7. SENECA
8. TONKAWA
9. PONCA
10. OTO AND MISSOURI

KAW   OSAGE

CHEROKEE

8   Pawhuska ●

9   Vinita ●

10   PAWNEE

● Choteau

Cantonment ●   UNASSIGNED   CREEK   Tulsa ●

CHEYENNE AND ARAPAHO   ★ Tahlequah

36   LANDS   IOWA   SAC   ▼ Fort Gibson

Iowa ● Village   AND   ★ Okmulgee

Darlington ●   KICKAPOO   FOX

▼ Fort Reno   ● Webbers Falls

WICHITA

Seger Colony ●   AND   POTTAWATOMIE

CADDO   AND   SEMINOLE   ★ Wewoka

SHAWNEE

GREER   COMANCHE   CHOCTAW

COUNTY   KIOWA AND   McAlester ●

Fort Sill ▼   CHICKASAW   ★ Tuskahoma

APACHE

● Atoka

Tishomingo ★

Eagletown ●

Durant ●

INDIAN TERRITORY, 1866–1889

© 1976 by the University of Oklahoma Press

33. INDIAN TERRITORY, 1866–1889

New treaties concluded in Washington, D.C., in 1866 with each of the Five Civilized Tribes, in addition to providing for the abolition of slavery and the recognition of citizens' rights for the freedmen of the Indian tribes, provided land in the western part of Indian Territory for the settlement of tribes from Kansas, Nebraska, and elsewhere.

The Choctaw-Chickasaw treaty ceded the Leased District to the United States for $300,000. The Creek treaty ceded the western half of Creek lands—3,250,000 acres—for $975,168—approximately 30 cents an acre. The Seminoles ceded all their land—2,169,080 acres, for $325,362—15 cents an acre. The Seminoles further agreed to purchase 200,000 acres of land, a part of the tract recently acquired by the United States from the Creeks. (Actually, the Seminoles purchased an additional tract in 1881, enlarging their new home to 375,000 acres.)

The Cherokee treaty provided that friendly Indian tribes might be settled on the Cherokee Outlet at a price agreed upon by the Cherokees and the purchasers. The Cherokee Strip and the Neutral Lands (Map 22), both in Kansas, were to be sold to the highest bidder for the benefit of the Cherokees, at an average price no lower than $1.25 an acre.

Settlements on land ceded by the Creeks and Seminoles also were limited to "such other civilized Indians as the United States may choose to settle thereon."

Each of the Five Civilized Tribes agreed to admit two railroads—one rail line running east to west, the other north to south across tribal lands.

Tribal settlements in the Cherokee Outlet in 1889 were as follows: east of the Arkansas River, Osage and Kaw; west of the Arkansas, Oto and Missouri, Ponca, and Tonkawa. On Creek and Seminole land were the Sac and Fox, Pottawatomie and Shawnee, Iowa, and Kickapoo tribes.

The Comanche, Kiowa, and Apache tribes occupied a reservation more than 3,000,000 acres in extent in the southeastern part of the Leased District. The Cheyenne and Arapaho Reservation was west of the 98th meridian and south of the Cherokee Outlet.

The region between the North Fork of the Red River and the 100th meridian, about 2,300 square miles in extent, was still in dispute between Texas and the United States. Texas had organized the area as Greer County and admitted more than 8,000 homesteaders.

The Cherokee Outlet comprised over 6,000,000 acres not occupied by Indian groups. "No Man's Land" had no legal settlers. Greer County was settled only in part. A fourth region, the "Unassigned Lands," contained 1,887,796 acres, which became the first area opened to white settlement in 1889. It was near the center of the present state.

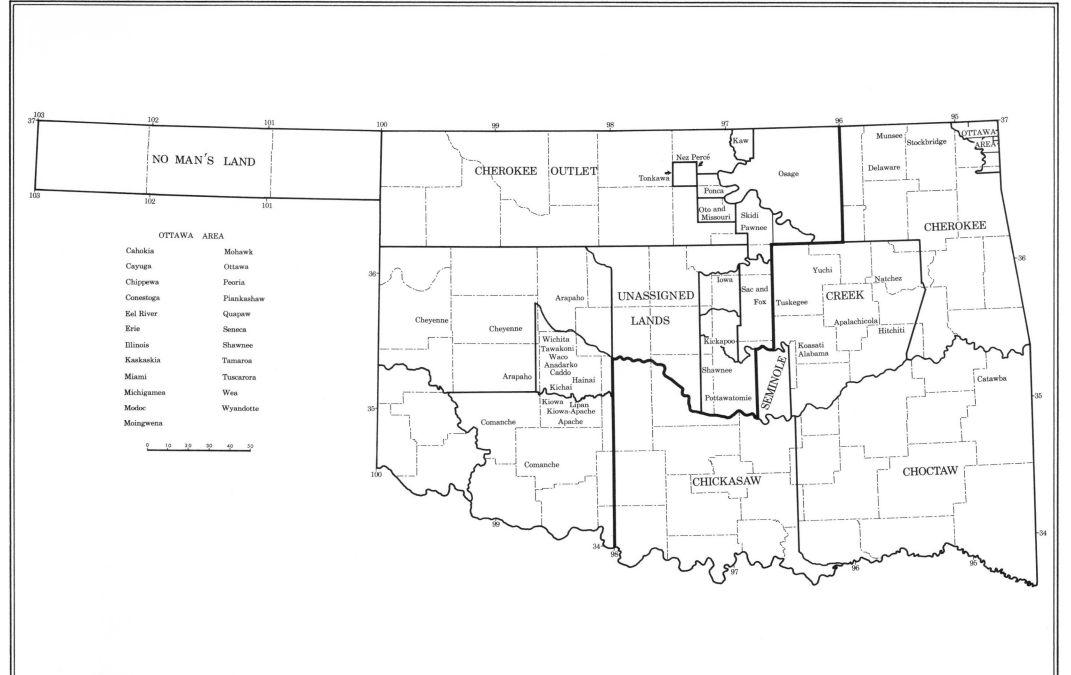

NO MAN'S LAND

CHEROKEE OUTLET

Kaw

Nez Percé

Tonkawa

Ponca

Osage

Munsee
Stockbridge

Delaware

OTTAWA
AREA

CHEROKEE

Oto and
Missouri

Skidi
Pawnee

OTTAWA AREA

Cahokia	Mohawk
Cayuga	Ottawa
Chippewa	Peoria
Conestoga	Piankashaw
Eel River	Quapaw
Erie	Seneca
Illinois	Shawnee
Kaskaskia	Tamaroa
Miami	Tuscarora
Michigamea	Wea
Modoc	Wyandotte
Moingwena	

Iowa

UNASSIGNED

LANDS

Sac and
Fox

Tuskegee

Yuchi

CREEK

Natchez

Arapaho

Cheyenne

Cheyenne

Apalachicola
Hitchiti

Wichita
Tawakoni
Waco
Anadarko
Caddo
Hainai
Kichai

Kickapoo

Koasati
Alabama

Arapaho

Shawnee

SEMINOLE

Catawba

Kiowa Lipan
Kiowa-Apache
Apache

Pottawatomie

Comanche

Comanche

CHICKASAW

CHOCTAW

0 10 20 30 40 50

TRIBAL LOCATIONS IN OKLAHOMA

© 1976 by the University of Oklahoma Press

34. TRIBAL LOCATIONS IN OKLAHOMA

The Indian Removal Act of 1830 was followed by many cessions of land and removals of other eastern Indians besides the Five Civilized Tribes. In 1831 the Senecas of the Sandusky Valley exchanged their Ohio land for 67,000 acres lying north of the new Cherokee Nation. Soon afterward a mixed band of Senecas and Shawnees ceded their land near Lewiston, Ohio, and received 60,000 acres adjoining the Seneca tract in Indian Territory. In 1833 a band of Quapaws moved from the Red River to a tract of 96,000 acres, also north and east of the Cherokees.

After the Civil War space was found in the district of northeastern Indian Territory for additional bands: Ottawas, Weas, Peorias, Kaskaskias, Piankashaws, and Miamis. Fragments of other tribes affiliated with these bands were brought in with them in some instances. The little Oregon band, the Modocs, brought in from Fort McPherson, Nebraska, in 1873, was settled on a tract of 4,040 acres, purchased from the Shawnees.

Two hundred Wyandotte Indians moved in with the Senecas in 1857. Driven north by guerrilla bands during the Civil War, both Senecas and Wyandottes returned in 1865. Two years later the Wyandottes obtained a reservation of 21,246 acres along the northern boundary of the Seneca tract.

Detached groups of Indians other than the Five Tribes set-tled permanently on the lands of these Indians in eastern Indian Territory from time to time. For example, the Choctaws admitted nineteen Catawbas from North Carolina in 1851 and granted full rights of citizenship to fourteen of them in 1853. Other members of the tribe settled in the Creek Nation. Catawbas belong to the Siouan linguistic stock, detached from kindred tribes on the Plains before written history appeared in that part of North America. The Biloxis of the Gulf Coast and the Winnebagos of Wisconsin are other Siouan tribes found by Europeans east of the Mississippi.

Two groups of Delaware Indians live in Oklahoma. A band from the Brazos in Texas came to the Wichita Agency in 1859. Their descendants live in communities near Anadarko and Carnegie. Another band moved by contract into the Cherokee Nation from their reservation in Kansas in 1867.

The Creek Indians, of Muskhogean linguistic stock, were accustomed from early times to adopting fragment groups into the tribe. The Creek Nation in Oklahoma contained Indians from the Koasati, Hitchiti, Natchez, Apalachicola, Alabama, Tuskegee, and Yuchi (Euchee) tribes. All of these except the Yuchis belong to the Muskhogean language group.

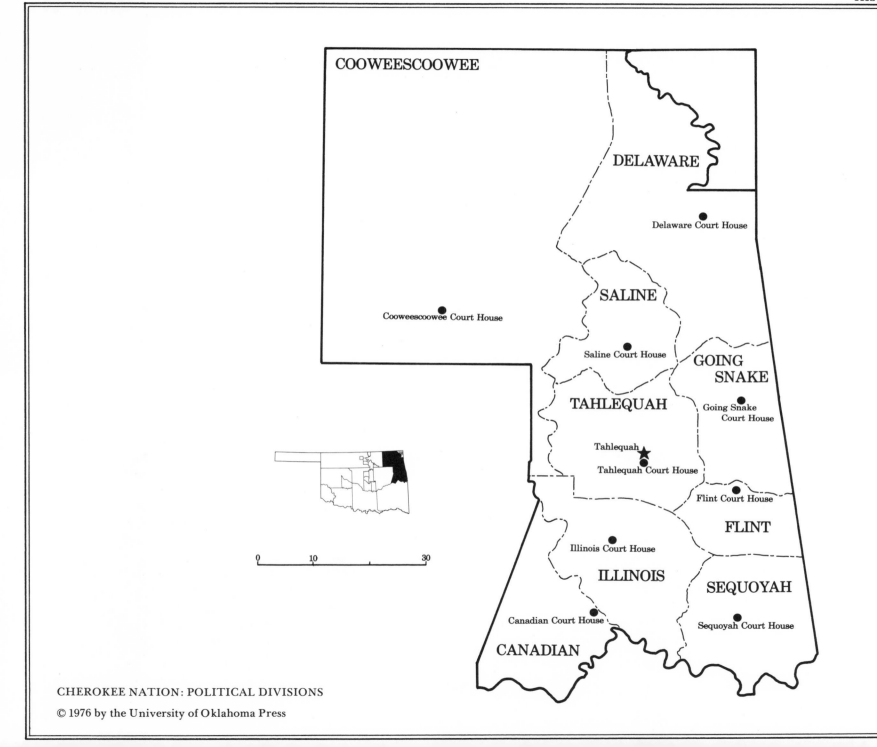

COOWEESCOOWEE

DELAWARE

Delaware Court House

SALINE

Cooweescoowee Court House

Saline Court House

GOING
SNAKE

TAHLEQUAH

Going Snake
Court House

Tahlequah ★
Tahlequah Court House

Flint Court House

FLINT

Illinois Court House

ILLINOIS

SEQUOYAH

Canadian Court House

Sequoyah Court House

CANADIAN

0   10   30

CHEROKEE NATION: POLITICAL DIVISIONS

© 1976 by the University of Oklahoma Press

35. CHEROKEE NATION: POLITICAL DIVISIONS

The Cherokee Constitution of 1839, written at Tahlequah after the followers of John Ross were removed from their eastern homes, was based upon the basic law adopted twelve years earlier in Georgia. The legislative department was composed of two houses, the National Committee and the Council. (After the amendments of 1866 the upper house was called the Senate and the lower house the Council. The legislature as a whole was officially known as the National Council.)

Two members were elected from each district for two-year terms in the upper house, and three members, also for two years, in the lower house. After 1866, representation in the Council was based upon the number of voters in each district. No district had fewer than two members unless it contained fewer than one hundred voters. In 1889, Saline, Sequoyah, and Flint each elected three councilors; Canadian and Going Snake, four each; Tahlequah and Illinois, five each; Delaware, six; and Cooweescoowee, seven. Thus the Council had forty members and the Senate eighteen—two from each of the nine districts.

The executive department was headed by a principal chief elected for a term of four years. Judges of the Supreme Court and inferior courts were elected by the National Council to serve four-year terms. Trial by jury was guaranteed to every person accused of a crime.

Principal Chiefs of the Cherokee Nation, 1866–1907

1866–67	William P. Ross
1867–72	Lewis Downing
1872–75	William P. Ross
1875–79	Charles Thompson
1879–87	Dennis Wolf Bushyhead
1887–91	Joel Bryan Mayes
1891–95	C. Johnson Harris
1895–99	Samuel Houston Mayes
1899–1903	Thomas Mitchell Buffington
1903–1907	William C. Rogers

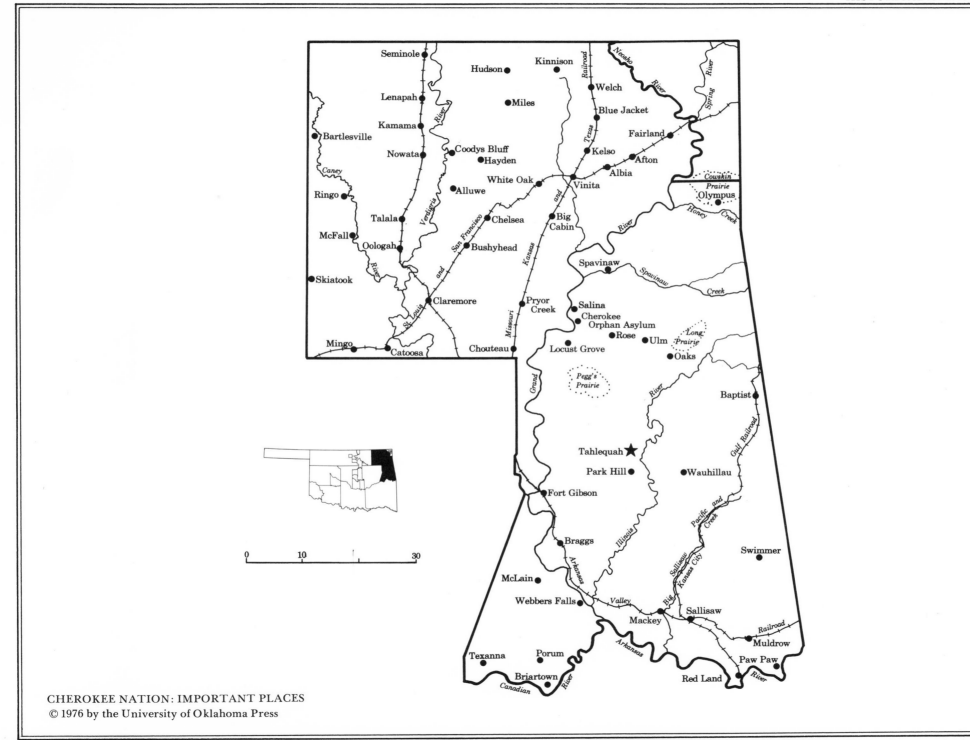

CHEROKEE NATION: IMPORTANT PLACES
© 1976 by the University of Oklahoma Press

36. CHEROKEE NATION: IMPORTANT PLACES

By 1889 the Cherokee Nation had four railroad lines and a rapidly growing population. White intruders were more numerous than Indians. Towns were located principally along the streams and the railroads. Vinita, Sallisaw, and Claremore enjoyed the advantages of two railroads, and the towns in the vicinity of Fort Gibson had both railroad and river connections.

Many of the towns were places of historic interest. Tahlonteeskee, the old capital of the Cherokees "West," no longer flourished; but Tahlequah, capital of the united tribe on the Illinois River, and nearby Park Hill held many remembrances for the older Indians.

The Three Forks area, where the Verdigris and the Grand empty into the Arkansas, was a region of long-continued exchange of goods between Indians and Europeans, important to Cherokees, Creeks, Seminoles, Osages, and many other Indians, as well as to traders and white settlers.

Settlers were moving to locations near John Bartle's store on Caney River, and Bartlesville was marked for growth and increasing trade. Settlers at Coodys Bluff crossed the Verdigris to trade in the stores at Nowata, which also had "spring-wagon customers" from Lenapah and Talala. Webbers Falls on the Arkansas, Locust Grove and Salina north of Fort Gibson on the Grand, and Briartown on the Canadian were old and well-established trade centers. Briartown, the Cherokee settlement farthest south, was Stand Watie's place of refuge during the Civil War when his daring raids north of the Arkansas River caused him to be sought by overwhelming military forces.

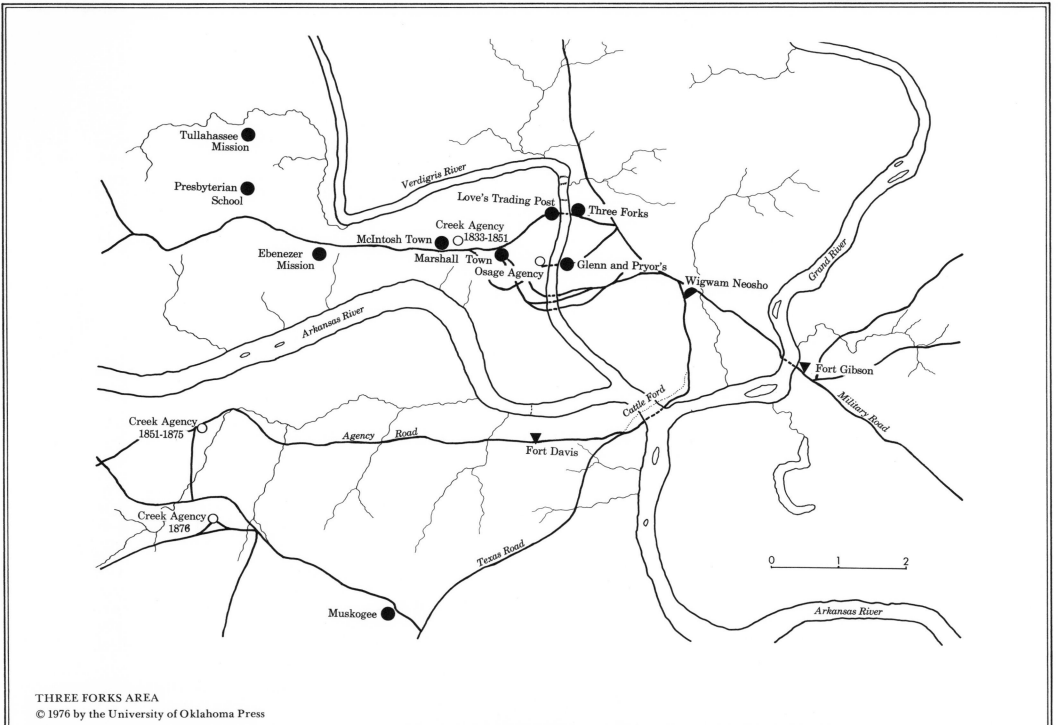

Tullahassee Mission

Presbyterian School

Verdigris River

Love's Trading Post

Three Forks

Creek Agency 1833-1851

McIntosh Town

Ebenezer Mission

Marshall Town

Osage Agency

Glenn and Pryor's

Wigwam Neosho

Grand River

Arkansas River

Fort Gibson

Military Road

Cattle Ford

Creek Agency 1851-1875

Agency Road

Fort Davis

Creek Agency 1876

Texas Road

Muskogee

Arkansas River

0   1   2

THREE FORKS AREA
© 1976 by the University of Oklahoma Press

No place in Oklahoma has a stronger appeal for students of history than the area surrounding Three Forks. For many years it was the center of exchange for products of the trappers—Indian, French, American pioneers, and others. Trading posts were established by men whose names were known in St. Louis and New Orleans, as well as to the Indians, who seldom ventured from the security of their remote homeland. Colonel Hugh Glenn and Jacob Fowler knew the place as traders and pioneer caravan leaders on the long trail to New Mexico. Nathaniel Pryor, the noted explorer of the upper Missouri with Lewis and Clark, was the partner of Colonel Glenn for a few years. Brand and Barbour, French and Rutherford, Jean Pierre Chouteau, Auguste Pierre Chouteau, Jesse B. Turley, and Benjamin Hawkins, a leader of the McIntosh Creeks, were all identified with the trading activities of the Three Forks area.

Fort Gibson, constructed in 1824, gave an impetus to trade and road building in the Three Forks region. Fort Davis had a brief existence as a Confederate stronghold during the Civil War. The Texas Road crossed the Arkansas below the mouth of the Verdigris, and an early cattle trail, prominent in the northern drive, made use of the same ford. Important Indian agencies were established from time to time in the area.

Great mission schools flourished and declined in the vicinity of Three Forks. Most famous, perhaps, was the academy at Tullahassee, where Alice Robertson attended classes and began the career which was to add fame to a great family. As the daughter of Ann Eliza Robertson and the granddaughter of Samuel Austin Worcester, Alice Robertson was expected to render effective public service. Her membership in Congress was only a small part of her useful career.

Bacone Indian College, founded by Almon C. Bacone as Indian University at Tahlequah in 1880, was moved near Muskogee and continued as a junior college. It has achieved a secure position in the field of Indian education. Among its famous alumni are Alexander Posey, the Creek poet, and Patrick Hurley, formerly United States secretary of war.

The Negro settlement at Marshall Town on the "Point" between the Arkansas and Verdigris rivers was a turbulent spot for many years, especially between 1878 and 1885. Cattle theft was common in the region, and occasionally some of the Cherokee cattlemen attempted to take the law into their own hands to recover their cattle and punish the thieves. Generally, light-horse police in the Muskogee District were black, and racial antipathy was added to the bad relations between the young Cherokee cattlemen and the Creek law officers. The clashes were frequent and sometimes fatal. In August, 1879, for example, a fight between the Cherokees and the black police resulted in the death of John Vann, a prominent member of the Indian tribe. The battle was a continuation of another clash, on the previous Christmas, in which a policeman was killed and three of his men wounded. An Indian police force established for the Five Civilized Tribes by an act of Congress was instrumental in finally bringing an end to the worst of the disorders.

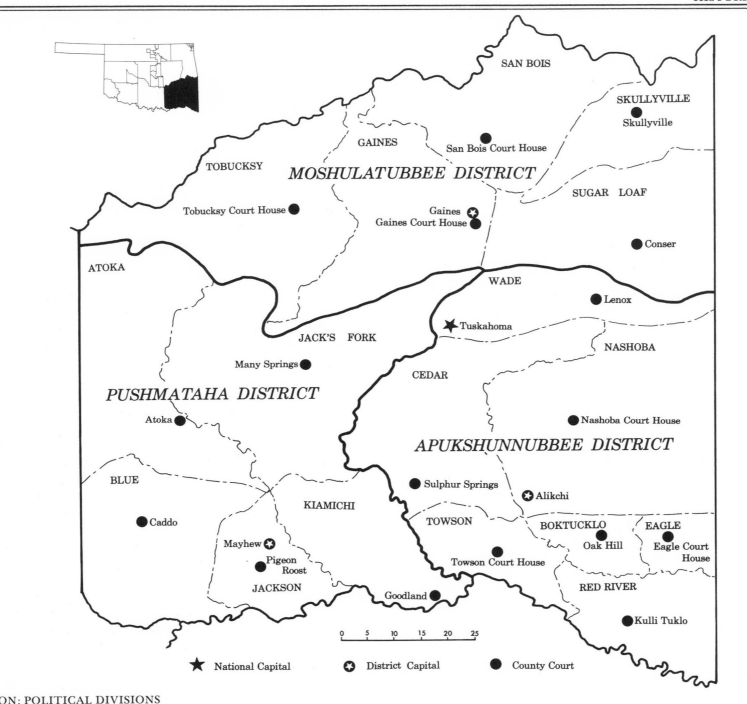

SAN BOIS

SKULLYVILLE
● Skullyville

GAINES
● San Bois Court House

TOBUCKSY

MOSHULATUBBEE DISTRICT

SUGAR LOAF

Tobucksy Court House ●

Gaines ✪
Gaines Court House ●

● Conser

ATOKA

WADE
● Lenox

★ Tuskahoma

JACK'S FORK

NASHOBA

Many Springs ●

CEDAR

PUSHMATAHA DISTRICT

● Nashoba Court House

Atoka ●

APUKSHUNNUBBEE DISTRICT

BLUE

KIAMICHI

● Sulphur Springs

Alikchi ✪

● Caddo

TOWSON

BOKTUCKLO

EAGLE

Mayhew ✪

Oak Hill ●

Eagle Court House

● Pigeon Roost

● Towson Court House

JACKSON

Goodland ●

RED RIVER

● Kulli Tuklo

0   5   10   15   20   25

★ National Capital   ✪ District Capital   ● County Court

CHOCTAW NATION: POLITICAL DIVISIONS
© 1976 by the University of Oklahoma Press

The Choctaws divided their land west of Arkansas into three districts: Okla Falaya, east of the Kiamichi and extending north from the Red River nearly 75 miles along the Arkansas boundary; Pushmataha, west of the Kiamichi to a line running north from the source of Island Bayou; and Moshulatubbee, the territory along the Arkansas and Canadian rivers, extending nearly 120 miles west of the Arkansas boundary. The name of Okla Falaya District was changed to Apukshunnubbee, and a fourth district on the west, assigned to the Chickasaws by the Treaty of Doaksville in 1837, was to become the Chickasaw Nation by the terms of a new treaty of separation in 1855.

The Choctaw Nation made many changes in its basic law between 1834 and 1860. The constitution written at Skullyville in 1857, which abolished the office of district chief and established a national governor, was opposed by a group which wrote a new constitution at Doaksville and set up a rival government. The compromise constitution of 1860 made use of the older organization, with district chiefs and courts, and established a new national government with a two-house General Council, a principal chief, and a Supreme Court.

As in the other governments of the Five Civilized Tribes, the Choctaw basic law was democratic, with wide suffrage and extensive eligibility of citizens to hold office. Sharp separation of legislative, executive, and judicial functions was provided in the constitution. The bill of rights included guarantees of trial by jury, religious liberty, and freedom of assembly.

Moshulatubbee District was divided into the following counties: Skullyville, Sugar Loaf, San Bois, Tobucksy, and Gaines. Apukshunnubbee District had seven counties: Red River, Boktucklo, Eagle, Towson, Cedar, Nashoba, and Wade. In Pushmataha District there were four original counties: Kiamichi, Blue, Atoka, and Jack's Fork. The General Council had authority to alter county boundaries, and in 1886 a new county was created from land organized under Blue and Kiamichi counties and named Jackson.

The elective officers of the counties were judge, sheriff, and ranger, with two-year terms. The sheriff could appoint deputies, and the county judge selected a citizen to serve as clerk and treasurer. The counties were units of local government and election districts for members of the Council.

Principal Chiefs of the Choctaw Nation, 1864–1907

1864–66	Peter P. Pitchlynn
1866–70	Allen Wright
1870–74	William Bryant
1874–78	Coleman Cole
1878–80	Isaac Garvin
1880–84	Jackson McCurtain
1884–86	Edmund McCurtain
1886–88	Thompson McKinney
1888–90	Ben F. Smallwood
1890–94	Wilson N. Jones
1894–96	Jefferson Gardner
1896–1900	Green McCurtain
1900–1902	Gilbert Dukes
1902–1907	Green McCurtain

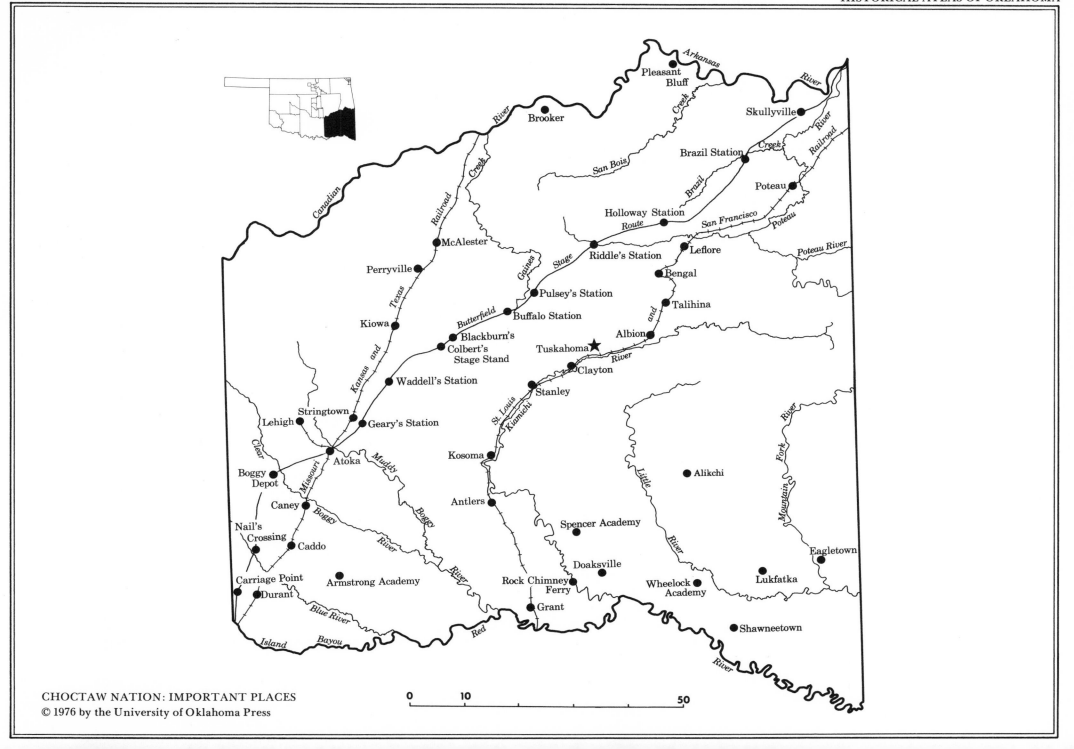

CHOCTAW NATION: IMPORTANT PLACES
© 1976 by the University of Oklahoma Press

39. CHOCTAW NATION: IMPORTANT PLACES

Beginning with the Treaty of Doak's Stand in 1820, the Choctaw Nation held land in the West that was recognized by the United States as their own; and after 1825, the Choctaw Nation was separate from Arkansas Territory. As western agent, Major William McClellan took steps in 1827 toward the construction of agency buildings at Skullyville, and within two years about 150 Choctaw Indians had moved to the district on the Arkansas River. With the general removal from Mississippi after the Treaty of Dancing Rabbit Creek in 1830, towns in the new Choctaw Nation developed rapidly.

Near Tuskahoma, which became the capital in 1834, a new council house was built, which was called Nanih Waiya, the name of the Choctaw sacred mound in Mississippi. Boggy Depot, on the Clear Boggy River near the western border of Pushmataha District, became a trade center of some importance.

At various times Boggy Depot served as the national capital, and, in addition to Skullyville and Tuskahoma, other towns were used as the seat of the government. Before the Civil War the Council had designated Fort Towson and Doaksville as the capital for brief periods; and in 1862 a constitutional amendment moved the capital to Armstrong Academy, which received the name Chahta Tamaha.

Doaksville became the largest town in the Choctaw Nation and, before the end of its prosperous era, the principal trade center of the entire Indian Territory. The United States had established a post office at Miller's Court House, which had been designated as a county seat in Arkansas Territory about a year before the boundary line of 1825 revealed that it was west of the territorial border. A post office was established at Doaksville in 1832, Skullyville, 1834, Perryville, 1841, and Boggy Depot, 1849.

Atoka, where the Missouri, Kansas and Texas Railway line crossed the old Butterfield Stage route, became one of the important trade centers of the Pushmataha District. Wheelock Mission, its stone church dating back to 1846, the oldest church building in Oklahoma, is one of the many places of historical significance in the Choctaw Nation.

Little River, with its principal tributary, Mountain Fork, is notable for its scenic beauty. The Kiamichi and Poteau rivers with their branches are also attractive examples of mountain streams surrounded by timbered hills.

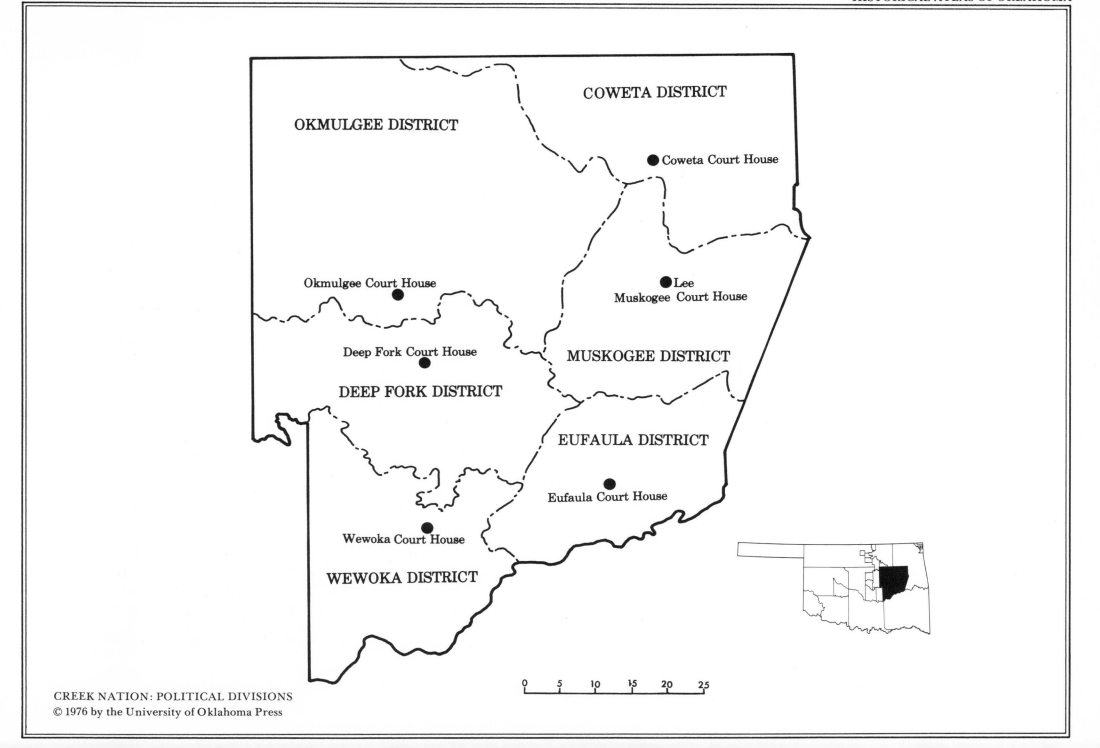

OKMULGEE DISTRICT

COWETA DISTRICT

● Coweta Court House

Okmulgee Court House ●

●Lee
Muskogee Court House

Deep Fork Court House ●

MUSKOGEE DISTRICT

DEEP FORK DISTRICT

EUFAULA DISTRICT

● Eufaula Court House

Wewoka Court House ●

WEWOKA DISTRICT

0   5   10   15   20   25

CREEK NATION: POLITICAL DIVISIONS
© 1976 by the University of Oklahoma Press

40. CREEK NATION: POLITICAL DIVISIONS

William McIntosh had begun the compilation of Creek laws before the tribe removed from Georgia. As early as 1840 the two districts in the West attempted united action in a General Council, with Roley McIntosh presiding as chief of the Arkansas District and Opothle Yahola sitting with him as chief of the Canadian District. The years 1859 and 1860 saw a number of interesting constitutional experiments, but the internal conflict of the era put an end to all legal progress.

On October 12, 1867, a brief written constitution was adopted by a vote of the Creek people. The National Council, composed of the House of Kings and the House of Warriors, was given the power to formulate and pass laws. Each town was entitled to elect one member of the House of Kings, while members of the lower house were apportioned among the towns roughly on the basis of population. The principal chief, with his appointed private secretary, was given the function of law enforcement. The erudite messages of semiliterate chiefs are to be explained only by their skill in the selection of secretaries.

The constitution of 1867 divided the Creek Nation into six districts. The National Council elected a judge for each district, the principal chief appointed six district attorneys with the approval of the Council, and the voters of each district elected a captain and four privates to serve as a light-horse police force. District officers were chosen for a term of two years. The principal chief, a second chief to succeed him in the event of his death in office, and members of the National Council were elected, each to serve for four years in his office.

Trial by jury was provided for civil and criminal cases. All suits at law in which the amount in dispute was more than $100 were tried by the Supreme Court, composed of five justices named by the National Council for terms of four years.

Perhaps the most distinctive feature of the Creek government was its use of the town as the unit of elections and administration. After the Creeks removed to the West, the people no longer restricted their residence to the towns, but the older system of governmental units was preserved.

Principal Chiefs of the Creek Nation, 1867–1907

1867–75	Samuel Chocote
1875–76	Locher Harjo
1876–79	Ward Coachman
1879–83	Samuel Chocote
1883–87	Joseph M. Perryman
1887–95	Legus Perryman
1895	Edward Bullette
1895–99	Isparhecher
1899–1907	Pleasant Porter

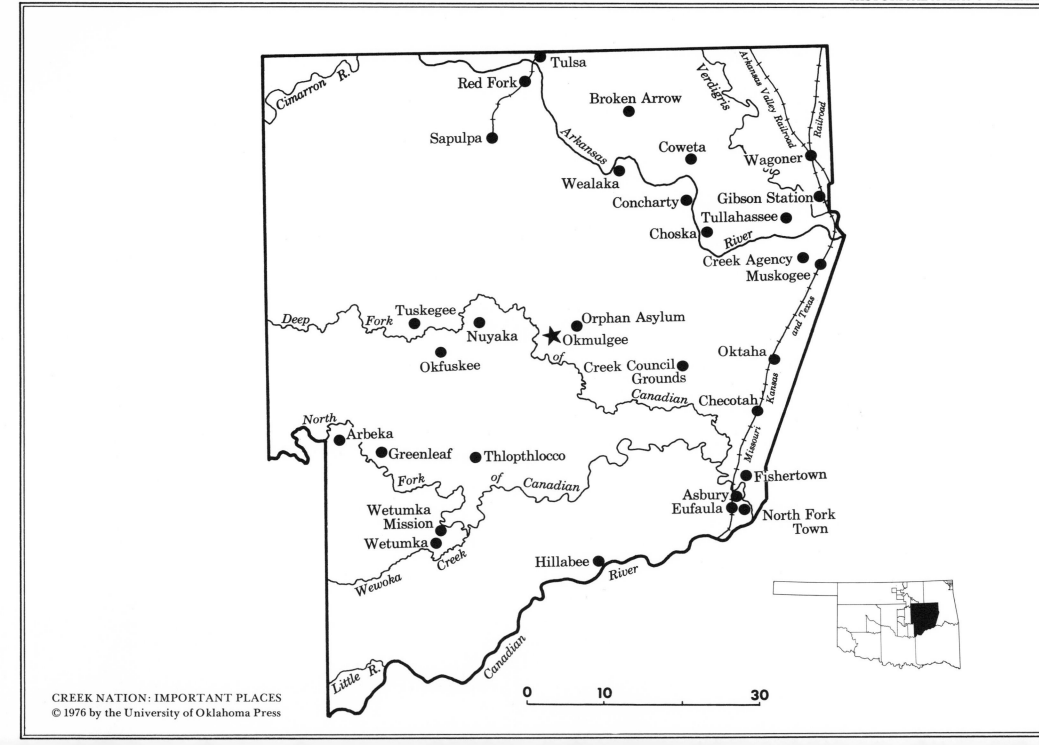

Cimarron R.

Tulsa

Red Fork

Broken Arrow

Sapulpa

Arkansas

Coweta

Verdigris

Arkansas Valley Railroad

Railroad

Wagoner

Wealaka

Concharty

Gibson Station

Tullahassee

Choska

River

Creek Agency

Muskogee

Deep   *Fork*   Tuskegee

Orphan Asylum

Nuyaka

Okmulgee

Okfuskee

Creek Council
Grounds

of

Canadian

Oktaha

Missouri Kansas and Texas

Checotah

North

Arbeka

Greenleaf

Thlopthlocco

Fork   *of*   *Canadian*

Fishertown

Asbury

Eufaula

North Fork
Town

Wetumka
Mission

Wetumka

Creek

Wewoka

Hillabee

River

Canadian

Little R.

0   10   30

CREEK NATION: IMPORTANT PLACES
© 1976 by the University of Oklahoma Press

41. CREEK NATION: IMPORTANT PLACES

The earliest Creek settlements were determined by the Texas Road and certain areas of fertile land that attracted wild game as well as farmers to the Three Forks area and the forks of the Canadian. The McIntosh Creeks—Chilly McIntosh, William's son; Jane Hawkins, the old chief's daughter-in-law; and other adherents of the Cowetan who headed the removal party—occupied land near Three Forks and along the Verdigris River to the north. Here the Creek immigrants settled with their families and slaves and contested the Cherokees for the western half of the lower Grand River valley.

A second region of dense settlement spread westward from North Fork Town, occupying the deep, black soil of the Canadian, North Canadian, and Deep Fork bottoms. At the forks of the Canadian an important mission school was established in 1847—Asbury Mission—and several towns grew up and flourished in the vicinity. North Fork Town was important until the Missouri, Kansas and Texas railroad was built through the area in 1871. A station was constructed at Eufaula, and the older towns moved to the railroad. North Fork Town and Micco Post Office vanished completely, and Eufaula prospered.

The substantial four-story building of the Eufaula Boarding School, rebuilt on the site of Asbury after the Civil War and again after the school was burned in 1888, was to remain in use until the 1950's, when most of the Creek children were enrolled in the public schools of the area.

The federal census of 1890 recorded a population of 1,200 in Muskogee, 500 in Eufaula, and 136 in Okmulgee. At that time, 9,291 Creek Indians, 462 Cherokees, 172 Seminoles, 3,289 white citizens, and 4,621 Negroes—Creek freedmen and others—resided in the Creek Nation. The census also listed three Chinese residents.

The St. Louis and San Francisco Railroad (successor of the Atlantic and Pacific) extended its line to Tulsa in 1882 and to Sapulpa in 1886. The Arkansas Valley Railroad crossed the Missouri, Kansas and Texas at Wagoner.

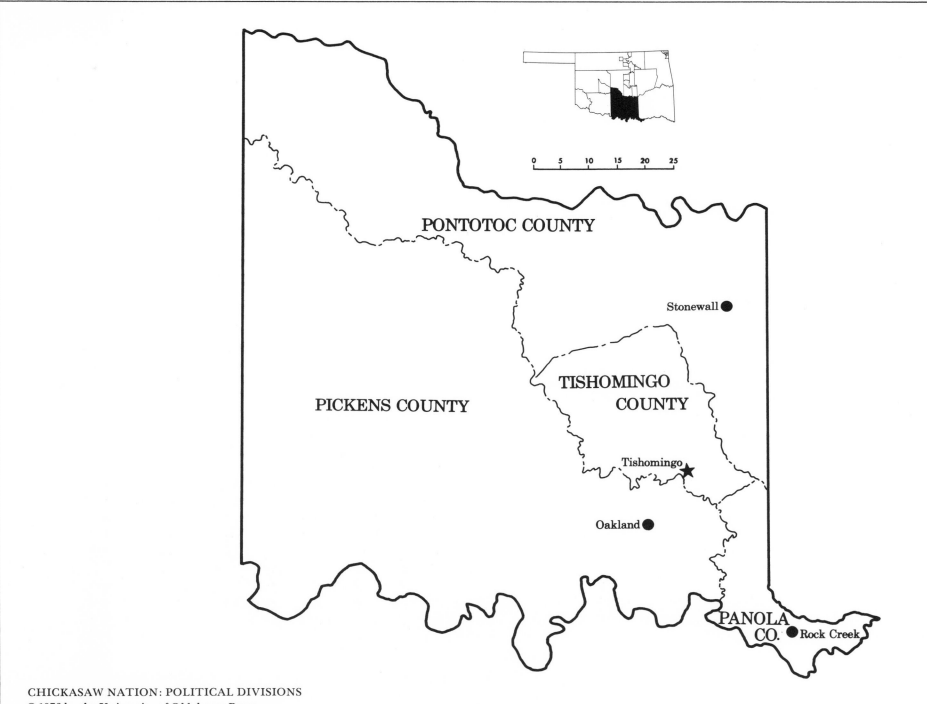

PONTOTOC COUNTY

Stonewall ●

TISHOMINGO
COUNTY

PICKENS COUNTY

Tishomingo ★

Oakland ●

PANOLA
CO. ● Rock Creek

0   5   10   15   20   25

CHICKASAW NATION: POLITICAL DIVISIONS
© 1976 by the University of Oklahoma Press

42. CHICKASAW NATION: POLITICAL DIVISIONS

The permanent separation of the Chickasaw Nation from the Choctaws in 1855 established boundaries for the smaller tribe as indicated on the map—Red River on the south, the 98th meridian from the Red to the Canadian River on the west, the Canadian River on the north, and directly southward from the Canadian to the source of Island Bayou, then along that stream to its confluence with the Red River. As compensation for the surrender of the land west of the 98th meridian in a permanent lease to the United States, the Chickasaws received $200,000 as their share of the lease money. For the first time since their arrival in the West, the Chickasaws were in a position to control their own public affairs without Choctaw domination.

The Chickasaws had constructed a council house at Good Spring on Pennington Creek as early as 1853. Cyrus Harris was elected governor, and the capital at Good Spring was renamed Tishomingo, in honor of a famous Chickasaw chief. The manuscript of the new constitution was lost before it could be printed, but the Council redrafted the document in 1857 and published it at Tishomingo.

In 1867 the Chickasaws adopted a new constitution. In many respects it was similar to the Choctaw basic law, with an extensive bill of rights, guarantees of personal liberty, and prohibition of polygamy. The two houses of the legislature were called the Senate and the House of Representatives and the chief executive officer was called the "governor of the Chickasaw Nation." Suffrage was provided for "free male persons of the age of nineteen years and upwards, who are by birth or adoption members of the Chickasaw Tribe of Indians."

Some very able men have served as governor of the Chickasaw Nation. In addition to Cyrus Harris, the list includes William R. Guy, Jonas Wolf, and Douglas H. Johnston. Charles D. Carter, who represented the Third District of Oklahoma in Congress for twenty years, and Homer Paul, a brilliant state senator from Pauls Valley, are among other Chickasaw Indians who have become distinguished in public life. Oklahoma Governor Johnston Murray had both Chickasaw and Choctaw blood through his mother, Alice Hearrell Murray, the niece of Governor Douglas H. Johnston.

Governors of the Chickasaw Nation, 1866–1907

1866–70	Cyrus Harris
1870–71	W. P. Brown
1871–72	Thomas J. Parker
1872–74	Cyrus Harris
1874–78	B. F. Overton
1878–80	B. C. Burney
1880–84	B. F. Overton
1884–86	Jonas Wolf
1886–88	William M. Guy
1888–92	William L. Byrd
1892–94	Jonas Wolf
1894–96	Palmer S. Mosley
1896–98	Robert M. Harris
1898–1902	Douglas H. Johnston
1902–1904	Palmer S. Mosley
1904–1907	Douglas H. Johnston

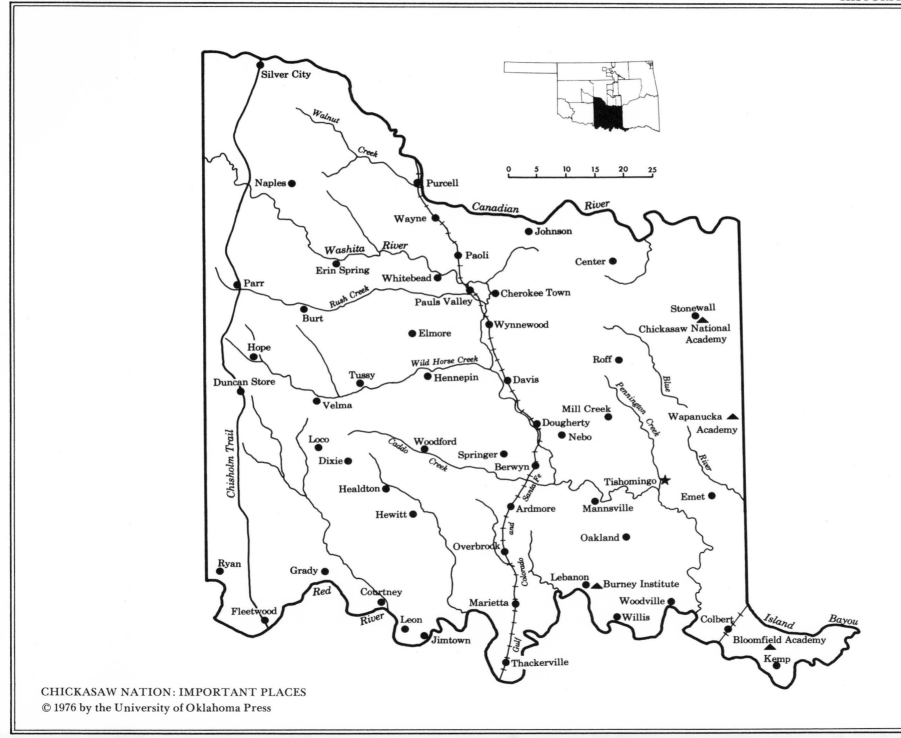

CHICKASAW NATION: IMPORTANT PLACES
© 1976 by the University of Oklahoma Press

43. CHICKASAW NATION: IMPORTANT PLACES

Many towns in the Chickasaw Nation are rich in historic interest. Purcell, Wayne, Pauls Valley, Davis, Ardmore, and Marietta on the Santa Fe Railway; Silver City, Duncan, and Fleetwood on the Chisholm Trail; Roff and Stonewall in the northeast, Ryan and Grady in the southwest, and Hennepin on Wild Horse Creek—each has a distinctive story. Bloomfield Academy, Wapanucka Academy, Burney Institute, and the Chickasaw National Academy; Colbert, near a well-known crossing of Red River; and Tishomingo, the Chickasaw capital, have all been important at some stage of Chickasaw development.

The Chickasaws established their capital at Good Spring on lower Pennington Creek when they were separated from the Choctaws in 1856. The place was given a new name, Tishomingo City, in honor of a famous tribal chief. Several stores, a cotton gin, a water mill, and a newspaper, the *Chickasaw and Choctaw Herald*, were established in the place. The capitol, erected in 1853, was replaced in 1896 by a building which has been in use since that time. The Chickasaw Manual Labor School for boys was opened near Good Spring (Tishomingo) in 1851.

Wapanucka Academy for girls was opened in 1852; Bloomfield Academy for girls, in 1852; Collins Institute (Colbert Institute), in 1854; and Burney Institute for girls, in 1859.

Captain Randolph B. Marcy removed Camp Arbuckle from its original location southeast of Purcell on the Canadian River and established Fort Arbuckle on Wild Horse Creek, west of Davis, in 1851. The ruins of chimneys and the walks between barracks are still to be seen on the site of Fort Arbuckle. Initial Point, the point of origin for the Oklahoma survey of ranges, townships, and sections, is approximately one mile south of the fort.

Purcell, Pauls Valley, and Ardmore became important shipping centers on the Atchison, Topeka and Santa Fe Railway and the Gulf, Colorado and Santa Fe (south of Purcell) after the building of the road through Oklahoma and Indian Territory, 1886–90.

Ben Colbert's ferry in the Chickasaw Nation was an important point on the Texas Road and on the East and West Shawnee cattle trails. The M. K. and T. railroad, entering the Indian Territory in 1870, crossed Cherokee, Creek, and Choctaw lands before entering the Chickasaw Nation. It reached Colbert's Ferry in January, 1873.

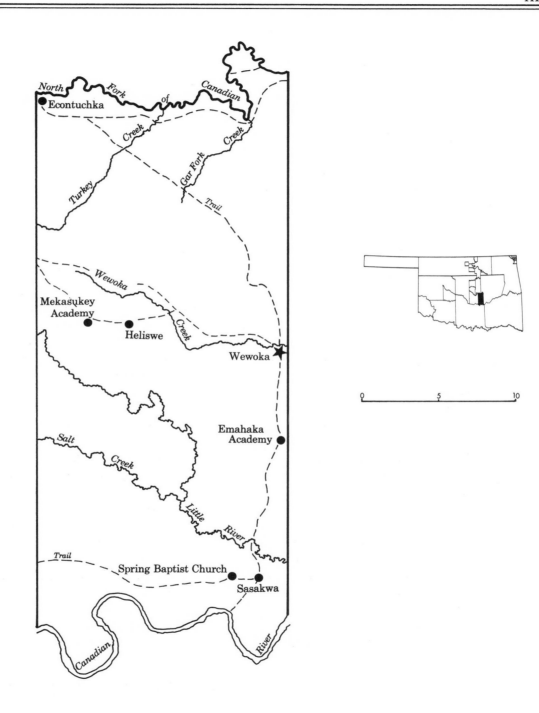

SEMINOLE NATION, 1889
© 1976 by the University of Oklahoma Press

In the reorganization of Indian boundaries after the Civil War, the Seminole Nation agreed (March 21, 1866) to cede all of its land to the United States for the sum of $325,362, "said purchase being at the rate of fifteen cents per acre." At the same time the Seminoles agreed to purchase from the Creek Nation, at 50 cents an acre, a new holding of 200,000 acres.

In order to obtain what they called "elbow room" between the various bands of Seminoles, the nation purchased in 1881 an additional 175,000 acres of land from the adjacent Creek Nation, at the rate of $1.00 an acre. After this addition, the Seminole Nation was slightly smaller than present Seminole County, Oklahoma.

Wewoka, the Seminole capital, was first settled by John Coheia (Gopher John) in 1845. This black, who as a youth was a slave, held a place of respect among the Seminoles as well as United States Army officers because of his skill as a scout and guide and also by reason of his financial responsibility. It was Gopher John who provided a loan of $1,500 in cash when Lieutenant E. R. S. Canby, conducting a Seminole party from Florida to the Indian Territory, was hard-pressed for subsistence funds. For this service, John was freed by the tribe from slavery.

Sasakwa, the home of John Jumper and business headquarters of Chief John F. Brown, was the location of the Sasakwa Female Academy from 1884–1894. The Seminole Council consolidated this academy with Emahaka in 1894.

The city of Seminole, center of a great petroleum development in the 1920's, had not appeared on the maps in 1889. The discovery of oil on the grounds of the Mekasukey Academy, the property of the Seminole Nation, provided a small income for each member of the tribe.

Principal Chiefs (Governors) of the Seminole Nation, 1866–1907

1866–81	John Chupco (chief of the "Northern Faction" until his death in 1881)
1866–77	John Jumper
1877–1902	John F. Brown
1902–1904	Hulputta Micco
1904–1907	John F. Brown

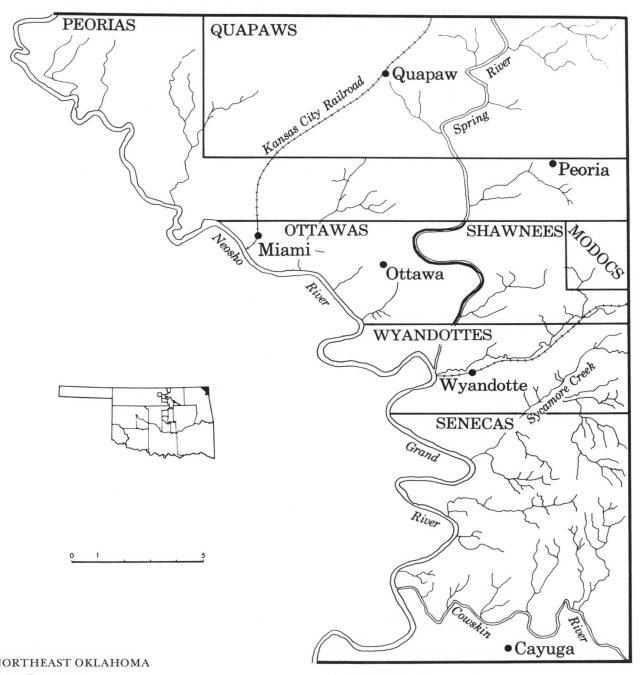

PEORIAS

QUAPAWS

•Quapaw

Spring River

Kansas City Railroad

•Peoria

OTTAWAS

Miami

Neosho

•Ottawa

SHAWNEES

MODOCS

River

WYANDOTTES

•Wyandotte

Sycamore Creek

SENECAS

Grand

River

Cowskin

River

•Cayuga

0 1 5

SMALL INDIAN GROUPS IN NORTHEAST OKLAHOMA
© 1976 by the University of Oklahoma Press

45. SMALL INDIAN GROUPS IN NORTHEAST OKLAHOMA

The Indians in the northeastern corner of Oklahoma were settled there at various times as a solution to the problems of tribes and fragments of tribes who had pressing needs for space.

Between 1828 and 1832 the Senecas of Sandusky, Ohio, negotiated for western land and received, in the final treaties, a tract of 70,000 acres at the bend of Grand River near the southwestern corner of Missouri. A mixed band of Seneca and Shawnee Indians at Lewiston, Ohio, exchanged their eastern lands for 60,000 acres just north of the Seneca tract; and in 1833 the band of Quapaws who had been living along Red River obtained a reservation of 96,000 acres north of the Seneca and Shawnee land. The Quapaw area, between the western boundary of Missouri and the Neosho River, extended half a mile north of the Kansas line.

In 1867 the Sandusky Senecas ceded 20,000 acres of their land for settlement of the Wyandottes. The Seneca-Shawnee band separated, the Senecas joining their kindred tribe from Sandusky. The northern half of the joint reservation was assigned to the Confederated Peorias, united with fragments of the Piankashaw (a branch of the Miami at one time), Kaskaskia, Wea, and Miami Indians. The Quapaws ceded to the United States their land north of the Kansas state line, and also a part of their reservation south of the thirty-seventh parallel, for the use of the Confederated Peorias.

The southwestern part of the old Seneca-Shawnee reservation, lying west of Spring River, was assigned in 1867 to the Ottawas of Kansas who wanted to maintain their tribal organization in preference to receiving land in severalty. The tract to which the Ottawas moved contained less than 15,000 acres. In 1891, when they finally accepted land in severalty, the Ottawas numbered 157. The Shawnees of the joint reservation, called Eastern Shawnees after their separation from the Senecas, continued to occupy the remainder of their tract.

After the Modoc revolt under Kintpuash ("Captain Jack"), and the execution of their leader in 1873, the Modocs were moved to Oklahoma during the following year. The Eastern Shawnees ceded 4,000 acres of their diminished reservation for the use of the Modocs. Sixty-eight Modocs received allotments in severalty beginning in 1890.

The land assigned to the small Indian groups in northeastern Oklahoma has natural advantages in scenic beauty. A large part of the area has deep, fertile soil.

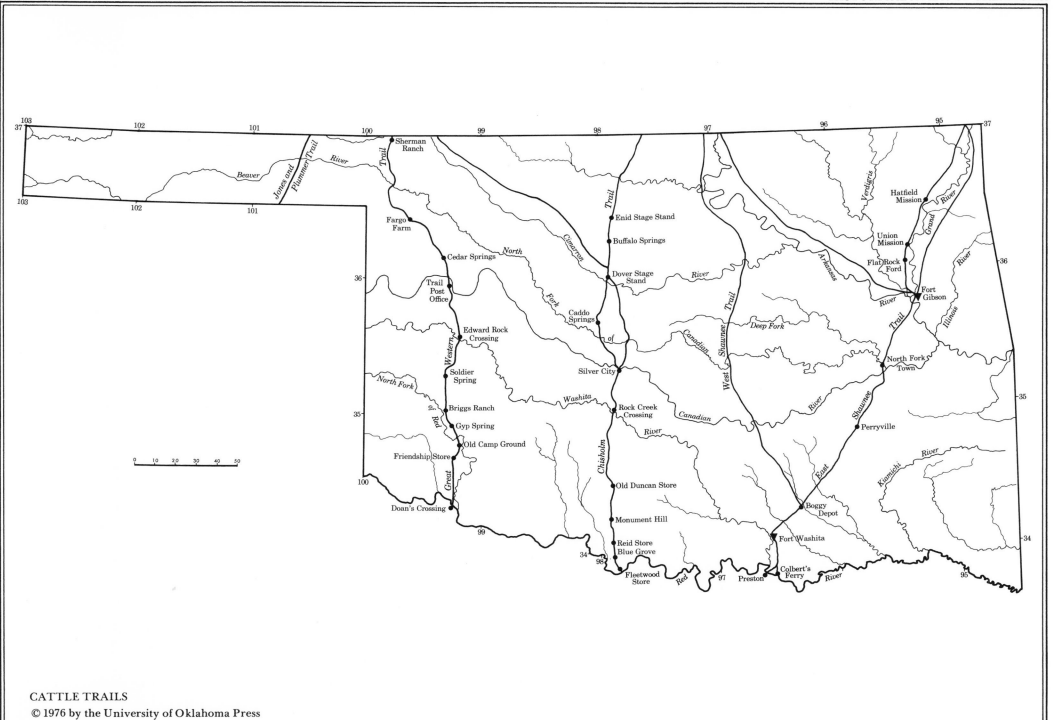

CATTLE TRAILS
© 1976 by the University of Oklahoma Press

46. CATTLE TRAILS

The trails of the great cattle drives from Texas through the Indian Territory became well-established routes for the transportation of cattle on the hoof. In 1866 the price of a fine steer in Texas was usually not more than $5; in Chicago or Newark the same beef animal would sell for a price ranging from $65 to $90. The great need of Texas ranchers was a means for delivering their cattle to a point where railroad lines made connections with markets.

Railroads in Missouri and eastern Kansas determined the route of the first northern drives. As the rails were pushed westward in Kansas, however, cattle trails leading to them also were established farther west.

The drives in 1866 followed the Texas Road, a trail filled with difficulties and dangers—deep streams that were hard to ford, Indians who resented cattle drives across their insufficient pasture lands, and rough, timbered areas where the wild Texas steers might cause endless delay by hiding in the brush. This was known as the East Shawnee Trail. From Fort Gibson a branch trail developed along the left bank of the Arkansas, and many Indian ranchmen of northeastern Indian Territory followed this route into Cowley County, Kansas.

The West Shawnee Trail left the Texas Road at Boggy Depot toward the northwest, crossing the Canadian near the site of Konawa, the North Canadian near the site of Shawnee, the Cimarron near the site of present-day Cushing, and continued to the west of the Arkansas, passing near the sites of Pawnee and Ponca City.

Eighty miles west of Colbert's Ferry the Chisholm Trail crossed Red River near Ringold, Texas, and extended north to the Kansas line. This famous route, slightly irregular because of the locations of the best fords, was roughly parallel to the 98th meridian and to the line followed later by the Rock Island railroad and U.S. Highway 81.

This great artery of the northern drive was named for Jesse Chisholm, the trader. Jesse was the son-in-law of the proprietor of Edwards' Post at the mouth of Little River. The Chisholm Ranch, near the site of Asher, drove cattle nearly one hundred miles to King Fisher's stagecoach station, where the Texas cattle passed on the way to Kansas. Jesse Chisholm, more interested in trade than livestock growing, hauled provisions south from Caldwell, Kansas, to supply the crews on the great cattle drives. The Cherokee Indian trader thus became the best-known person on the trail, and it was natural to designate the route by his name.

The Great Western Trail, crossing Red River within sight of Doan's Store, Texas, ran almost due north to Trail and Cedar Springs, then northwest to the crossing of Beaver Creek and to the Kansas line beyond Sherman Ranch. The Great Western was relatively free of timber, and the Indians were willing to exchange pasturage for beeves.

The northern objective was Dodge City, Kansas, which was called "the cow capital of the world" for a decade. Between 1866 and 1885 about 6,000,000 head of cattle were driven north from Texas to the Kansas railroad lines or to northern ranges in Nebraska, the Dakotas, Wyoming, or Montana. The Missouri, Kansas and Texas railroad, completed in 1872, the Santa Fe line completed across Oklahoma lands in 1886, and other lines from Texas to Kansas quickly reduced the cattle drives to local operations.

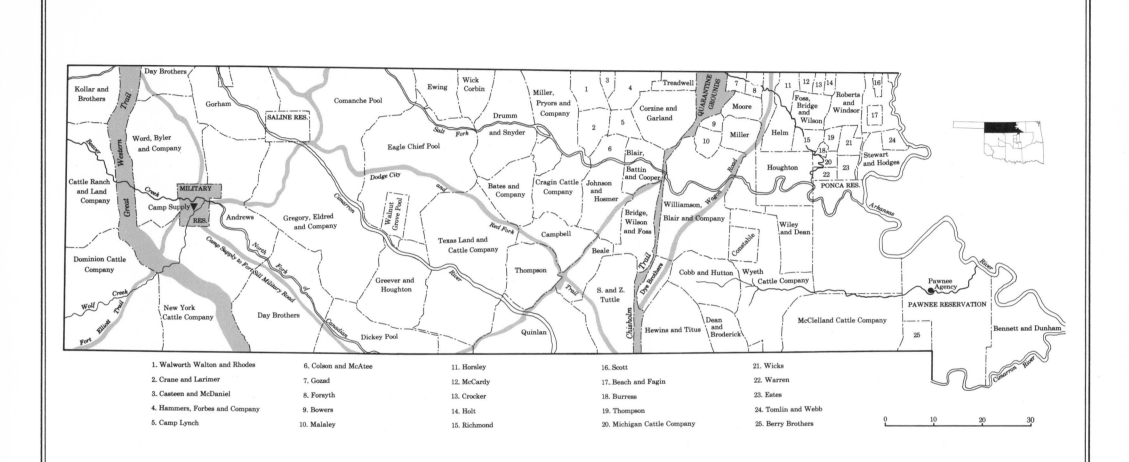

Kollar and Brothers
Day Brothers
Gorham
SALINE RES.
Comanche Pool
Ewing
Wick Corbin
Miller, Pryors and Company
3
1
4
Treadwell
QUARANTINE GROUNDS
7
8
11
12 13 14
Foss, Bridge and Wilson
Roberts and Windsor
16
Word, Byler and Company
Drumm and Snyder
Salt Fork
Corzine and Garland
Moore
17
Cattle Ranch and Land Company
MILITARY RES.
Camp Supply
Eagle Chief Pool
2
5
9
Miller
Helm
15
19
21
24
Dodge City
6
Blair, Battin and Cooper
10
Houghton
18
20
Stewart and Hodges
Andrews
Gregory, Eldred and Company
Cimarron
Walnut Grove Pool
Bates and Company
Cragin Cattle Company
Johnson and Hosmer
22
23
PONCA RES.
Dominion Cattle Company
Red Fork
Williamson, Blair and Company
Wiley and Dean
Arkansas
Camp Supply to Fort Sill Military Road
North Fork
Texas Land and Cattle Company
Campbell
Bridge, Wilson and Foss
Constable
Greever and Houghton
River
Thompson
Beale
Cobb and Hutton
Wyeth Cattle Company
Pawnee Agency
New York Cattle Company
Day Brothers
of
Canadian
S. and Z. Tuttle
Dye Brothers
PAWNEE RESERVATION
Wolf Creek
Fort Elliott Trail
Dickey Pool
Quinlan
Chisholm Trail
Hewins and Titus
Dean and Broderick
McClelland Cattle Company
25
Bennett and Dunham
Cimarron River

1. Walworth Walton and Rhodes
2. Crane and Larimer
3. Casteen and McDaniel
4. Hammers, Forbes and Company
5. Camp Lynch

6. Colson and McAtee
7. Gozad
8. Forsyth
9. Bowers
10. Malaley

11. Horsley
12. McCardy
13. Crocker
14. Holt
15. Richmond

16. Scott
17. Beach and Fagin
18. Burress
19. Thompson
20. Michigan Cattle Company

21. Wicks
22. Warren
23. Estes
24. Tomlin and Webb
25. Berry Brothers

0   10   20   30

LEASES OF THE CHEROKEE OUTLET
© 1976 by the University of Oklahoma Press

47. LEASES OF THE CHEROKEE OUTLET

After the Osages and other Plains Indians had moved to reservations on the Cherokee Outlet and the narrow "Cherokee Strip" north of the Kansas border had been ceded to the United States, there still remained 6,344,562 acres of unoccupied Cherokee land west of the 96th meridian.

The Cherokee Strip Live Stock Association was organized by a group of cattlemen during the years 1880 to 1883. Its principal purpose was to obtain from the Indian tribe a lease that would exclude nonmembers from grazing cattle on the Cherokee Outlet. In 1883 the organization succeeded in obtaining a five-year lease at the price of $100,000 a year—less than two cents an acre. The low price paid for exclusive grazing rights led to the charge that the Cherokee Council had accepted a bribe from the cattlemen. However, previous payments collected by the Cherokee tribe from individual cattlemen had never totaled more than $41,233.81, the amount collected in 1882.

The lease of 1883 was followed by a second agreement five years later at a more reasonable price—$200,000 a year for the entire unoccupied area. However, the legal right of the Cherokees to lease their western lands had been seriously questioned in many quarters and was to be flatly denied by two attorneys general of the United States—A. H. Garland of President Cleveland's cabinet and H. H. Miller of the Benjamin Harrison administration.

There is good evidence that the Cherokee Strip Live Stock Association was willing to purchase the land included in their lease at $3.00 an acre. The government of the United States, however, was moving rapidly toward the policy of opening the western half of the Indian Territory to white settlement. The Jerome Commission offered the Cherokees $1.25 an acre for their claims to the Outlet, and the Indians were in no position to bargain freely. The tribal officers reluctantly agreed to cede the unoccupied lands of the Cherokee Outlet for white settlement at the rate of $1.25 an acre. The agreement was approved by the Cherokee Council on January 4, 1892.

Members of the Cherokee Strip Live Stock Association, numbering more than one hundred, had obtained definite grazing lands within the area leased. The holdings had been surveyed, and each member had fenced his ground, built corrals, and put up shelters for his line-riders. Dean and Broderick, Greever and Houghton, McClellan Cattle Company, the Dominion Cattle Company, H. Kollar and Brother, Drumm and Snyder, Bennett and Dunham in the corner between the Cimarron and the Arkansas east of the Pawnees, and Dickey Brothers, with 22,500 cattle on a range that extended across the southern boundary of the Outlet into the Cheyenne and Arapaho Reservation—these were but a few of the well-known cattle companies that occupied for a brief time a portion of the Cherokee Outlet.

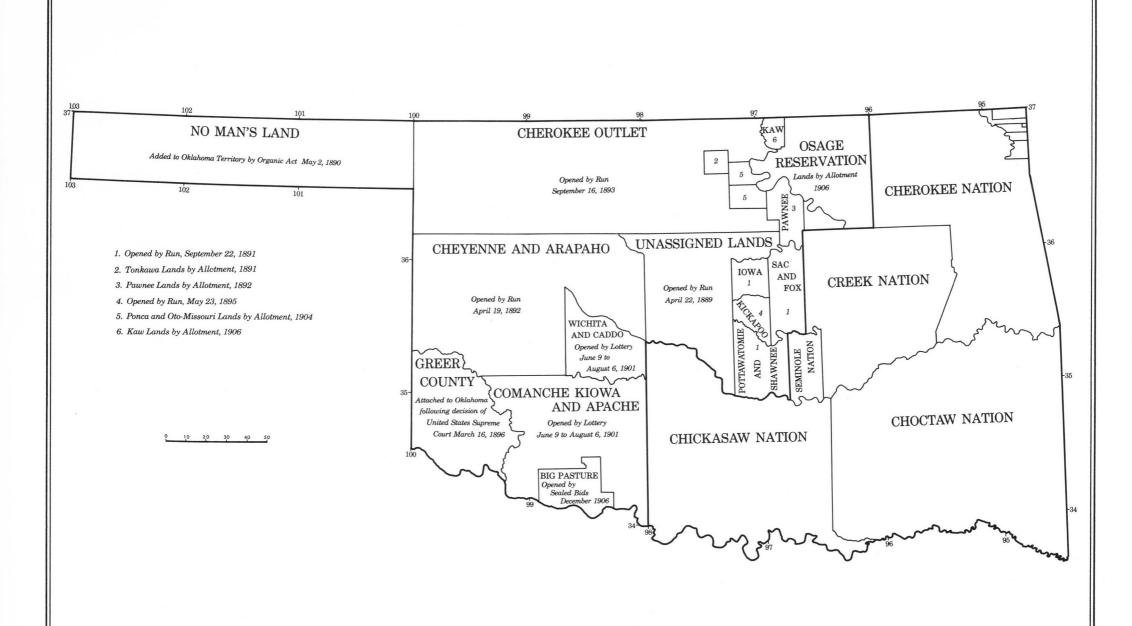

NO MAN'S LAND

Added to Oklahoma Territory by Organic Act May 2, 1890

CHEROKEE OUTLET

*Opened by Run
September 16, 1893*

KAW
6

2

5

5

OSAGE
RESERVATION

*Lands by Allotment
1906*

PAWNEE
3

CHEROKEE NATION

1. *Opened by Run, September 22, 1891*

2. *Tonkawa Lands by Allotment, 1891*

3. *Pawnee Lands by Allotment, 1892*

4. *Opened by Run, May 23, 1895*

5. *Ponca and Oto-Missouri Lands by Allotment, 1904*

6. *Kaw Lands by Allotment, 1906*

CHEYENNE AND ARAPAHO

UNASSIGNED LANDS

*Opened by Run
April 19, 1892*

*Opened by Run
April 22, 1889*

IOWA
1

SAC
AND
FOX

KICKAPOO

POTTAWATOMIE
AND
SHAWNEE

4

1

1

CREEK NATION

WICHITA
AND CADDO

*Opened by Lottery
June 9 to
August 6, 1901*

SEMINOLE
NATION

GREER
COUNTY

*Attached to Oklahoma
following decision of
United States Supreme
Court March 16, 1896*

COMANCHE KIOWA
AND APACHE

*Opened by Lottery
June 9 to August 6, 1901*

CHICKASAW NATION

CHOCTAW NATION

0 10 20 30 40 50

BIG PASTURE
*Opened by
Sealed Bids
December 1906*

LAND OPENINGS
© 1976 by the University of Oklahoma Press

48. LAND OPENINGS

Pressure for the opening of unoccupied Indian land to white settlement grew steadily from the end of the Civil War until the first run in 1889. After that first major breach in the policy of holding the land for the Indians, the runs for homesteads brought rapid growth of the new territory, Oklahoma.

During his third week in office President Benjamin Harrison issued a proclamation concerning settlement of the Unassigned Lands. At noon on April 22, 1889, eligible persons were authorized to enter the district. Homestead laws already in effect governed the opening, with the added restriction that any person who entered before the designated hour should forfeit his right to take up land. The customary reservation of sections sixteen and thirty-six in each township was provided.

Estimates of the number of settlers who made the first run vary widely. More than 9,000 homesteads were occupied, and the new towns, Guthrie and Oklahoma City, each grew to 10,000 before the first rush subsided. Probably the total number who made the run on April 22 was over 50,000.

The second and third openings of land in Oklahoma were east and west of the original territory. On September 22, 1891, the surplus lands of the Iowa, Sac and Fox, and the Shawnee-Pottawatomie tribes were opened to white settlement by run. About 20,000 persons contested for 7,000 quarter-sections, and all of the land was occupied in one afternoon.

The Cheyenne-Arapaho surplus lands were opened to settlement on April 19, 1892. The eastern half of the vast tract filled promptly, but much of the western part continued for several years to be used as grazing land for cattlemen. Most of it, however, was occupied before statehood by persons seeking farm homes.

The Cherokee Outlet opening on September 16, 1893, found 100,000 persons on the starting line. There, too, the quarter-sections in the western half were unoccupied—in some instances for several years—after the opening.

Kickapoo lands, not included in the second opening because the tribe had not agreed to the terms offered for their surplus, were opened to settlement on May 23, 1895. The reservation was between Deep Fork and the North Canadian, on the eastern border of the original territory opened to settlement.

In 1896 the United States Supreme Court denied the claim of Texas to Greer County, and Congress made the region a part of Oklahoma Territory. About 4,000 new homesteads were declared open for settlement in Greer County.

The surplus lands of the Kiowa-Comanche and the Wichita-Caddo reservations were opened to settlement in 1901 by lottery. Nearly 170,000 persons registered for the drawing, with 13,000 quarter-sections available for settlement.

Grazing land, 480,000 acres in extent, was reserved for surplus livestock of the Kiowa-Comanche and Wichita-Caddo Indians. The Big Pasture was opened to white settlement in 1906. After allotments had been provided for children born after the land opening of 1901, the remaining land was sold to the highest bidder among qualified homesteaders.

In 1904 and 1906 the lands of the Ponca, Oto and Missouri, Kaw, and the Osage tribes were distributed among the tribal citizens. These reservations were not opened to white settlement. Each member of the Osage tribe received more than 500 acres.

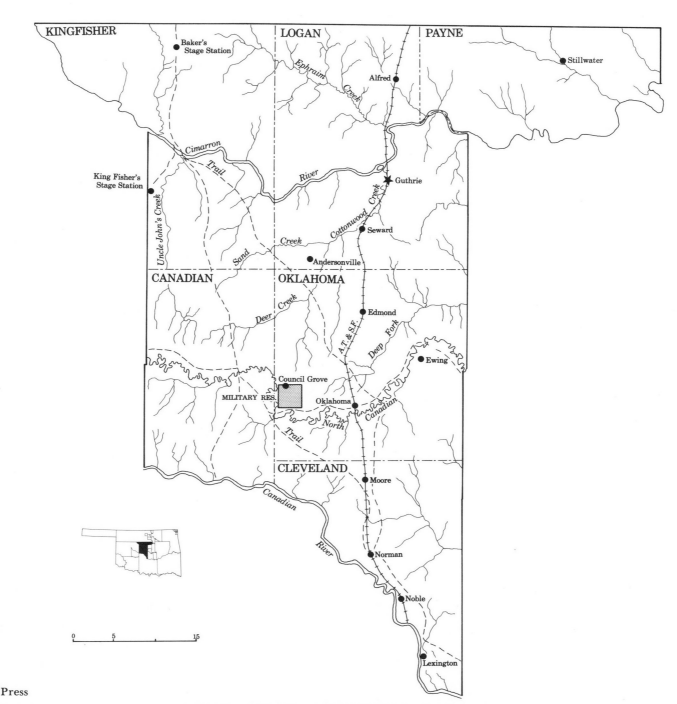

KINGFISHER

Baker's
Stage Station

LOGAN

PAYNE

Stillwater

Ephraim

Creek

Alfred

Cimarron

Trail

King Fisher's
Stage Station

River

Guthrie

Uncle John's Creek

Cottonwood Creek

Seward

Creek

Sand

Andersonville

CANADIAN

OKLAHOMA

Deer Creek

Edmond

A.T. & S.F.

Deep Fork

Ewing

Council Grove

MILITARY RES.

Oklahoma

Canadian

North

Trail

CLEVELAND

Moore

Canadian

River

Norman

Noble

0   5   15

Lexington

UNASSIGNED LANDS, 1889
© 1976 by the University of Oklahoma Press

49. UNASSIGNED LANDS, 1889

In the treaties of 1866 with the Creeks and Seminoles, the United States had obtained title to one-half of the Creek lands and all of the Seminole lands. The area was ceded with the restriction—stated explicitly in the Creek treaty and implied in the Seminole treaty—that the land acquired was for the use of Indians and freedmen.

Chief Pleasant Porter of the Creek Nation went to Washington in January, 1889, to negotiate with the government on the relinquishment of all restrictions upon the land ceded in 1866. An agreement was reached whereby the Creeks released the United States from the restrictions in return for $2,280,000. The Seminoles immediately asked for a similar agreement. The bargain was made, and Congress appropriated the necessary money.

The land of the Oklahoma District was included in the area thus cleared for white settlement. It included the major parts of six present-day Oklahoma counties—a total of 1,887,796.47 acres. Portions of the Canadian, North Canadian, Cimarron, Deep Fork, and Little rivers were in the district, as well as the rich bottomland of these streams and such tributaries as Cottonwood and Uncle John's creeks. Thin soil, above the second bottoms, useful chiefly for grazing, was also plentiful. Probably very few if any persons in 1889 suspected the great wealth in petroleum beneath the surface.

A considerable part of the higher ground was prairie. In some regions, however, there was a growth of scrub timber—blackjack on the ridges and cottonwood along the streams. In the valleys some excellent oak, walnut, and black gum trees were available for lumber. Timber for fence posts could be found in widely separated areas, and heavy beams were cut in Cottonwood and Stillwater bottoms, among other places, for railroad and wagonroad bridges.

Beginning with the run of April 22, 1889, the larger towns appeared on the Santa Fe Railway. Guthrie and Oklahoma City were far ahead of the others; but Lexington, Norman, and Edmond were marked for early growth. Stillwater received its mail by stagecoach from Perry, on the Santa Fe, until a branch railroad line was built south from Skedee. Freight also was hauled from Perry to Stillwater.

The county names shown on the map were adopted after the organization of Oklahoma Territory in 1890. The east line of Cleveland, Oklahoma, and Logan counties was moved six miles farther east after the addition of the Iowa and Pottawatomie lands in 1891; and the counties on the west, Canadian and Kingfisher, almost doubled their area when the Cheyenne and Arapaho Reservation was opened to settlement in 1892.

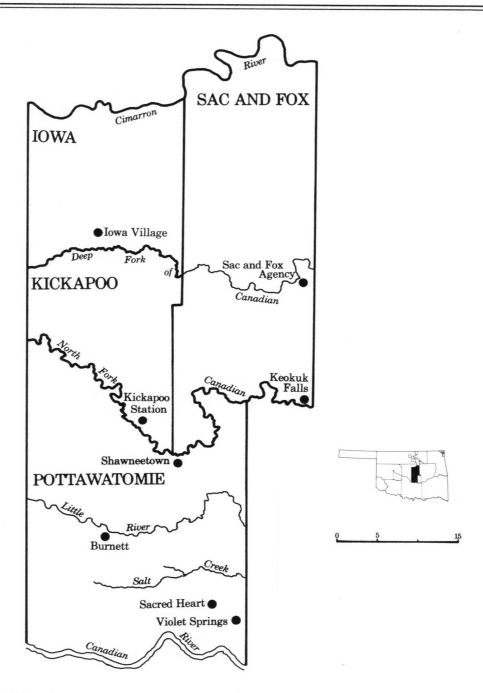

SAC AND FOX

IOWA

River

Cimarron

● Iowa Village

Deep Fork of

KICKAPOO

Sac and Fox
Agency ●

Canadian

North Fork

Canadian

Kickapoo
Station
●

Keokuk
Falls
●

Shawneetown ●

POTTAWATOMIE

Little River

Burnett ●

Salt Creek

Sacred Heart ●

Violet Springs ●

Canadian River

0   5   15

IOWA, SAC AND FOX, KICKAPOO, POTTAWATOMIE LANDS
© 1976 by the University of Oklahoma Press

50. IOWA, SAC AND FOX, KICKAPOO, POTTAWATOMIE LANDS

After Congress passed the Organic Act setting up the government of Oklahoma Territory on May 2, 1890, the first addition of settlers to the jurisdiction of the territorial officers came with the land opening to the east. Surplus lands of the Kickapoos were not included because the Jerome Commission had not reached an agreement with that tribe. Hence, the second run for homesteads, on September 22, 1891, was confined to the lands of the Iowas, Sac and Foxes, and Pottawatomies, with the Kickapoo Reservation a small enclave of unsettled land after the run.

Twenty thousand persons made the race for the seven thousand homesteads (1,120,000 acres) available. Since there was some excellent soil for farming, ample grazing land, timber for firewood, and water for all ordinary demands of settlers with livestock, it is not remarkable that the region was occupied quickly. Before sunset on the day of the opening, every claim was staked—and in some instances two or more claimants had appeared.

At Tecumseh and Chandler, selected as county seats of the two counties planned for the area, townsites were also opened by run. The experiment was a failure. In the claims for town lots many disputes arose, and at Tecumseh one death occurred during the struggle of riders for advantage in the crowded rush of the horses.

About 200,000 acres were available for settlement in the separate Kickapoo run of May 23, 1895. The Indians had received allotments totaling 22,640 acres, and school land was withheld.

Violet Springs, opposite the Seminole western boundary near the Sacred Heart Mission, and Keokuk Falls on the North Canadian River, also near the Seminole border, were centers of illegal whisky sales to the Indians for many years. Both places had lurid records for general disorder, including theft of livestock and, occasionally, murder. In 1898 the mob burning of two Seminole boys, Lincoln McGeisey and Palmer Sampson, was closely connected with the disreputable activities of the border towns.

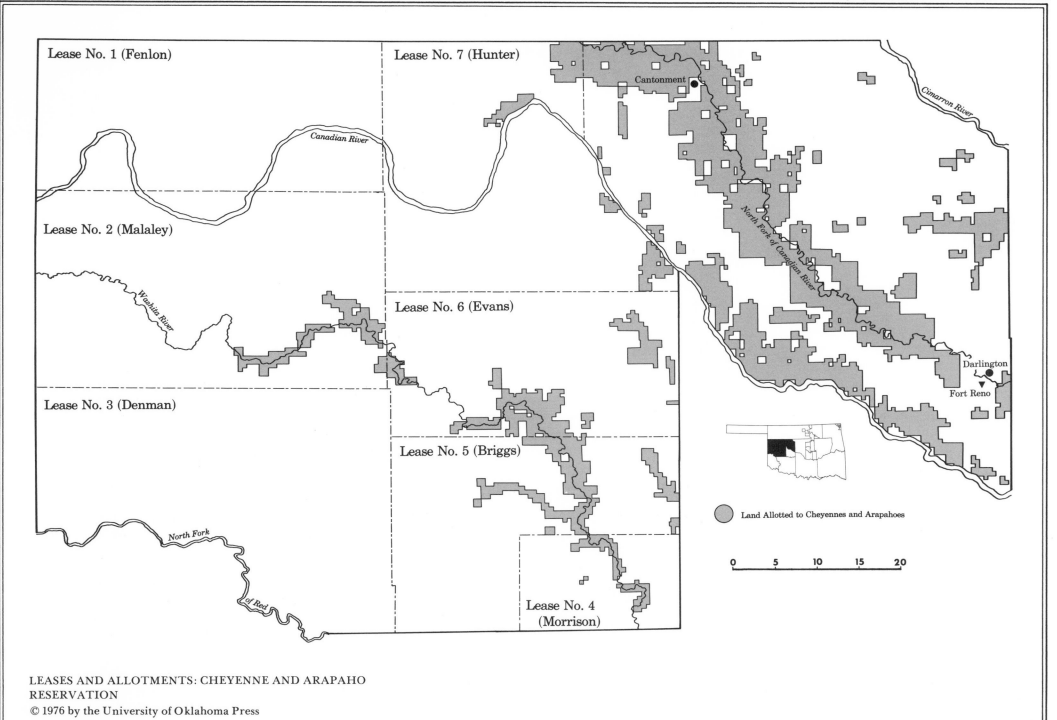

Lease No. 1 (Fenlon)

Lease No. 7 (Hunter)

Cantonment

Cimarron River

Canadian River

Lease No. 2 (Malaley)

North Fork of Canadian River

Washita River

Lease No. 6 (Evans)

Darlington

Fort Reno

Lease No. 3 (Denman)

Lease No. 5 (Briggs)

North Fork

Land Allotted to Cheyennes and Arapahoes

of Red

Lease No. 4
(Morrison)

0   5   10   15   20

LEASES AND ALLOTMENTS: CHEYENNE AND ARAPAHO
RESERVATION
© 1976 by the University of Oklahoma Press

51. LEASES AND ALLOTMENTS: CHEYENNE AND ARAPAHO RESERVATION

In December, 1882, a Cheyenne and Arapaho council sent the commissioner of Indian affairs a written request to be permitted to lease their grazing lands. John D. Miles, Cheyenne and Arapaho agent, was authorized by the chiefs to proceed with the leases without waiting for a reply from officials at Washington. Tentative agreements were signed promptly with seven cattlemen who were eager to obtain exclusive grazing rights.

Lewis M. Briggs of Kansas, Hampton B. Denman of Washington, D.C., Albert G. Evans and Robert D. Hunter of St. Louis, Edward Fenlon and William E. Malaley of Kansas, and Jesse Morrison of Darlington, Indian Territory, leased areas varying from 140,000 to 570,000 acres. The lessees were entitled to fence their lands, cutting timber on the leased area for posts. All fences constructed were to become the property of the tribe at the expiration of the lease, which was made for a period of ten years. Annual rental was set at two cents an acre.

Henry M. Teller, secretary of the interior for President Arthur, injected confusion into the tentative agreements by refusing to approve the contracts and at the same time suggesting that the cattlemen who had leases might expect protection. The lessees paid the tribal authorities $30,000 in silver as the first installment on their agreement.

The confusion that resulted from Secretary Teller's ambiguous position grew steadily worse through the latter half of the Arthur administration. Wire cutting and raids on cattle herds became common. Not only obscure ranchers, who might try to gain advantage from the confusion for a quick increase in their herds, but established cattlemen, such as the Dickey Brothers of the Cherokee Outlet, were ready to fight for their rights—as they understood them. President Cleveland in 1885 ordered all cattle removed from the Cheyenne and Arapaho lands.

Before the reservation was opened to white settlement on April 19, 1892, each member of the tribe received an allotment of 160 acres. The lands thus distributed to 3,320 Indians (up to March 20, 1892) totaled 529,682.06 acres. The United States agreed to pay $1,500,000 for the surplus lands, with a substantial per capita distribution of silver dollars as evidence of good faith. Between July 19 and October 1, 1891, nearly 3,000 members of the tribe came to the agency at Darlington and received payment—seventy-five silver dollars each.

The Indians selected their allotments generally in the eastern half of the reservation and in the valleys of the Washita, Canadian, or North Canadian rivers.

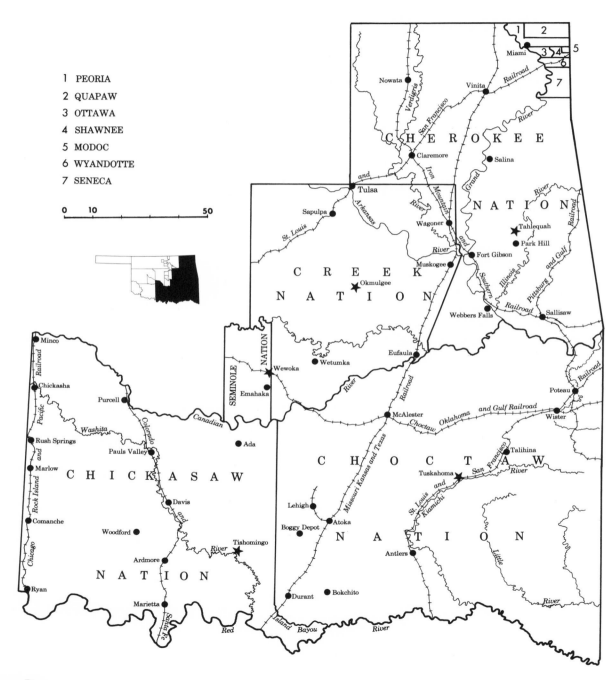

1 PEORIA
2 QUAPAW
3 OTTAWA
4 SHAWNEE
5 MODOC
6 WYANDOTTE
7 SENECA

0   10   50

CHEROKEE NATION

Nowata
Vinita
Miami
Claremore
Salina
Tulsa
Sapulpa
Tahlequah
Wagoner
Park Hill
Muskogee
Fort Gibson
CREEK NATION
Okmulgee
Webbers Falls
Sallisaw

Minco
Wewoka
SEMINOLE NATION
Wetumka
Eufaula
Emahaka
Chickasha
Poteau
Purcell
McAlester
Wister
Rush Springs
Washita
Ada
CHICKASAW
Marlow
Lehigh
CHOCTAW
Talihina
Davis
Tuskahoma
Comanche
Boggy Depot
Atoka
Woodford
NATION
Ardmore
Tishomingo
Antlers
NATION
Ryan
Durant
Bokchito
Marietta
Red

INDIAN TERRITORY, 1889
© 1976 by the University of Oklahoma Press

At the time of opening the Unassigned Lands to settlement in 1889—the basis of a newly organized territory a year later—the east side was still governed by the councils and chiefs of the Five Civilized Tribes. To the northeast of the Cherokee Nation, seven small Indian bands occupied specific areas reserved for them by the government of the United States (Map 45). In some instances these groups contained fragments of separate tribes.

Four of the five large tribes were governed under written constitutions. The fifth tribe, the Seminoles, had simple laws relatively free from verbiage, which had been codified for conducting tribal business in the United States courts. This Seminole law code had served the purpose of a written constitution under such great chiefs as John Chupco and John F. Brown.

All of the Indian basic laws were combinations—derived from the federal Constitution, the laws of the American states, and the older tribal customs of the Indians themselves. The Cherokee Constitution was written by the leaders of the tribe before removal to the West. In the land assigned to them west of Arkansas Territory, John Ross and his advisers adapted their basic law to the combined parties—Cherokees East and Cherokees West. The statesmanship of the great chief was equal to the difficult task of fusing two hostile factions under familiar laws based upon fundamental justice.

The Creek Constitution, with its House of Kings, House of Warriors, and elective chiefs, gave particular weight to the town as a unit of government. The Choctaws, outstanding among the tribes in trade and general economic advancement and progressive in education, were governed under well-written basic laws by a series of great chiefs and other competent officials. The Chickasaws, smaller than their kindred tribe, have appeared to some scholars the best governed of all the Indian nations. The Seminole Nation, also small by comparison with the Creeks from whom they were separated, displayed unquestionable talent for government and a strong, persistent tendency toward self-determination.

All of the tribes were strongly democratic. The Cherokees set the age for suffrage at eighteen, more than a century earlier than the first state of the United States to adopt that reform—Georgia.

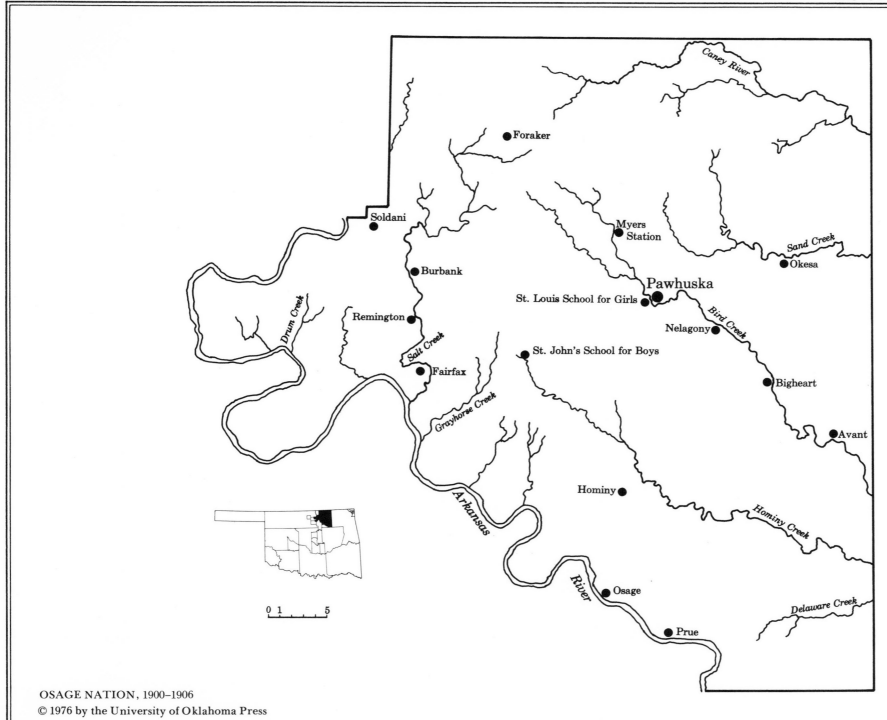

Caney River

● Foraker

Myers
Station ●

Sand Creek

● Okesa

● Burbank

Soldani
●

Drum Creek

St. Louis School for Girls ●

Pawhuska
●

Bird Creek

Nelagony ●

Remington ●

Salt Creek

St. John's School for Boys ●

● Fairfax

Bigheart ●

Grayhorse Creek

● Avant

Hominy ●

Hominy Creek

Arkansas

River

● Osage

Delaware Creek

● Prue

0 1   5

OSAGE NATION, 1900–1906
© 1976 by the University of Oklahoma Press

53. OSAGE NATION, 1900–1906

By an act of Congress on June 5, 1872, a part of the Cherokee Outlet was assigned to the Osage and Kaw Indians. The region included all the land of the Outlet between the 96th meridian on the east and the Arkansas River on the west. The separate reservation of the Kaw Indians within this area occupied 100,141 acres in the northwest corner, along the Arkansas River. The Osage lands comprised 1,466,167 acres. The Osage Agency was established at Pawhuska, and the agency of the Kaws, a sub-agency of the Osage, at Washunga.

A large part of the land in the Osage Nation has thin, poor soil, unsuitable for farm crops. The bluestem grass on many thousand acres, however, provided excellent pasturage for cattle, and since each member of the tribe received an equal share of the total area, the Osages were not miserably poor even before oil and gas were discovered on their property. Their trust fund, held by the United States government, had grown to $8,189,807 by 1891, and there was strong demand for their pasture leases.

It would not be accurate to state that nobody suspected the presence of mineral wealth in the Osage Nation in 1900. Edwin B. Foster had obtained a ten-year oil-and-gas lease in 1896 on the tribe's entire holding, and at the end of that contract the lease was renewed by its owner, the Indian Territory Illuminating Oil Company.

Actual discoveries of oil and gas were made in 1904 and 1905 on Bird Creek and Salt Creek and in the Arkansas bottom. In 1906 more than 5,000,000 barrels of petroleum were produced in the Osage Nation. The tribal government retained for its people the entire income from oil and gas production. In forty years these citizens received about $300,000,000 in royalties, which gave them a higher per capita income than any other people on earth.

Most important of the sources for the study of the Osage country is John Joseph Mathews' *The Osages*. Muriel H. Wright also gave interesting accounts of the Osages and Kaws in her *Guide to the Indian Tribes of Oklahoma*.

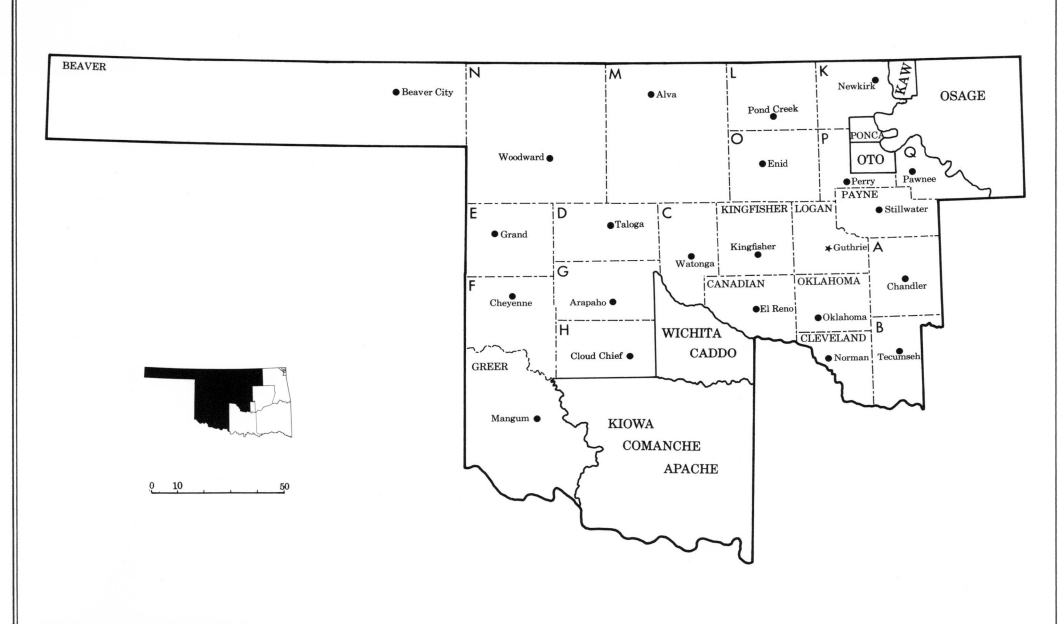

BEAVER

N ● Beaver City

KAW

OSAGE

M ● Alva

L

K ● Newkirk

● Pond Creek

O

P

PONCA

● Woodward

OTO

Q

● Enid

● Perry ● Pawnee

PAYNE

E

D

C

KINGFISHER LOGAN

● Stillwater

● Grand ● Taloga ● Kingfisher ★ Guthrie A

● Watonga

G

CANADIAN OKLAHOMA ● Chandler

F

● Cheyenne ● Arapaho ● El Reno ● Oklahoma B

H CLEVELAND

● Cloud Chief WICHITA CADDO ● Norman ● Tecumseh

GREER

● Mangum KIOWA

COMANCHE

APACHE

0 10   50

OKLAHOMA TERRITORY, 1890–1899
© 1976 by the University of Oklahoma Press

54. OKLAHOMA TERRITORY, 1890–1899

Congress gave the territory west of the Five Civilized Tribes a formal government by means of the Organic Act of May 2, 1890. The direct and immediate application of this law was to the Unassigned Lands and No Man's Land in the northwest. As areas on the east, west, and north of the central district were added by successive land openings, the territorial courts and other agencies of government were expanded.

On March 16, 1896, the United States Supreme Court decided that Greer County between the 100th meridian and the North Fork of Red River was not a part of the state of Texas. Since the Organic Act placed the southern and western boundaries of Oklahoma Territory at the Texas border, the decision made the area in dispute a part of the new territory. In May, 1896, Congress passed an act concerning the status of homesteads in Greer County, obtained under the authority of Texas, and declared the area a county of Oklahoma Territory.

The total population of Oklahoma's seven counties in 1890 was 60,417. Logan County recorded 14,254 persons, by comparison with 12,794 in Oklahoma County. Beaver County, in the Panhandle, had 2,982. By 1896 the number of counties had increased to twenty-three, and by 1900 the population had grown to 400,000. As counties were added after the several runs, they were designated by letters until names could be officially adopted: A and B counties on the eastern border of the original Oklahoma District, C through H in the Cheyenne-Arapaho area, and K through Q in the Cherokee Outlet.

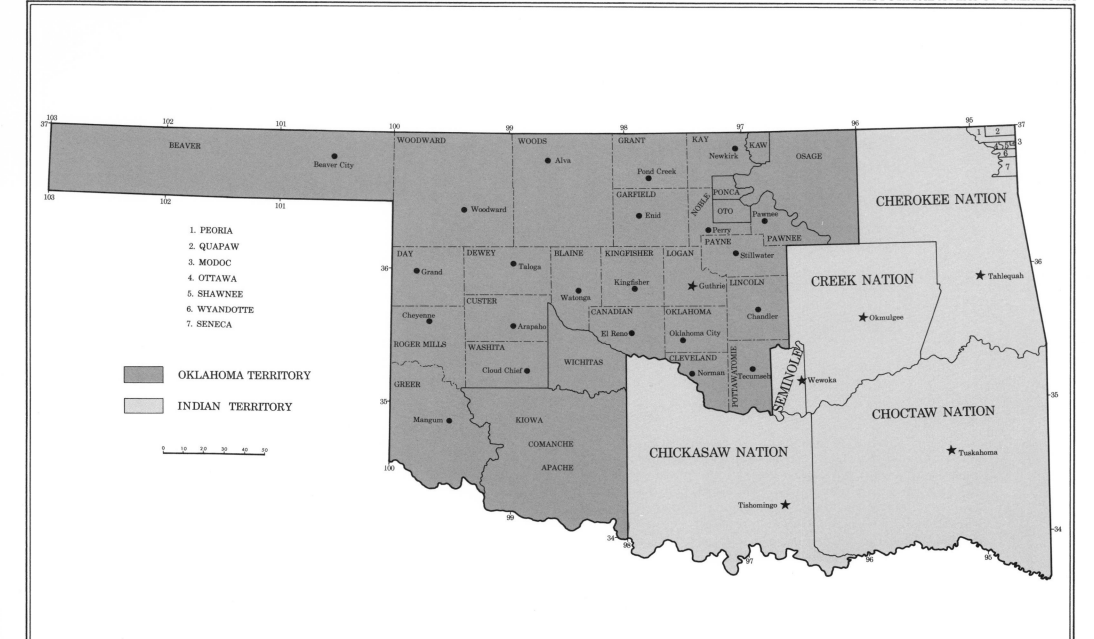

1. PEORIA
2. QUAPAW
3. MODOC
4. OTTAWA
5. SHAWNEE
6. WYANDOTTE
7. SENECA

OKLAHOMA TERRITORY

INDIAN TERRITORY

OKLAHOMA TERRITORY–INDIAN TERRITORY, 1900

© 1976 by the University of Oklahoma Press

55. OKLAHOMA TERRITORY–INDIAN TERRITORY, 1900

By 1900 all twenty-three counties of Oklahoma Territory were known by names rather than by letters, had organized county governments, designated county seats, and were continuing to increase in population. All of the Panhandle was included in Beaver County, and Beaver City was designated as the county seat. Most of the western half of the Cherokee Outlet was divided between the two large counties of Woods and Woodward. All of the land added to Oklahoma Territory by the Supreme Court decision of 1896 remained as a single county, Greer, with the county seat at Mangum. Each of these four large counties was sparsely populated, and there was a considerable amount of land in each that had not been claimed. The Kaw and Osage reservations on the northeast, the Wichita, Caddo, Kiowa, Comanche, and Apache lands in the south, and the Oto-Missouri and Ponca reservations along the Arkansas River were still unoccupied by white settlers.

The Chickasaw and Choctaw nations occupied the land south of the Canadian River and between the 98th meridian and the Arkansas boundary. The Seminole, Creek, and Cherokee nations were east of Oklahoma Territory and north of the Canadian and Arkansas rivers. The northeastern corner of Indian Territory was still divided among the peoples of seven different tribes, but small groups from several Plains tribes had also been settled in the area.

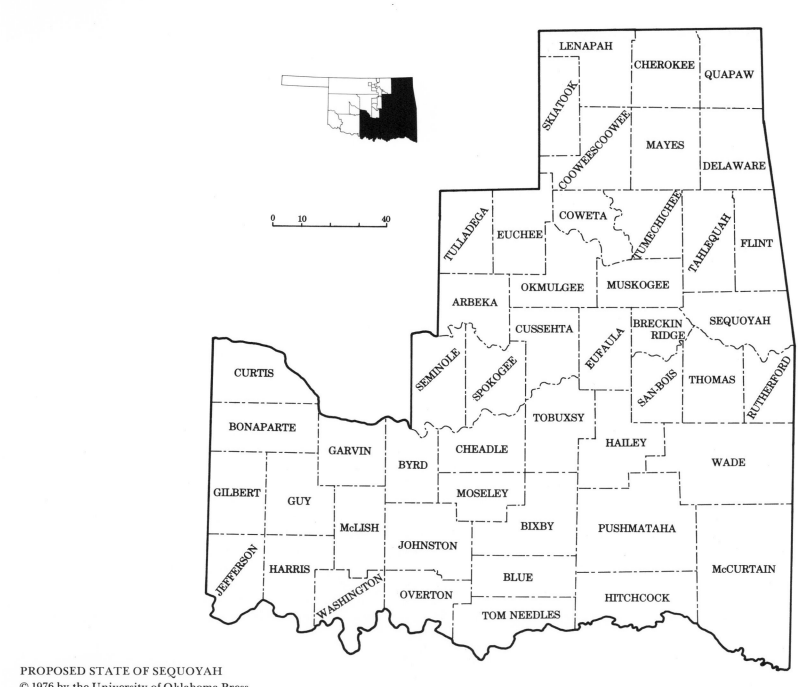

LENAPAH

CHEROKEE

QUAPAW

SKIATOOK

COOWEESCOOWEE

MAYES

DELAWARE

TULLADEGA

EUCHEE

COWETA

TUMECHICHEE

TAHLEQUAH

FLINT

OKMULGEE

MUSKOGEE

ARBEKA

CUSSEHTA

BRECKIN RIDGE

SEQUOYAH

SEMINOLE

SPOKOGEE

EUFAULA

SAN-BOIS

THOMAS

RUTHERFORD

CURTIS

TOBUXSY

HAILEY

WADE

BONAPARTE

GARVIN

BYRD

CHEADLE

GILBERT

GUY

MOSELEY

McLISH

BIXBY

PUSHMATAHA

JOHNSTON

JEFFERSON

HARRIS

BLUE

McCURTAIN

WASHINGTON

OVERTON

HITCHCOCK

TOM NEEDLES

0   10   40

PROPOSED STATE OF SEQUOYAH

© 1976 by the University of Oklahoma Press

56. PROPOSED STATE OF SEQUOYAH

The citizens of the Five Civilized Tribes and other residents of the east side in 1905 favored establishing a separate state for their section. Oklahoma Territory had expanded to the Red River on the south and the 37th parallel on the north. Its territorial officers included many persons who were experienced in politics before coming to Oklahoma. The leaders of the Indian nations apparently feared that the west side would dominate them if the two territories were combined.

The Sequoyah Convention met at Muskogee in the summer of 1905. The convention was composed of seven delegates from each of twenty-six districts and one delegate-at-large from each of the Five Civilized Tribes. The Indian leaders quickly demonstrated their grasp of political management by electing the president and five vice-presidents of the convention.

The Creek principal chief, Pleasant Porter, was elected president of the convention. William H. Murray, speaker for the Chickasaws; Charles N. Haskell, for the Creeks; W. C. Rogers, for the Cherokees; Green McCurtain, for the Choctaws; and John F. Brown, for the Seminoles, were all elected vice-presidents. The chairman of the drafting committee was W. W. Hastings, a well-known Cherokee. When the convention had completed the proposed basic law, it was submitted to the voters of Indian Territory. On November 7, 1905, the constitution was ratified by the voters, 56,279 to 9,073—more than six to one.

A bill to admit the state of Sequoyah was introduced on December 4 in the national House of Representatives and was tabled. Porter McCumber of North Dakota introduced a similar bill into the Senate, with similar results. The question of single or double statehood was to be settled not by the voice of the people most concerned but by partisan considerations in the Fifty-eighth Congress.

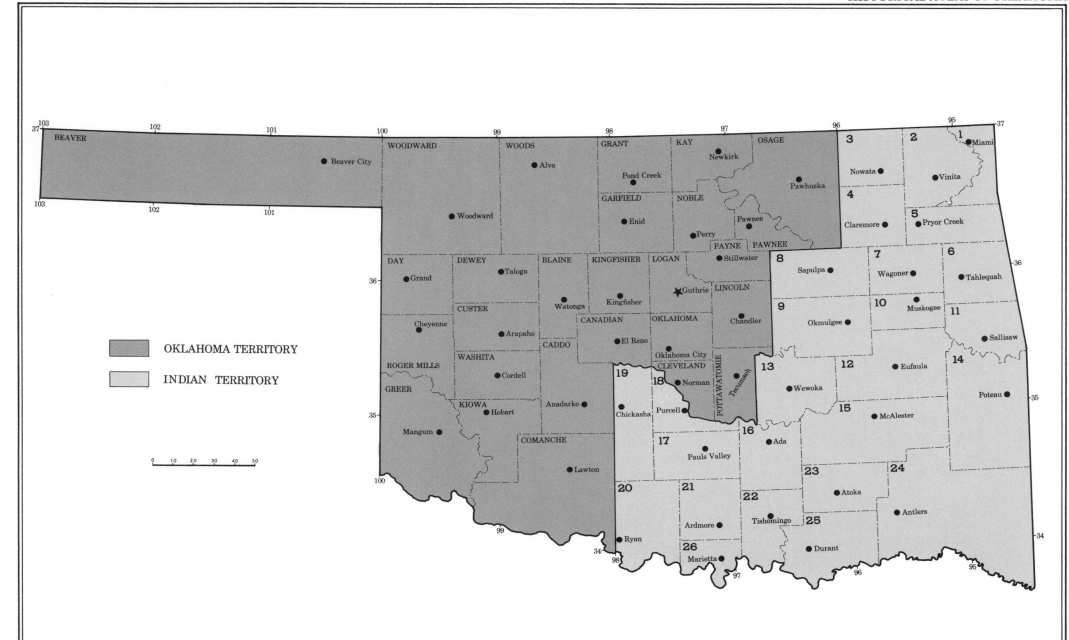

BEAVER

WOODWARD

WOODS

GRANT

KAY

OSAGE

3

2

1

• Miami

• Beaver City

• Alva

Newkirk
•

Pawhuska
•

Nowata
•

Vinita
•

Pond Creek
•

GARFIELD

NOBLE

4

Claremore
•

5

• Pryor Creek

• Woodward

Enid
•

Pawnee
•

Perry
•

DAY

DEWEY

BLAINE

KINGFISHER

LOGAN

PAYNE

PAWNEE

8

7

6

Stillwater
•

Sapulpa
•

Wagoner
•

Tahlequah
•

• Grand

• Taloga

Watonga
•

Kingfisher
•

Guthrie
LINCOLN

9

10

Muskogee
•

11

CUSTER

CANADIAN

OKLAHOMA

Chandler
•

Okmulgee
•

Sallisaw
•

• Cheyenne

Arapaho
•

CADDO

El Reno
•

CLEVELAND

13

12

Eufaula
•

14

ROGER MILLS

WASHITA

Oklahoma City
•

POTTAWATOMIE

Wewoka
•

Poteau
•

• Cordell

Norman
•

19

18

Tecumseh

15

McAlester
•

GREER

KIOWA

Anadarko
•

Chickasha
•

Purcell
•

16

Ada
•

• Mangum

• Hobart

17

Pauls Valley
•

23

24

COMANCHE

20

21

Atoka
•

• Lawton

22

25

Antlers
•

26

Ardmore
•

Tishomingo
•

Ryan
•

Durant
•

Marietta
•

OKLAHOMA TERRITORY

INDIAN TERRITORY

0 10 20 30 40 50

COUNTIES OF OKLAHOMA TERRITORY
AND RECORDING DISTRICTS OF INDIAN TERRITORY, 1906
© 1976 by the University of Oklahoma Press

57. COUNTIES OF OKLAHOMA TERRITORY
AND RECORDING DISTRICTS OF INDIAN TERRITORY, 1906

One of the difficult problems facing the "Twin Territories," especially after the federal census of 1900, was the question of "single" statehood or "double" statehood. Advocates of separate states for the west side and the east side—Oklahoma Territory and Indian Territory—worked diligently to promote their view, but many members of Congress were reluctant to accept statehood for Oklahoma on any terms, and the majority were opposed to the admission of two states between Kansas and Texas.

In 1901 the surplus lands of the reservations south of the Canadian in Oklahoma Territory, with the exception of the area classified as the Big Pasture, were to be opened by means of a lottery. The Big Pasture was opened for settlement by sealed bids in 1906. The Ponca and Oto-Missouri reservations were to be divided among the three adjoining counties, the Indians receiving title to all of the land. The Kaws and Osages also were to receive equal shares in the division of their lands. Each Osage citizen was entitled to more than 500 acres of land. By 1906, Oklahoma Territory had increased from twenty-three to twenty-seven counties. The county seat of Washita County was moved from Cloud Chief to Cordell.

Indian Territory was divided into twenty-six recording districts with a city or town designated as the recording center. The boundaries of the Five Nations were not recognized in forming the recording districts. It was necessary for each Indian, or tribe member, to record the land he wished to claim for his own.

In June, 1906, President Theodore Roosevelt signed the Enabling Act which provided for the creation of a single state from the "Twin Territories."

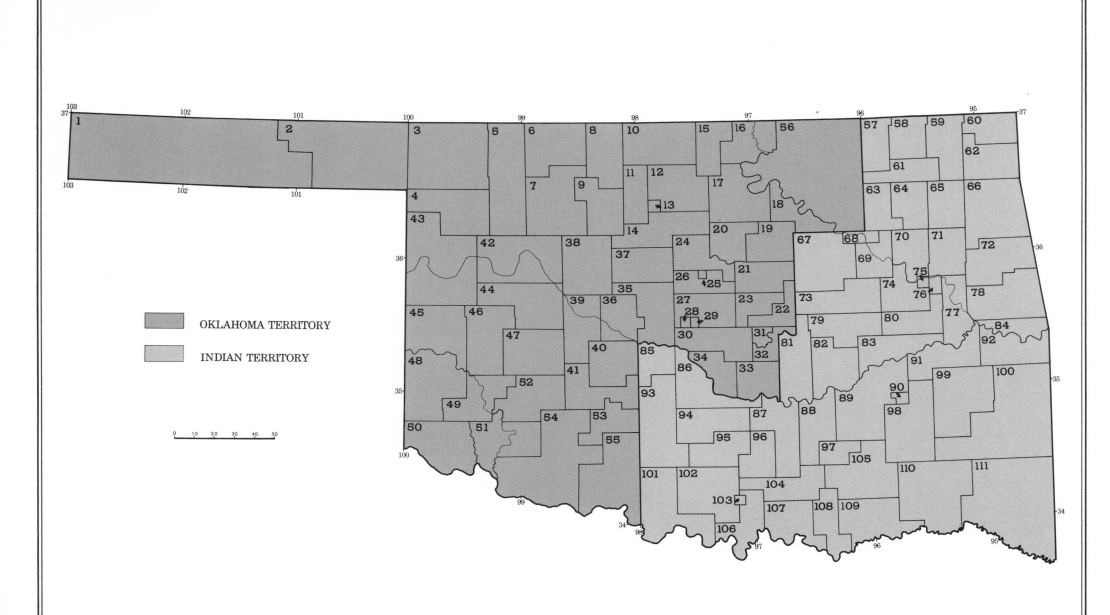

CONVENTION DELEGATE DISTRICTS
© 1976 by the University of Oklahoma Press

58. CONVENTION DELEGATE DISTRICTS

The Oklahoma Enabling Act passed by Congress in 1906 provided for the election of 112 delegates to write the constitution for the proposed new state. The governor, chief justice, and secretary of state of the Territory of Oklahoma were instructed to "apportion the Territory of Oklahoma into fifty-six districts, as nearly equal in population as may be, except that such apportionment shall include as one district the Osage Indian Reservation." Two delegates were to be elected "from said Osage district," and one delegate each from the other fifty-five districts in the Territory of Oklahoma.

The commissioner to the Five Civilized Tribes and two judges of the United States courts for the Indian Territory, as the apportionment board, were instructed to divide the Indian Territory into fifty-five districts, "as nearly equal in population as may be." Each of the fifty-five districts was entitled to elect one delegate.

In both territories the elections were ordered to be conducted "in the same manner as is prescribed by the laws of the Territory of Oklahoma regulating elections for Delegates to Congress." The election districts were numbered 1 to 56 in Oklahoma Territory and 57 to 111 in the Indian Territory.

Eligible voters were defined as follows: "All male persons over the age of twenty-one years, who are citizens of the United States, or who are members of any Indian nation or tribe in said Indian Territory and Oklahoma, and who have resided within the limits of said proposed State for at least six months next preceding the election."

The Enabling Act provided further: "The Capital of said State shall temporarily be at the city of Guthrie, in the present Territory of Oklahoma and shall not be changed therefrom previous to Anno Domini nineteen hundred and thirteen."

The convention, which met at Guthrie, contained able and experienced men representing a wide variety of occupations and interests. Ninety-nine were Democrats, twelve were Republicans, and one—Frank J. Stowe of the 95th District—regarded himself as an Independent.

The Constitution was ratified by the people on September 17, 1907, by a vote of 180,333 to 73,059.

OKLAHOMA COUNTIES, 1907

© 1976 by the University of Oklahoma Press

59. OKLAHOMA COUNTIES, 1907

Article XVII, Section 8, of the Constitution of Oklahoma concerned the formation of counties and the designation of county seats. Boundaries of seventy-five counties were defined and their respective county seats designated, these counties to become operational at the time of statehood, November 16, 1907.

Shortly after the formation of Oklahoma Territory, some counties were formed and identified by either letter or name (Maps 54 and 55). In some instances the Constitutional Convention changed the name or area of a territorial county, designated a new county seat, or abolished the county altogether. In general, however, the territorial counties were left as they had developed and were defined as shown by the following example:

Cleveland County:—Said county shall be and remain as it now exists under the Territory of Oklahoma, until hereafter changed under the provisions of the Constitution. Norman is hereby designated the County Seat of Cleveland County.

The boundaries of several counties were defined by using township and range lines only as, for example, Adair:

Adair County:—Beginning on the township line between townships nineteen (19) and twenty (20) North, at its intersection with the range line between ranges twenty-three (23) and twenty-four (24) East; thence east along said township line to intersection with the Arkansas State line: thence southward along said Arkansas State line to its intersection with the township line between townships thirteen (13) and fourteen (14) North; thence west along said township line to its intersection with the range line between ranges twenty-three (23) and twenty-four (24) East; thence north along said range line to the point of beginning. Westville is hereby designated the County Seat of Adair County.

The boundaries of many counties were complicated by using township and range lines in conjunction with rivers, as, for example, Greer:

Greer County:—Beginning on the State line between Texas and Oklahoma at its intersection with the township line between townships six (6) and seven (7) North; thence east along said township line to its intersection with the range line between ranges twenty-three (23) and twenty-four (24) West; thence north along said range line to its intersection with the township line between townships seven (7) and eight (8) North; thence east along said township line to its intersection with the center line of the North Fork of Red River; thence down along the center line of said North Fork of Red River to its intersection with the range line between ranges nineteen (19) and twenty (20) West; . . . thence west along said township line to its intersection with the center line of the Salt Fork of Red River; thence down along the center line of said river to its intersection with the east and west center section line of township three (3) North; thence west along said center section line to its intersection with the range line between ranges twenty-three (23) and twenty-four (24) West; thence south along said range line to its intersection with the base line; thence west along said base line to its intersection with the State line between Texas and Oklahoma; thence westward and northward along said State line to the point of beginning.

The largest county formed was Osage, with a total area of 2,293 square miles; the smallest was Marshall, with an area of 360 square miles. Osage County comprised the former Osage Reservation, the only reservation to remain intact as a single county. Cimarron County, the most western Panhandle county, is the only county in the United States bordering three states.

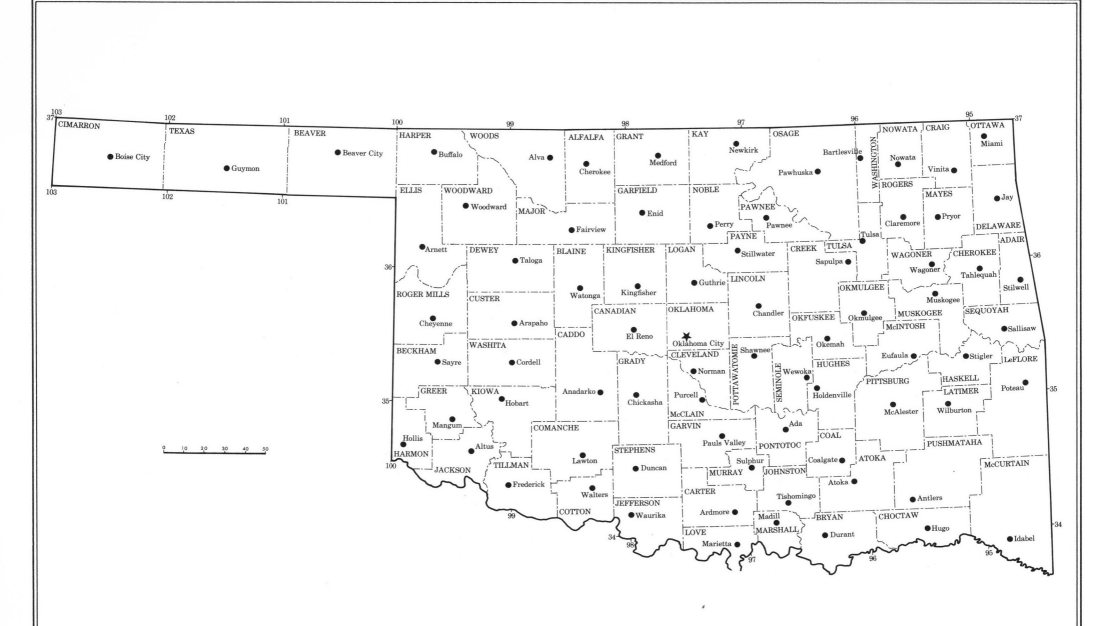

OKLAHOMA COUNTIES, 1970

© 1976 by the University of Oklahoma Press

60. OKLAHOMA COUNTIES, 1970

Article XVII, Sections 4 and 5, of the Oklahoma Constitution provided for the creation of new counties and the altering of county boundaries as given in Section 8 when and if the people so desired. Section 6 stated the method to be used for the removal of county seats.

Between 1907 and 1910 two new counties were formed, bringing the total number of counties in the state to seventy-seven. Harmon County was formed from the southwestern part of Greer County, and Hollis was designated as the county seat. The people in the southern part of Comanche County voted to form a new county, naming it Cotton, and approved Walters as the county seat. Two other attempts were made to establish new counties, one by the voters in southern Kiowa County, the other by the people of eastern Payne County, but each failed to receive the required 60 per cent of votes cast.

County boundary changes have been made in relatively few places. The most notable adjustments were made between Caddo and Grady counties and Love and Jefferson counties.

There have been several county seat "fights," and eight counties have changed the location of their county governments since 1907.

County Seat Changes, 1907–70

County	County Seat, 1907	County Seat, 1970
Adair	Westville	Stilwell
Coal	Lehigh	Coalgate
Cimarron	Kenton	Boise City
Delaware	Grove	Jay
Ellis	Grand	Arnett
Grant	Pond Creek	Medford
Jefferson	Ryan	Waurika
Pottawatomie	Tecumseh	Shawnee

In 1910, as the result of a special election, the state capital was moved from Guthrie to Oklahoma City.

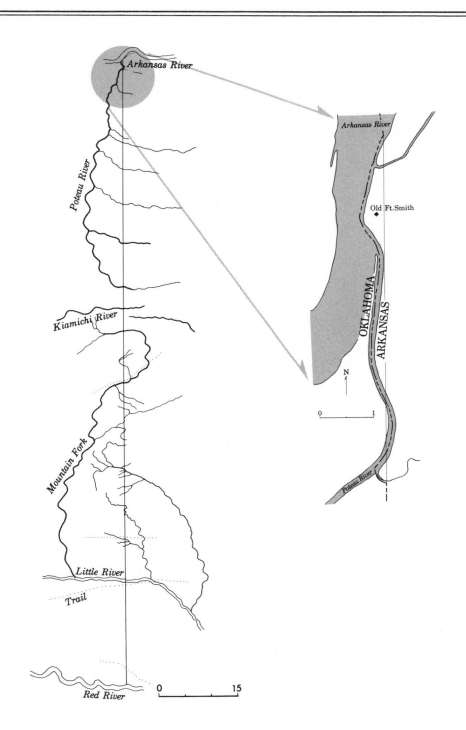

Arkansas River

Arkansas River

Old Ft. Smith

Poteau River

Kiamichi River

Mountain Fork

OKLAHOMA

ARKANSAS

N

0   1

Poteau River

Little River

Trail

Red River

0   15

FORT SMITH BOUNDARY

61. FORT SMITH BOUNDARY

James S. Conway started his survey of the Arkansas-Choctaw boundary at Fort Smith on November 2, 1825, and completed it on December 7, when his party reached Red River. Using his field notes, he finished the map of the boundary and on July 1, 1826, certified it as follows:

> I do hereby certify that the above Plat of the line forming the eastern boundary of the Choctaw Lands in the Territory of Arkansas has such marks and bounds both natural and artificial as are represented thereon and described in the field notes thereof and returned with this 'Plat' into the office of the secretary of War [Map 21].

A final adjustment was made in the Arkansas-Choctaw line between the years 1905 and 1909. An act of Congress provided for the transfer of Choctaw land amounting to about 130 acres to the state of Arkansas. Sebastian County annexed the land, and the City Council of Fort Smith accepted it as a part of the corporation. The transfer was made as a means of providing city administration for a shanty-town area in the Indian Territory that had become a refuge for criminals. Sales of land as city property amounted to $23,188.25, which was paid to the Choctaw and Chickasaw tribes. The area transferred from Oklahoma to Arkansas, sometimes referred to as the "Choctaw Strip," lies between the Poteau and Arkansas rivers on the west and the original Oklahoma-Arkansas boundary on the east.

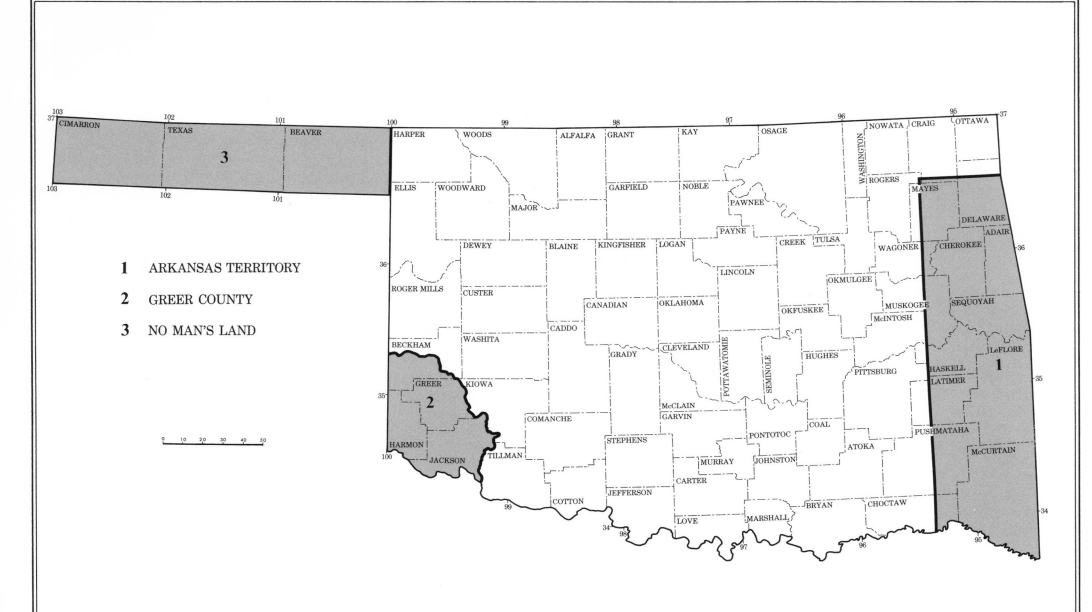

1 ARKANSAS TERRITORY

2 GREER COUNTY

3 NO MAN'S LAND

AREAS INVOLVED IN QUESTIONS OF TITLE

© 1976 by the University of Oklahoma Press

62. AREAS INVOLVED IN QUESTIONS OF TITLE

1. *Arkansas Territory*. On May 26, 1824, an act of Congress located the western boundary of Arkansas Territory as extending forty miles west from the southwest corner of Missouri and from that point due south to Red River. This act was in direct conflict with a treaty between the United States and the Choctaw Indians dated October 18, 1820, which had ceded to the Choctaws all territory embraced within the present state of Oklahoma lying south of the Canadian and Arkansas rivers. On October 13, 1827, the Arkansas Territory legislature organized Lovely County with Nicksville as the county seat. Lovely County was to include the land west of the Arkansas River and north of the Canadian River located within the Arkansas Territory boundaries. Previously, however, on February 12, 1825, a treaty had been made between the United States and the Creek Indians giving this area of land to the Creeks. On May 28, 1828, all of the land north and east of the Arkansas River located in the then Territory of Arkansas was ceded by the United States to the Cherokees. On October 17, 1828, an act of the Arkansas Territory legislature abolished the counties that had been organized west of the present Arkansas-Oklahoma boundary, and the area was recognized as a part of the Choctaw, Creek, or Cherokee nations.

2. *Greer County*. The original Greer County included all of the land in present-day Oklahoma located south and west of the North Fork of Red River. This area was claimed by both Texas and the United States. On February 8, 1860, the Texas legislature created Greer County, Texas. Only a few families moved into the area, and it remained very sparsely settled. No post office was established within Greer County until 1886. On March 16, 1896, the Supreme Court of the United States adjudged this area to be a part of Indian Territory. Soon thereafter it was attached to Oklahoma Territory, organized as a county, and opened for settlement. Those who had previously settled in the area were permitted to retain their land. At the time of the Oklahoma Constitutional Convention the area was divided among Beckham, Greer, and Jackson counties. After statehood the part that had been designated Greer County was further divided to form Harmon County (Maps 59, 60).

3. *No Man's Land*. No Man's Land, or the Panhandle, as it is generally known, is the only part of the present state of Oklahoma that was never a part of Indian Territory. Legally it was known as the "Public Land Strip." The area became a part of the United States when the independent nation of Texas asked to be admitted as a state. Since Texas desired to enter the United States as a slave state, it was necessary that all land north of 36°30′ north latitude be ceded to the United States in accordance with the Missouri Compromise of 1850. Accordingly, No Man's Land was ceded to the United States on November 25, 1850. Because of the lawlessness in the area, as well as the desire by several settlers to gain clear title to the land, an attempt was made in March, 1887, to organize the Public Land Strip as Cimarron Territory. A full complement of officers was elected, Beaver City was selected as the capital of the Territory of Cimarron, and a territorial legislature held a meeting. The federal government, however, failed to recognize the organization. The Organic Act of April 22, 1899, added No Man's Land to Oklahoma Territory as county number 7. Later the area was named Beaver County. At the time of the Constitutional Convention, No Man's Land was divided into three counties, Beaver, Texas, and Cimarron (Map 59).

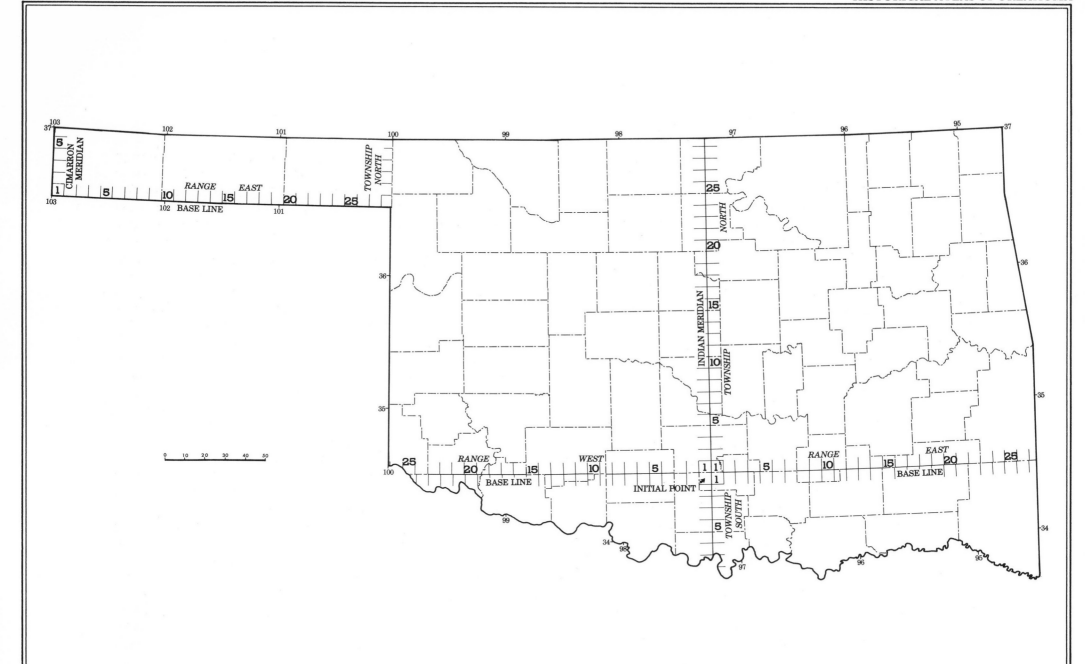

TOWNSHIPS AND RANGES
© 1976 by the University of Oklahoma Press

63. TOWNSHIPS AND RANGES

All land in Oklahoma, with the exception of the Panhandle, is surveyed from Initial Point, located in Murray County. Initial Point was established in 1870 by Ehud N. Darling. Darling was surveying the lands of the Choctaw and Chickasaw nations as described in the treaty of June 22, 1855. By the treaty of April 28, 1866, these Indians agreed to the survey and subdivision of their land east of 98th meridian, using the public-land survey system of the United States.

The 1871 report of the commissioner of the General Land Office contains this statement:

> The surveyors were instructed to select a suitable initial point in the center of the Chickasaw lands, or in the vicinity of Fort Arbuckle, and perpetuate it by a suitable monument, and from this point to establish a principal meridian and base line to be known by the designation of the Indian Base Line and Meridian.

The point chosen was about one mile south of Fort Arbuckle, probably because Fort Arbuckle was a convenient and well-known location. The land was then divided into townships north and south and ranges east and west of Initial Point. Each township and range is six miles in length; thus each encloses a square of six miles by six miles, or a total area of thirty-six-square miles. There are twenty-nine townships north and nine south, twenty-seven ranges east and twenty-six west of Initial Point.

Initial Point for the Panhandle was designated as 103° west longitude and 36°30′ north latitude, or the southwestern corner of the area. The 36°30′ parallel was designated as the Cimarron Base Line and 103d meridian west as the Cimarron Meridian. All townships in the Panhandle are north and all ranges east of the Initial Point, there being twenty-eight ranges east and six townships north.

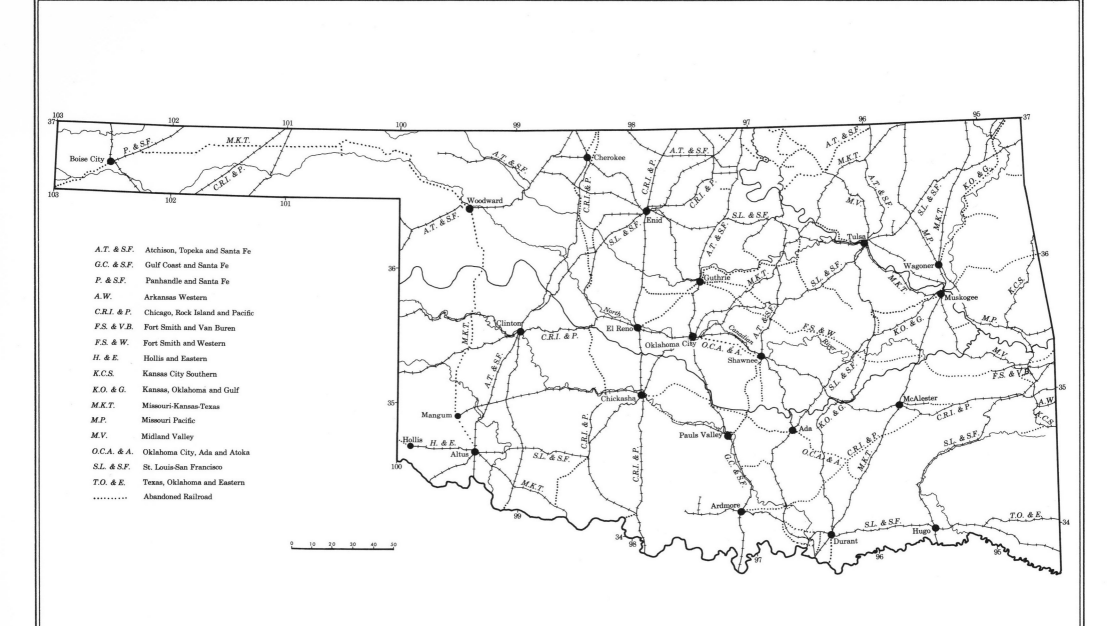

A.T. & S.F.	Atchison, Topeka and Santa Fe
G.C. & S.F.	Gulf Coast and Santa Fe
P. & S.F.	Panhandle and Santa Fe
A.W.	Arkansas Western
C.R.I. & P.	Chicago, Rock Island and Pacific
F.S. & V.B.	Fort Smith and Van Buren
F.S. & W.	Fort Smith and Western
H. & E.	Hollis and Eastern
K.C.S.	Kansas City Southern
K.O. & G.	Kansas, Oklahoma and Gulf
M.K.T.	Missouri-Kansas-Texas
M.P.	Missouri Pacific
M.V.	Midland Valley
O.C.A. & A.	Oklahoma City, Ada and Atoka
S.L. & S.F.	St. Louis-San Francisco
T.O. & E.	Texas, Oklahoma and Eastern
··········	Abandoned Railroad

RAILROADS IN OKLAHOMA, 1870–1974
© 1976 by the University of Oklahoma Press

64. RAILROADS IN OKLAHOMA, 1870–1974

Plans for railroad building at the time of the Civil War included connecting the Great Lakes with the Missouri River, the Missouri Valley with the Gulf Coast, and the Mississippi River with California. Indian Territory was in the path of the second and third of these major plans. The first railroad line to the Pacific became a reality when the Union Pacific, building west from Omaha, and the Central Pacific, building east from Sacramento, met at Ogden, Utah, in 1869.

The Union Pacific planned a southern branch to connect eastern Kansas with the Gulf of Mexico, following the route of the old Texas Road. In 1869 the Missouri, Kansas and Texas Railway Company, chartered by the state of Kansas, acquired the properties of this southern branch, and by 1873 had extended the line from Chetopa, Kansas, across Indian Territory to the Red River near Colbert's Ferry. Crossing the Arkansas River on a bridge 840 feet long, this first line in the land of the Five Civilized Tribes ran southwest through Muskogee, Eufaula (North Fork Town), McAlester, Atoka, and Durant.

The Atlantic and Pacific (St. Louis and San Francisco) had constructed a line from St. Louis to Seneca, Missouri, on the border of Indian Territory by April 1, 1871. This road extended its line southwest toward the Creek Nation. It formed a junction with the M. K. and T. at Vinita on September 1, and stopped construction until 1882. By that time it had been reorganized as the St. Louis and San Francisco Railroad Company. It bridged the Arkansas River by 1886 and established an important cattle shipping center at Red Fork on the right bank. Between 1882 and 1887 the same company constructed a line from Fort Smith, Arkansas, through the Choctaw Nation to the Red River south of Hugo.

The Chicago, Rock Island and Pacific Railroad built south from Caldwell, Kansas, in 1890, approximately along the line of the Chisholm Trail across the Cherokee Outlet and the Unassigned Lands to the border of the Chickasaw Nation. In 1902 the Rock Island Company bought the properties of the Choctaw, Oklahoma and Gulf Railroad, which gave El Reno a connection with Oklahoma City, Shawnee, Wewoka, McAlester, and Wister Junction. Since the principal fuel for locomotives at that time was coal, access to the eastern Oklahoma mines was an important consideration for the M. K. and T., the Rock Island, and other roads.

The Atchison, Topeka and Santa Fe, which was in operation before the opening of the Unassigned Lands, played a large part in the runs for homesteads and the location of townsites. The growth of population in the Twin Territories and the development of industry and agriculture were closely dependent upon railroads in Oklahoma, as in other parts of the American West.

By 1916, even before railroad construction was completed in Oklahoma, abandonment of unprofitable lines had begun. This phenomenon, due in part to the competition of highways and pipe lines, was paralleled by abandonment in the nation at large. The most recent (1975) abandonment of a long line was of the M. K. and T. in western Oklahoma. This route extended northward from Altus to Woodward and then westward across the Panhandle to a point near Keyes in Cimarron County.

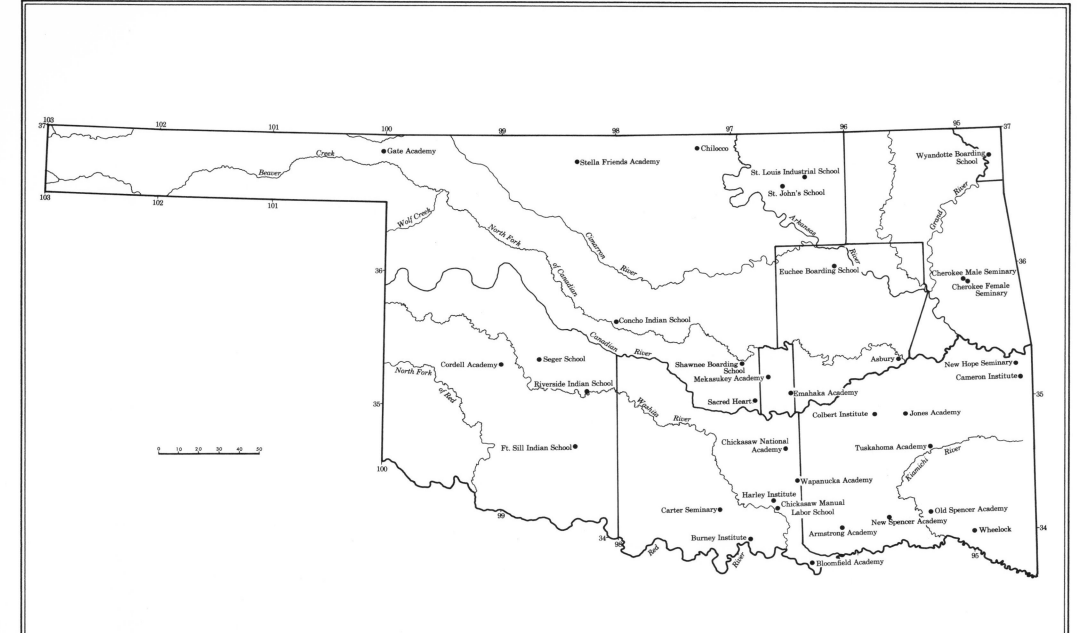

37 103 | 102 | 101 | 100 | 99 | 98 | 97 | 96 | 95 | 37

Creek
Beaver

● Gate Academy

● Stella Friends Academy

● Chilocco

Wyandotte Boarding School

St. Louis Industrial School

St. John's School

103 | 102 | 101

Wolf Creek

North Fork

Cimarron River

of Canadian

Arkansas River

Grand River

36

● Euchee Boarding School

Cherokee Male Seminary

Cherokee Female Seminary

36

● Concho Indian School

Canadian River

North Fork

● Cordell Academy

● Seger School

Shawnee Boarding School ●
Mekasukey Academy ●

● Asbury

New Hope Seminary ●
Cameron Institute ●

35

● Riverside Indian School

of Red

Washita River

Sacred Heart ●

Emahaka Academy ●

Colbert Institute ● ● Jones Academy

35

Ft. Sill Indian School ●

Chickasaw National Academy ●

Tuskahoma Academy ● Kiamichi River

100

Wapanucka Academy ●

Harley Institute ●
Chickasaw Manual Labor School ●

Old Spencer Academy ●

New Spencer Academy ●

99

● Carter Seminary

Armstrong Academy ●

● Wheelock

34

34 98

Burney Institute ●

Red River

95

Bloomfield Academy ●

34

0 10 20 30 40 50

OKLAHOMA ACADEMIES

© 1976 by the University of Oklahoma Press

65. OKLAHOMA ACADEMIES

The earliest formal education available in Oklahoma was that provided by the Indian schools. Churches established some of the schools, and missionary societies supplemented the meager funds provided by Congress for tribal education. In the mission schools religious training was combined with instruction in reading, writing, and numbers. The national councils of the Five Civilized Tribes gave attention to the problem of training some of their bright young people for college.

Among the notable academies that grew out of missions were Sacred Heart, Asbury, Tullahassee, Wheelock, and Bloomfield. In the Choctaw Nation the Education Act of 1842 was followed by the establishment and rapid growth of several academies. Spencer Academy, built in an attractive location ten miles from Fort Towson, was designed to accommodate one hundred boys. The school gave special attention to manual training and agriculture. New Hope School for Girls was situated five miles southeast of Fort Coffee. Armstrong, fifty miles west of Fort Towson, Fort Coffee Academy for Boys, occupying buildings formerly used by the garrison, and Chuala Female Seminary at Pine Ridge, one mile from Doaksville, were other schools supported by the Choctaws.

After the John Ross faction of the Cherokees moved west, the Cherokee Male Seminary, near Tahlequah, and the Female Seminary, near Park Hill, were constructed, largely as a result of the great chief's influence. Bloomfield Academy, established by the Methodist missionary John H. Carr in the Chickasaw Nation, opened its first classes in 1852. As a frontier preacher, the founder had ridden the circuits of the Southwest for eighteen years, and as a carpenter he directed all the work of construction on the campus at Bloomfield for fifteen years. He also made practically all the coffins for deceased Indians of the community.

In Oklahoma Territory the schools for Indian children at Riverside, on the Washita near Anadarko, at Fort Sill, at Pawhuska (St. Louis Industrial School), and at Concho were widely known. These schools taught beginners, with age limits from five or six to nineteen or twenty. At Chilocco many of the Indian boys and girls were admitted to studies beyond the elementary grades. At Riverside and Chilocco the older pupils engaged in such "practical" pursuits as dressmaking and cooking (for girls) and the care of livestock, carpentry, and bricklaying (for boys).

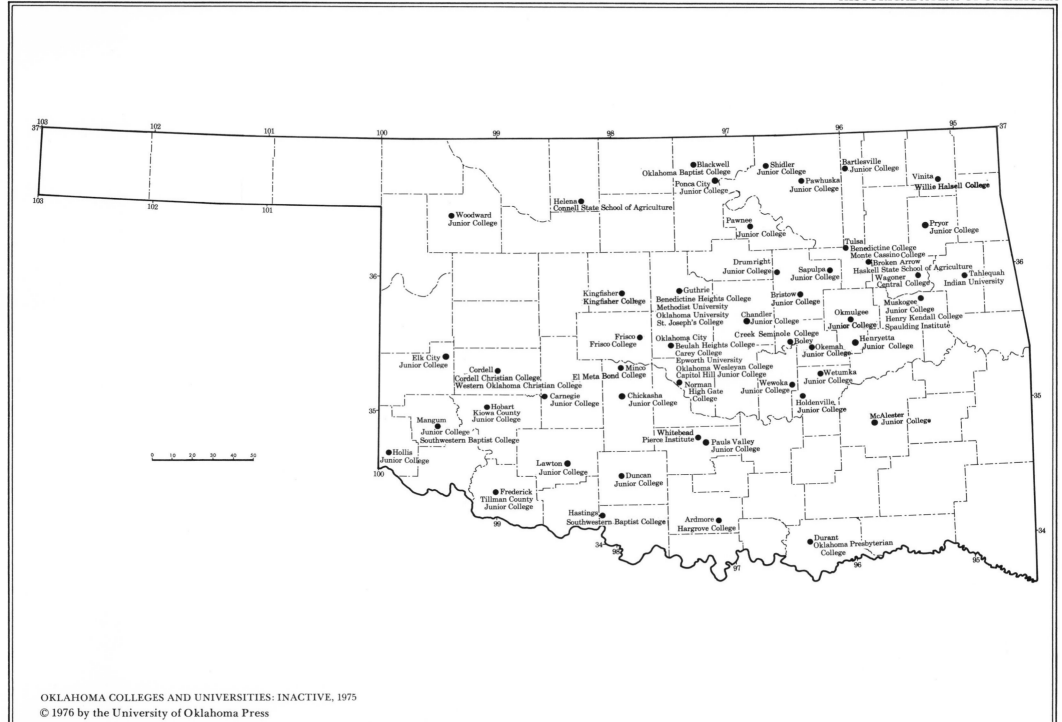

103 37
102
101
100
99
98
97
96
95 37

●Blackwell
Oklahoma Baptist College
Ponca City
Junior College

●Shidler
Junior College

Bartlesville●
Junior College

Vinita●
Willie Halsell College

Helena●
Connell State School of Agriculture

●Pawhuska
Junior College

Woodward●
Junior College

Pawnee●
Junior College

●Pryor
Junior College

Tulsa●
Benedictine College
Monte Cassino College
●Broken Arrow
Haskell State School of Agriculture

36

Drumright●
Junior College

Sapulpa●
Junior College

Wagoner●
Central College
●Tahlequah
Indian University

Kingfisher●
Kingfisher College

●Guthrie
Benedictine Heights College
Methodist University
Oklahoma University
St. Joseph's College

Bristow●
Junior College

Muskogee●
Junior College
Henry Kendall College
Spaulding Institute

Frisco●
Frisco College

Oklahoma City●
Beulah Heights College
Carey College
Epworth University
Oklahoma Wesleyan College
Capitol Hill Junior College

Chandler●
Junior College

Okmulgee●
Junior College

Creek Seminole College
●Boley

●Henryetta
Junior College

Okemah●
Junior College

Elk City●
Junior College

●Minco
El Meta Bond College

Cordell●
Cordell Christian College
Western Oklahoma Christian College

Norman●
High Gate
College

●Wetumka
Junior College

Wewoka●
Junior College

Carnegie●
Junior College

●Chickasha
Junior College

Holdenville●
Junior College

35

Mangum●
Junior College
Southwestern Baptist College

●Hobart
Kiowa County
Junior College

McAlester●
Junior College

Hollis●
Junior College

●Whitebead
Pierce Institute

●Pauls Valley
Junior College

Lawton●
Junior College

●Duncan
Junior College

Frederick●
Tillman County
Junior College

Hastings●
Southwestern Baptist College

Ardmore●
Hargrove College

●Durant
Oklahoma Presbyterian
College

0 10 20 30 40 50

OKLAHOMA COLLEGES AND UNIVERSITIES: INACTIVE, 1975

© 1976 by the University of Oklahoma Press

A number of colleges and universities have been reorganized under new names and in some instances moved to new locations as steps in permanent development. Others have entirely disappeared from the scene.

Kingfisher College, founded in 1894, maintained its separate existence with remarkably high academic standards for thirty-three years. It was absorbed by the University of Oklahoma in 1927. Henry Kendall College, established at Muskogee in 1894, was moved to Tulsa thirteen years later and became the University of Tulsa in 1920. Epworth University, founded at Oklahoma City in 1904, was moved to Guthrie for a few years, returning to Oklahoma City in 1919 as Oklahoma City College.

Indian University, founded at Tahlequah in 1880, was moved to Bacone, near Muskogee, the next year, and in 1910 was renamed for its founder, Almon C. Bacone. Oklahoma Presbyterian College, Durant, was chiefly a school for Indian girls.

The state schools of agriculture at Helena and Broken Bow ceased to operate in 1917, when Governor Robert L. Williams vetoed their appropriations. Among the church schools that were discontinued were Southwestern Baptist College at Mangum, St. Joseph's at Guthrie, Monte Cassino at Tulsa, Oklahoma Wesleyan at Oklahoma City, and Oklahoma Baptist at Blackwell.

The establishment of municipal junior colleges provides clear proof of Oklahoma's optimism, as well as its genuine interest in education. But the financial hazards are many and the mortality rate high. Several local school districts established junior colleges that have since been discontinued, among them Shidler, Pawhuska, Pawnee, Bartlesville, Woodward, Bristow, Sapulpa, Okmulgee, Muskogee, Okemah, Wewoka, Duncan, Hobart, Mangum, Hollis, Carnegie, Holdenville, Wetumka, and Frederick. The Capital Hill Junior College was under the control of the Oklahoma City school district.

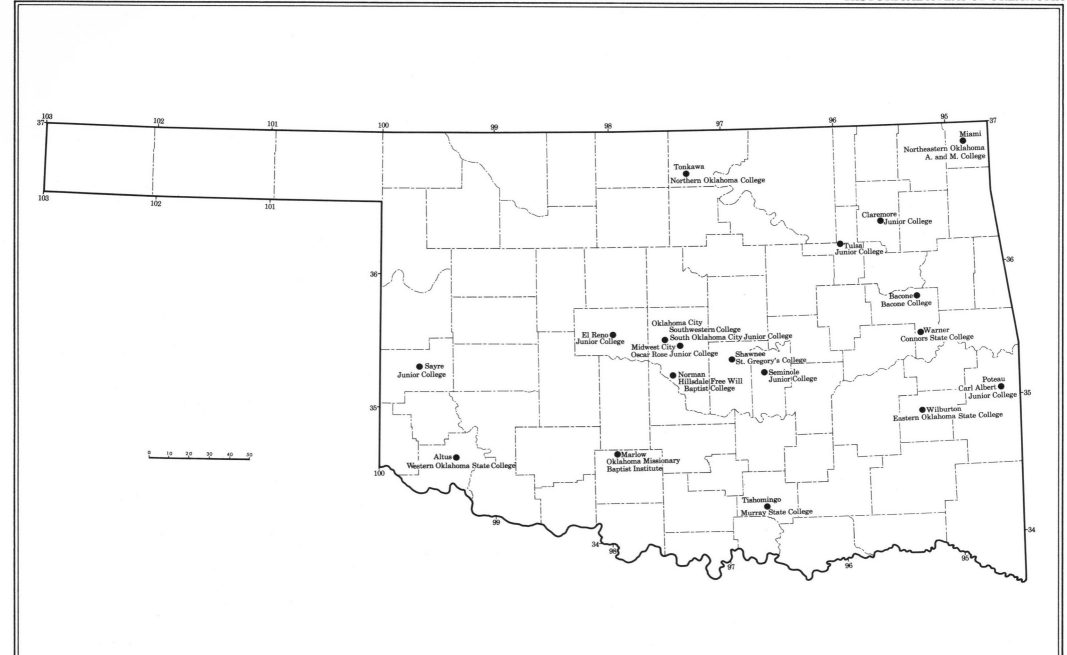

103 102 101 100 99 98 97 96 95

Miami
Northeastern Oklahoma
A. and M. College

Tonkawa
Northern Oklahoma College

Claremore
Junior College

Tulsa
Junior College

Bacone
Bacone College

El Reno
Junior College

Oklahoma City
Southwestern College
South Oklahoma City Junior College

Warner
Connors State College

Midwest City
Oscar Rose Junior College

Shawnee
St. Gregory's College

Sayre
Junior College

Norman
Hillsdale Free Will
Baptist College

Seminole
Junior College

Poteau
Carl Albert
Junior College

Wilburton
Eastern Oklahoma State College

Altus
Western Oklahoma State College

Marlow
Oklahoma Missionary
Baptist Institute

Tishomingo
Murray State College

0 10 20 30 40 50

OKLAHOMA JUNIOR COLLEGES: ACTIVE

67. OKLAHOMA JUNIOR COLLEGES: ACTIVE

The eight junior colleges owned and operated by the state are Claremore Junior College (formerly Oklahoma Military Academy), Claremore; Connors State College of Agricultural and Applied Science, Warner; Eastern Oklahoma State College (formerly Oklahoma School of Mines), Wilburton; Murray State College, Tishomingo; Northeastern Oklahoma A. and M. College, Miami; Northern Oklahoma College, Tonkawa (established in 1901 as the University Preparatory School, it became Oklahoma Business Academy in 1920 and was changed to the current name in 1941); Tulsa Junior College, Tulsa; and Western Oklahoma State College, Altus. Tulsa Junior College was established by legislative action in 1970. The college at Altus, which was started as a community college in 1925, was added to the state system by the Oklahoma legislature in 1972.

The six community colleges formerly financed by district funds, are now financed by the state. These six colleges are El Reno Junior College, El Reno; Oscar Rose Junior College, Midwest City; Carl Albert Junior College, Poteau; Sayre Junior College, Sayre; Seminole Junior College, Seminole; and South Oklahoma City Junior College, Oklahoma City. The junior colleges at El Reno, Poteau, Sayre, and Seminole were established in the 1930's, when many other junior colleges were being started. For the first few years each of these four operated in conjunction with the high school, often in the same building with classes instructed by the same teachers.

Five Oklahoma junior colleges are classed as independent. These are Bacone College, Bacone; Hillsdale Free Will Baptist College, Norman; Oklahoma Missionary Baptist Institute, Marlow; St. Gregory's College, Shawnee; and Southwestern College, Oklahoma City. Bacone College, founded in Tahlequah in 1880, was known as Indian University. It moved to the present site a year later but did not change its name until 1910. St. Gregory's College was established in Shawnee after the buildings of Sacred Heart Academy, in the southern part of Pottawatomie County, were destroyed by fire. Hillsdale College was first organized in Tecumseh as Tecumseh College. After being closed for a few years, it was reopened in Tulsa, moved to Wagoner, and then shifted to Oklahoma City before moving to its present campus. All the independent junior colleges are closely related to church organizations.

The junior colleges having the largest enrollments are Tulsa Junior College, Oscar Rose Junior College, and South Oklahoma City Junior College. Although all the junior colleges offer credit that is transferable to the senior colleges or universities, they also give the students many opportunities to study specialized courses and activities that lead to terminal certification and junior-college degrees.

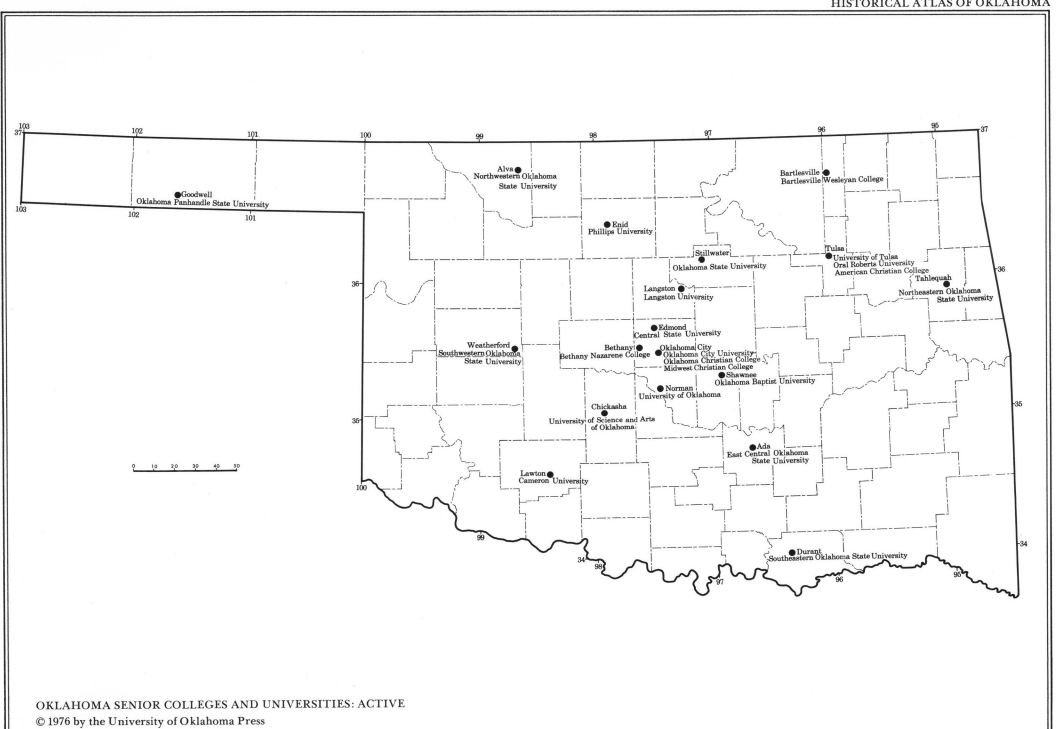

Alva ●
Northwestern Oklahoma
State University

Goodwell
Oklahoma Panhandle State University

Bartlesville ●
Bartlesville Wesleyan College

● Enid
Phillips University

Stillwater ●
Oklahoma State University

Tulsa ●
University of Tulsa
Oral Roberts University
American Christian College

Langston ●
Langston University

Tahlequah ●
Northeastern Oklahoma
State University

● Edmond
Central State University

Weatherford ●
Southwestern Oklahoma
State University

Bethany ●
Bethany Nazarene College

Oklahoma City ●
Oklahoma City University
Oklahoma Christian College
Midwest Christian College

● Shawnee
Oklahoma Baptist University

● Norman
University of Oklahoma

Chickasha ●
University of Science and Arts
of Oklahoma

Ada ●
East Central Oklahoma
State University

Lawton ●
Cameron University

Durant ●
Southeastern Oklahoma State University

0 10 20 30 40 50

OKLAHOMA SENIOR COLLEGES AND UNIVERSITIES: ACTIVE

© 1976 by the University of Oklahoma Press

Higher education in Oklahoma had its beginnings before statehood. The first territorial legislature in 1890 provided for the establishment of the University of Oklahoma at Norman, the Agricultural and Mechanical College in Payne County, and a normal school at Edmond. By November 9, 1891, the normal school was ready for its first classes with an enrollment of nineteen. Preparatory students were admitted to all three of the schools and for several years outnumbered college students.

During the term of the third territorial governor, William C. Renfrow, the legislature established the Northwestern Normal School at Alva and the Agricultural and Normal University for Negroes at Langston. Southwestern Normal School at Weatherford was authorized by the legislature in 1901.

The first legislature of the new state considered the problem of providing colleges in eastern Oklahoma to balance those schools already established in the western part of the state. Southeastern Normal School at Durant, Northeastern Normal School at Tahlequah, and East Central Normal School at Ada, were established in rapid succession.

The state normal schools became state colleges as demand rose for more advanced education. In 1974 twelve state-supported colleges and universities were offering academic degrees. They include the University of Oklahoma, Norman; Oklahoma State University, Stillwater; Northeastern Oklahoma State University, Tahlequah; East Central Oklahoma State University, Ada; Southeastern Oklahoma State University, Durant; South-western Oklahoma State University, Weatherford; Northwestern Oklahoma State University, Alva; Central State University, Edmond; Langston University, Langston; University of Sciences and Arts of Oklahoma (formerly Oklahoma College of Liberal Arts, Oklahoma College for Women), Chickasha; Oklahoma Panhandle State University, Goodwell; and Cameron University, Lawton.

Colleges founded by religious organizations are maintained at Bartlesville (Bartlesville Wesleyan College), Bethany (Bethany Nazarene College), Enid (Phillips University), Oklahoma City (Oklahoma City University, Oklahoma Christian College, and Midwest Christian College), Shawnee (Oklahoma Baptist University), and Tulsa (University of Tulsa, Oral Roberts University, and American Christian College).

Some of the church-related institutions were first established in cities other than where they are now located and with different names. For example, Henry Kendall College moved from Muskogee to Tulsa and became the University of Tulsa; Oklahoma Baptist University is linked directly to Baptist colleges that once existed in Hastings, Mangum, and Blackwell; the predecessors of Oklahoma City University are Epworth University, of Oklahoma City, which moved to Guthrie and became Methodist University before returning to Oklahoma City, first as Oklahoma City College and then as Oklahoma City University.

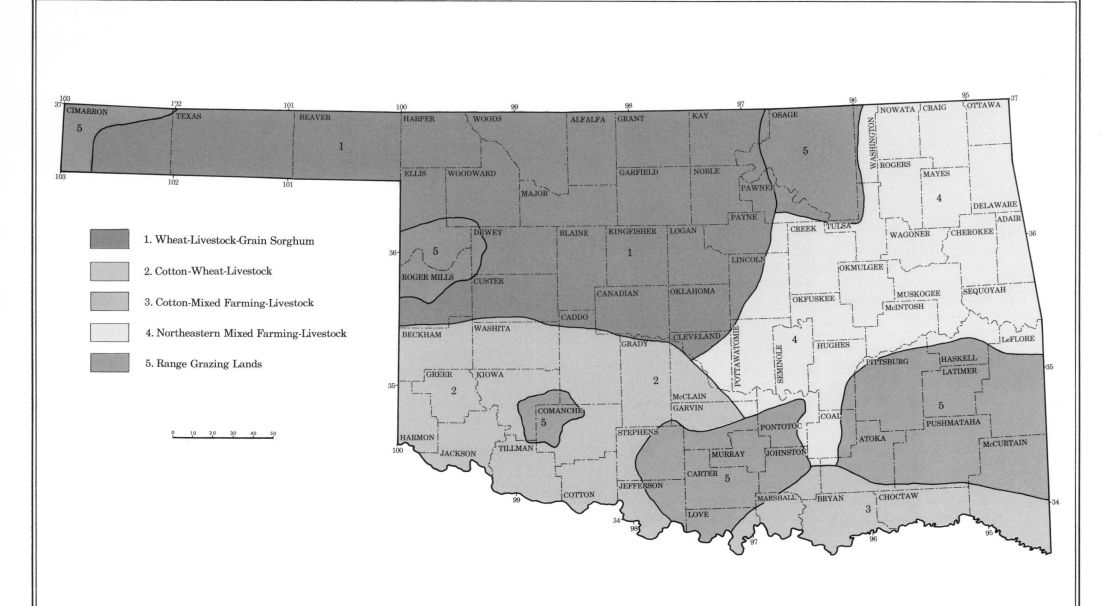

1. Wheat-Livestock-Grain Sorghum

2. Cotton-Wheat-Livestock

3. Cotton-Mixed Farming-Livestock

4. Northeastern Mixed Farming-Livestock

5. Range Grazing Lands

AGRICULTURAL REGIONS OF OKLAHOMA

© 1976 by the University of Oklahoma Press

Most of the early settlers of Oklahoma, both Indian and white, were primarily interested in agricultural activities. Many of the Indians who moved over the "Trails of Tears" into eastern Oklahoma had long been engaged in growing various crops. When they settled in their new land, they tried to continue farming. Large cotton plantations developed on the Red River plains, and well-cultivated and well-stocked farms were fairly numerous in the Three Forks and Ozark areas. Most of the pioneers who later moved into the Unassigned Lands, the Cherokee Outlet, and the various reservations as they were opened to settlement were farmers. Often the agricultural activities resulted in failure because the settlers did not know how to farm in the environment into which they had moved.

Oklahoma can be divided into five agricultural land-use areas, chiefly on the bases of climate, soils, and topography. In each area the farmers grow about the same groups of crops in about the same way. Boundaries between the areas are not clearly defined lines but rather are zones in which a somewhat gradual transition takes place. Livestock is the common denominator for all the agricultural regions since the most common land use in all parts of Oklahoma is for pasture.

Six areas of Oklahoma—the western Panhandle, the western Canadian River valley, the Osage Hills, the Wichita Mountains, the Arbuckle Mountain area, and the Ouachita Mountains—grow very few crops other than hay. All these areas are too rugged or too dry for intensive or even extensive cultivation. Wheat is the dominant crop in the northwestern quarter of the state. Farms are large, and much of the work is mechanized. Winter wheat makes good pasture during the winter season; thus the grazing of feeder stock is common throughout the area. Grain sorghums are the second most important crop of the northwest. In southwestern Oklahoma cotton competes with wheat for land use, especially in those sections where water is available for irrigation; grain sorghums to be used for feed are the third crop of the southwest. In the region south of the Ouachita Mountains more acres are planted in soybeans than in cotton, but the crop having the greatest acreage is hay. Peanuts are also a common product of this region. In the northeastern part of Oklahoma grain sorghum, corn, wheat, and soybeans are important crops. The northeastern region is also an area of specialty crops, such as vegetables, fruits, and berries. Again, however, more land is planted in hay than in any other crop. Like the northwestern part of the state, livestock grazing is common in all the other regions.

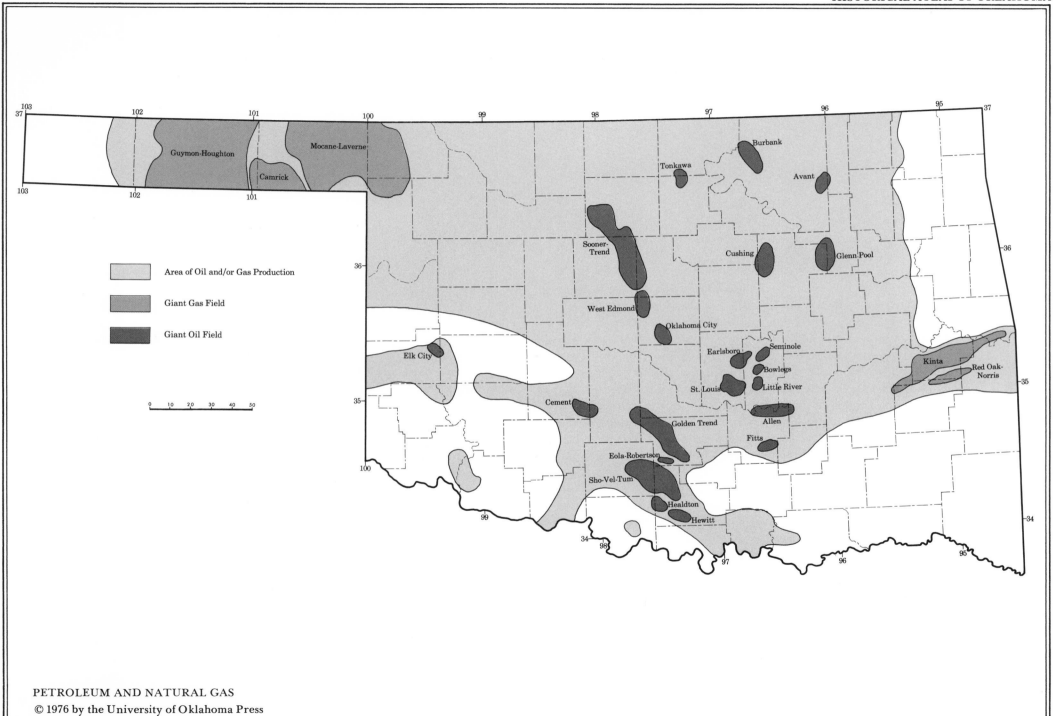

Area of Oil and/or Gas Production

Giant Gas Field

Giant Oil Field

Guymon-Houghton

Mocane-Laverne

Camrick

Burbank

Tonkawa

Avant

Sooner-Trend

Cushing

Glenn Pool

West Edmond

Oklahoma City

Seminole

Earlsboro

Bowlegs

Kinta

St. Louis

Little River

Red Oak-Norris

Elk City

Cement

Allen

Golden Trend

Fitts

Eola-Robertson

Sho-Vel-Tum

Healdton

Hewitt

0 10 20 30 40 50

PETROLEUM AND NATURAL GAS

© 1976 by the University of Oklahoma Press

70. PETROLEUM AND NATURAL GAS

Oklahoma has long been one of the principal petroleum and natural-gas-producing states of the nation. Many maps made by early explorers and settlers identified several places as oil springs. The following material is taken from or based upon the Oklahoma Geological Survey publication *Geology and Earth Resources of Oklahoma.*

No authentic records of the first discovery of oil in Oklahoma are available, but early settlers found oil springs in northeastern Oklahoma and reported a burning spring northeast of McAlester. In 1859 a well being drilled for salt near Salina accidentally produced oil, which was sold as lamp oil. Of wells drilled in search of petroleum, the first commercial well (one that makes a reasonable profit above the cost of drilling, equipping, and producing) was completed at Bartlesville in about 1896. The earliest production of oil in Oklahoma was thirty barrels, in 1901.

A giant oil field is one that has an ultimate recovery of more than 100 million barrels. There are twenty-two such fields in the state. Oklahoma's yearly production of about 225 million barrels of crude oil, valued at nearly $675 million, is 7 percent of the total United States annual output and ranks Oklahoma in fourth place as an oil-producing state. Production in the state is from approximately 81,000 wells in sixty-seven counties, and 46 percent comes from the giant oil fields. A giant gas field is one that has an ultimate recovery of more than 1 trillion cubic feet. Annual Oklahoma gas production of 1.4 trillion cubic feet, valued at about $200 million, is 8 percent of the total United States output. Only two other states produce more gas each year. Of the 8,150 gas-producing wells, many also produce liquid hydrocarbons that can be separated from the gas in gas-processing plants.

By the end of 1972 more than 293,000 wells had been drilled in Oklahoma in search of oil and gas, and about 82,260 wells were producing. Daily average production of oil per well was 7.7 barrels. The value of crude oil and natural gas produced during 1972 was $1.11 billion, about 91 percent of the state's total mineral production. Total cumulative production from 1901 through 1972 was 11 billion barrels of oil, 35 trillion cubic feet of natural gas, and 1 billion barrels of natural-gas liquids. The total value of these products was $29.4 billion. Oil and gas have been produced in seventy-three of the seventy-seven counties.

In 1972 Oklahoma established two depth records in the drilling of wells for oil and gas. The deepest well in the world was drilled to a total depth of 30,050 feet and was plugged back to a shallower depth for completion as a gas well. Another well was completed as a gas well from an interval extending to 24,548 feet, establishing it as the deepest producer in the world. Both of these wells are in Beckham County. They were drilled as a part of the intensive exploration program designed to find natural-gas reserves known to exist at great depths in major sedimentary basins of the world.

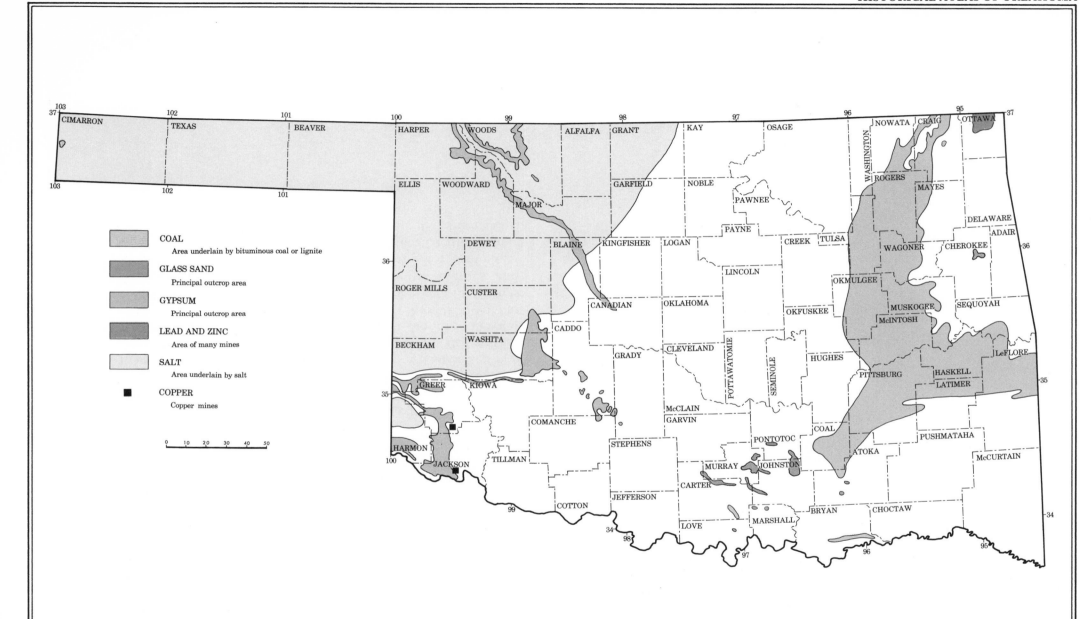

COAL
Area underlain by bituminous coal or lignite

GLASS SAND
Principal outcrop area

GYPSUM
Principal outcrop area

LEAD AND ZINC
Area of many mines

SALT
Area underlain by salt

COPPER
Copper mines

MINERAL RESOURCES OTHER THAN PETROLEUM AND
NATURAL GAS
© 1976 by the University of Oklahoma Press

71. MINERAL RESOURCES OTHER THAN PETROLEUM AND NATURAL GAS

The mineral wealth of Oklahoma is enormous and is fairly evenly distributed throughout the state. Mineral industries are active in seventy-six of the seventy-seven counties. The annual mineral production of the state, including petroleum and natural gas, is valued at more than $1 billion, approximately 5 percent of the mineral wealth of the entire United States. Oklahoma is the fourth-leading mineral producer in the nation. Total production since statehood is valued in excess of $28 billion. Although petroleum accounts for about 94 percent of the state's yearly output, nonpetroleum mineral resources represent a vast reserve of future wealth.

Coal, copper, granite, gypsum, cement, helium, stone (limestone, dolomite, sandstone, chat), sand and gravel, and zinc are the principal nonpetroleum resources that are being or have been mined. Minerals of lesser value at present are salt, tripoli, glass sand, bentonite, volcanic ash, clay, lime and lead (not all these minerals are shown on Map 71). Uranium and iron ore are among the untapped mineral resources. Among the states Oklahoma ranks fifth in the production of gypsum and third in helium. The single helium plant is located in Cimarron County, near Keyes.

Large reserves of bituminous coal are distributed over an area of 10,000 square miles in eastern Oklahoma. The coal ranges from low to high volatile. At present it is burned as an energy source in electric power plants and is converted to coke for use in steel manufacture. More than 200 million tons of coal have been mined from hundreds of Oklahoma mines since mining began in 1872. A recent estimate indicated remaining reserves of more than 3.2 billion tons. Ten Oklahoma companies are now producing coal at the rate of about 2.5 million tons per year.

In the past, mined open pit, or strip pit, coal lands have been left without any serious effort to restore or reclaim the land surface, but restoration is now required by Oklahoma's Mining Lands Reclamation Acts of 1968 and 1971. Newly mined lands must be graded to a gently rolling surface, revegetated, and have their acid-forming minerals buried. In addition, most Oklahoma coal operators voluntarily set aside the original topsoil and then spread it over the leveled "spoil banks." These reclamation requirements greatly reduce one of the major environmental problems that have been associated with the recovery of this much needed energy resource.

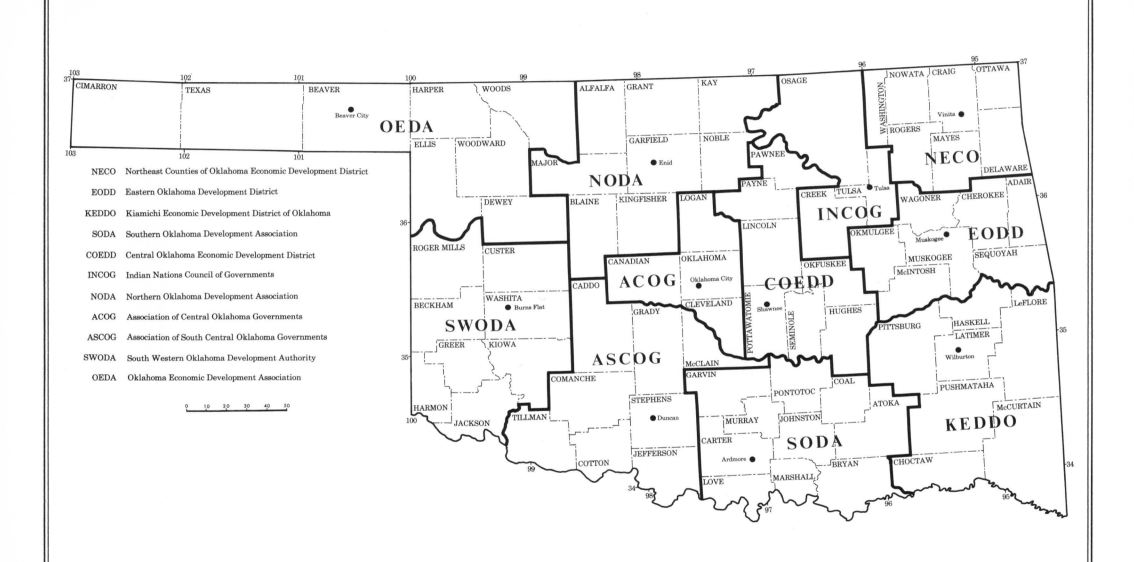

NECO   Northeast Counties of Oklahoma Economic Development District

EODD   Eastern Oklahoma Development District

KEDDO   Kiamichi Economic Development District of Oklahoma

SODA   Southern Oklahoma Development Association

COEDD   Central Oklahoma Economic Development District

INCOG   Indian Nations Council of Governments

NODA   Northern Oklahoma Development Association

ACOG   Association of Central Oklahoma Governments

ASCOG   Association of South Central Oklahoma Governments

SWODA   South Western Oklahoma Development Authority

OEDA   Oklahoma Economic Development Association

SUB-STATE PLANNING DISTRICTS
© 1976 by the University of Oklahoma Press

72. SUB-STATE PLANNING DISTRICTS

Senate Bill 290 of the 1969 Oklahoma Legislature provided that the Oklahoma Industrial Development and Park Commission divide Oklahoma into several Sub-State Planning Districts. On December 9, 1970, the eleven districts, as shown on Map 72, were delineated. The functions of the various Sub-State Planning Districts, as approved by the governor of the state of Oklahoma on May 21, 1971, are:

1. To foster citizen participation in identifying, planning for and implementing goals, objectives and programs.
2. To assist in improving communication between citizens, local and federal responsiveness to local needs.
3. To serve as a mechanism for improving state and federal responsiveness to local needs.
4. To undertake programs and activities which make government more effective.
5. To provide information about District issues and their possible impact on local governments.
6. To serve as a coordination point for processing federal grant applications for local units of government within the district.

7. To serve as a district clearing house for OMB Circular A-95 operations as specified and in concurrance with the State Clearinghouse, Office of Community Affairs and Planning.
8. To serve as a focal point for dissemination of technical information available from state and federal agencies.
9. To serve as a mechanism for local units of government to obtain state and federal assistance in technical, administrative and financial areas.
10. To serve as the coordination office for integrating comprehensive planning efforts into a district plan and assisting the Office of Community Affairs and Planning in integrating these plans into the State planning function.
11. To coordinate the planning efforts in the following areas:
    a. Law enforcement
    b. Health planning
    c. Community development
    d. Economic development
    e. Manpower planning
    f. Other specific areas as directed by the Office of Community Affairs and Planning

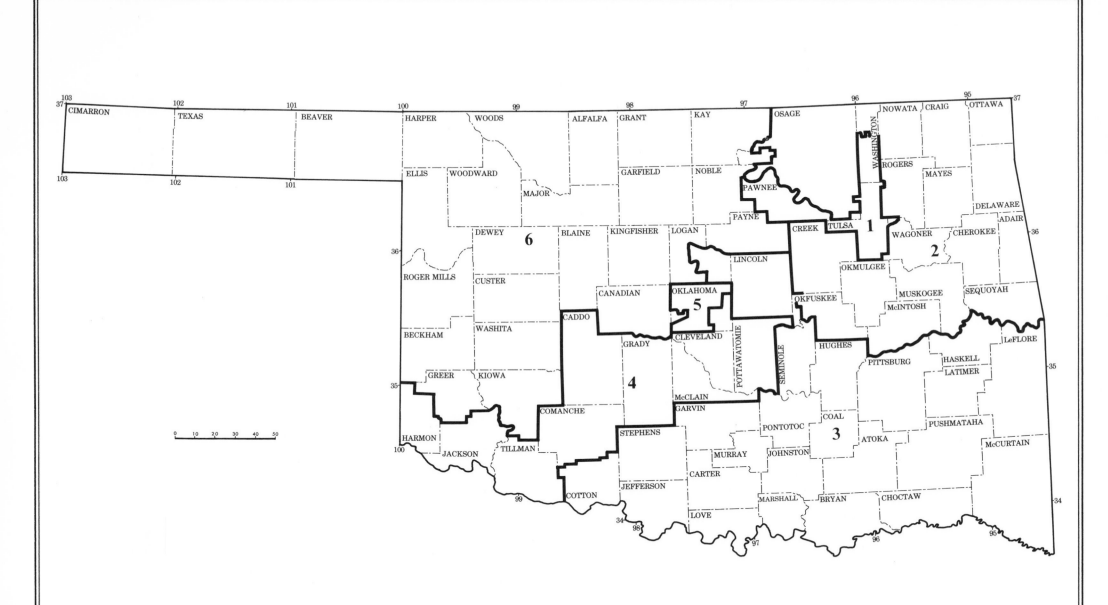

73. CONGRESSIONAL DISTRICTS, 1970

The Enabling Act for Oklahoma statehood, signed by President Theodore Roosevelt on June 16, 1906, provided that the new state should send five members to the lower house of the United States Congress until the next regular apportionment act, as provided by the federal Constitution. The first legislature of Oklahoma divided the state into five congressional districts.

After the federal census of 1910, the new apportionment, based upon Oklahoma's population of 1,657,155, gave the state eight representatives. Governor Lee Cruce had to decide between calling a special session of the legislature to form new districts and ordering the election of three congressmen-at-large. After giving the matter careful thought, Cruce directed that the voters should be given an opportunity to elect three members-at-large. The unnecessary expense of a special session was put forward as a major reason for the Governor's decision, but perhaps party politics was the deciding factor.

Although defeated in the two races for governor, the Republicans had provided strong opposition and in 1908 had won three of the five congressional seats. However, the combined pluralities of the three Republican districts was only 6,503 compared with 25,155 combined Democratic pluralities in the other two districts. In 1910, James S. Davenport won a seat for the Democrats, displacing Charles E. Creager, and in 1912 the Democrats elected the three representatives-at-large, in addition to three candidates running in the districts.

From 1914 to 1951, Oklahoma had eight congressional districts. In 1932, on the basis of its population of 2,396,040, the state was entitled to nine representatives, and Will Rogers of Oklahoma City was elected congressman-at-large. On the basis of the 1940 census the office was abolished, after Will Rogers had been re-elected four times. Reapportionment after the census of 1950 reduced Oklahoma's membership to six.

Owing to the unequal distribution of population within Oklahoma and because of rulings made by the United States Supreme Court, it was necessary that new congressional district boundaries be defined following the census of 1970. District 5, which includes much of Oklahoma City and most of Oklahoma County, is the smallest in area and yet has the largest population. District 6 has the largest area but the smallest population. All six districts, however, have comparable populations.

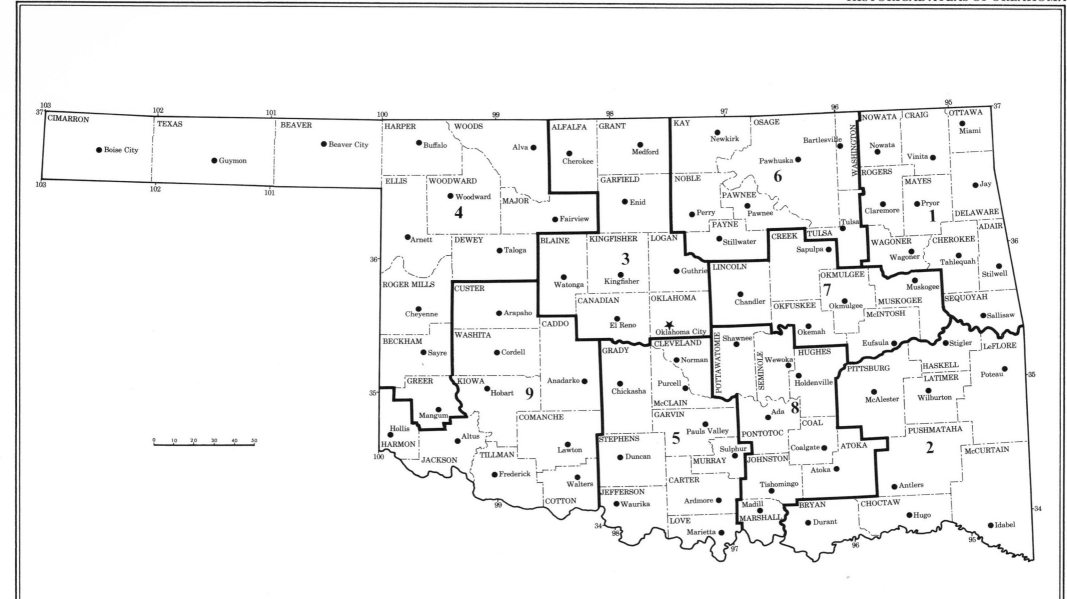

SUPREME COURT JUDICIAL DISTRICTS
© 1976 by the University of Oklahoma Press

74. SUPREME COURT JUDICIAL DISTRICTS

Oklahoma has three judicial districts for the Court of Criminal
Appeals (the Northern, Southern, and Eastern), and nine Supreme Court judicial districts, as shown on Map 74. By 1970
there was a wide disparity in the population of the several Supreme Court districts, the third and sixth each containing more
than three times as many people as the eighth district.

Population, Supreme Court Judicial Districts, 1970

1. 207,637	4. 105,887	7. 183,069
2. 166,557	5. 264,907	8. 141,422
3. 672,782	6. 594,516	9. 240,184

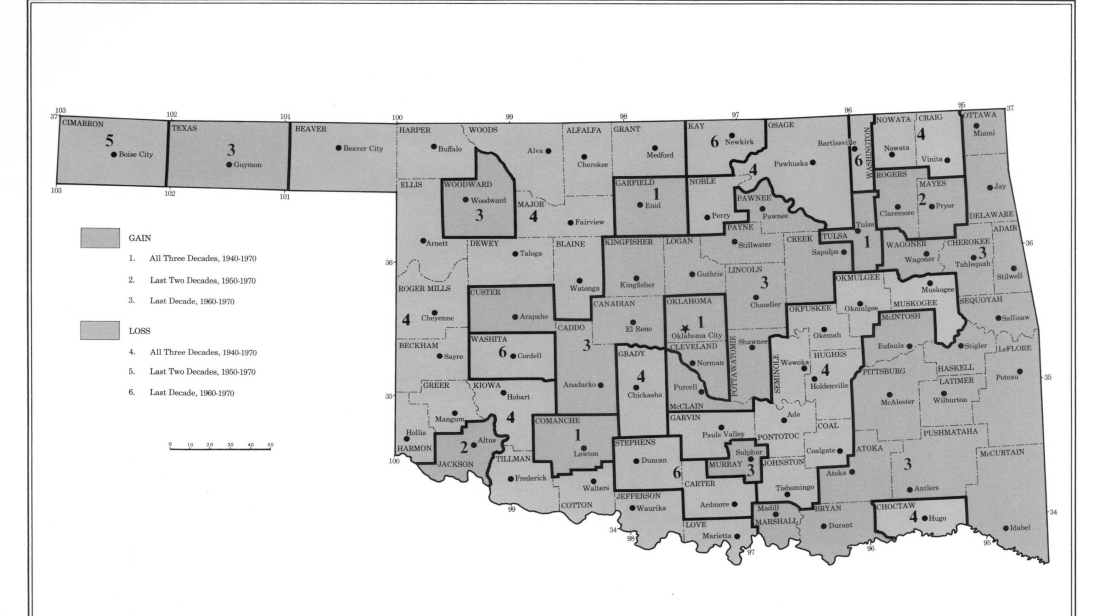

GAIN

1. All Three Decades, 1940-1970

2. Last Two Decades, 1950-1970

3. Last Decade, 1960-1970

LOSS

4. All Three Decades, 1940-1970

5. Last Two Decades, 1950-1970

6. Last Decade, 1960-1970

POPULATION: GAIN/LOSS, 1940–1970

© 1976 by the University of Oklahoma Press

75. POPULATION: GAIN/LOSS, 1940–1970

Oklahoma was settled in a different way from any other state. Soon after the purchase of Louisiana Territory, the land that now forms Oklahoma was set aside as a home for Indians. No white people were to be permitted to settle or live in this Indian country. At first all of Oklahoma, except the Panhandle, was allotted to the Five Civilized Tribes. As a result of the Civil War these tribes lost their western lands. Parts of these western lands were formed into reservations for various Plains tribes. National politics and political pressures then developed for the opening of areas such as the Unassigned Lands to white settlement. Eventually all Indians were assigned certain areas or sections of land, whites and blacks were permitted to settle throughout Indian and Oklahoma Territory, and all previous Indian lands, as well as the Panhandle, were formed into the state of Oklahoma.

Because of the methods used in settling Oklahoma Territory and the fact that farm size was limited to 160 acres, many of the counties in western Oklahoma became overpopulated. At the time of the openings people came to Oklahoma for various reasons, but chiefly because they could get land at a very low cost or make a new start in business. Later many came to work in the coal or lead and zinc mines, the oil fields, or other mineral industries. The decline in mineral industries and the "dry years" that resulted in many failures in agricultural areas caused a significant number of people to move from the state. From 1930 to 1950 Oklahoma lost population; since 1950 there has been a gradual increase.

The counties shown on Map 74 as having lost population for the last three decades are for the most part (1) agricultural counties in the western part of the state or (2) counties having declining oil production in the central part of Oklahoma. In the agricultural counties farms have been enlarged and machines have taken over much of the work. Also much cropland has been returned to pasture, and grazing has become the dominant activity. The population of Harper and Ellis counties has decreased during each decade since 1910. Alfalfa, Beaver, Cotton, Jefferson, and Major counties have had population decreases for the past fifty years.

The population of the urban centers of Oklahoma, like those of the entire United States, have continued to increase as rural population declines. Oklahoma and Tulsa counties have had the greatest increase because of the growth of the two major cities as manufacturing, distribution, financial, and retail centers. Cleveland County population has increased because some of the towns and cities in the county serve as "bedroom" towns for Oklahoma City and because of the growth of the University of Oklahoma. Much of the population growth in Garfield County centers around Enid, an important agricultural and manufacturing center. Fort Sill, one of the nation's principal military posts, is located in Comanche County. Lawton, the third-largest city in Oklahoma, is also in Comanche County, adjacent to Fort Sill. It is a large retail and distribution center.

Increased growth in population in eastern Oklahoma during the 1960–70 decade was due to highway improvements, the construction of large lakes for water power and recreation, and the development of small industries in many smaller towns.

Population of Oklahoma

Year	Total Population	Increase or Decrease Number	Percent
1910	1,657,155		
1920	2,028,283	371,128	22.4
1930	2,396,040	367,757	18.1
1940	2,336,434	−59,606	−2.5
1950	2,233,351	−103,083	−4.9
1960	2,328,284	94,933	4.3
1970	2,559,253	230,969	9.9

75. POPULATION: GAIN/LOSS, 1940–1970

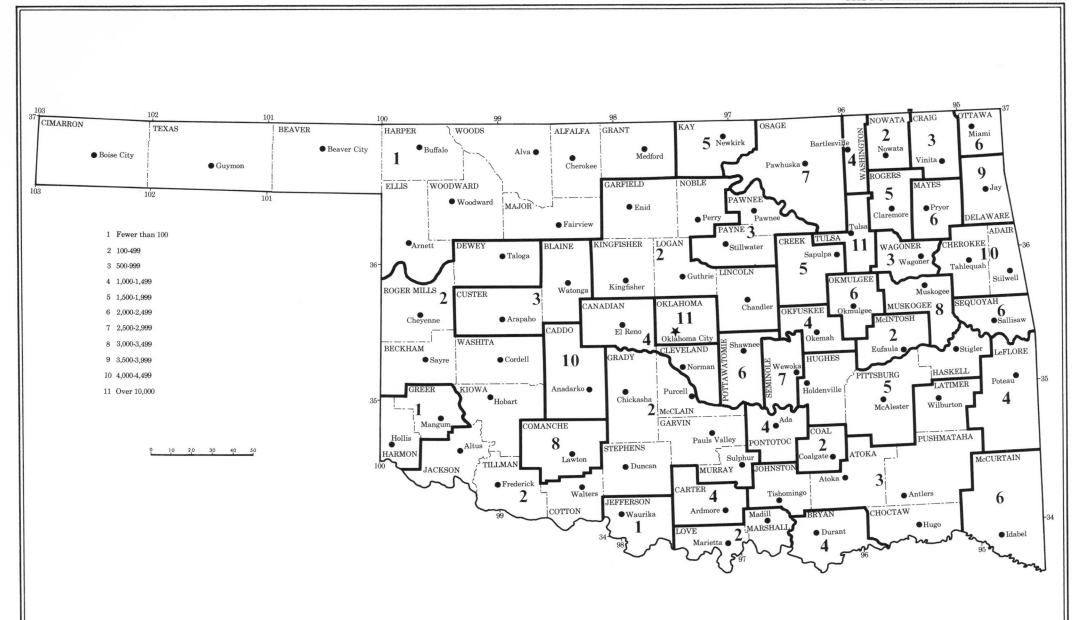

1 Fewer than 100
2 100-499
3 500-999
4 1,000-1,499
5 1,500-1,999
6 2,000-2,499
7 2,500-2,999
8 3,000-3,499
9 3,500-3,999
10 4,000-4,499
11 Over 10,000

POPULATION: DISTRIBUTION OF INDIANS, 1970

© 1976 by the University of Oklahoma Press

The 1970 census of the United States shows the total Indian population of the nation to be 792,730 with 98,468 Indians listed as residents of Oklahoma. Arizona, with an Indian population of 95,812, and California with 91,018, ranked second and third respectively among the fifty states.

As indicated on Map 76, the Indian population of Oklahoma is not evenly distributed throughout the state. Only seven Indians live in Beaver County and twelve in Cimarron County. The total Indian population of the Panhandle is only sixty-nine. Oklahoma and Tulsa counties, with totals of 10,341 and 11,041 respectively, have the largest Indian populations. In general, however, the greatest numbers of Indians are concentrated in the old Indian Territory area and in those parts of Oklahoma where the Cheyenne-Arapaho and the Comanche-Kiowa-Apache reservations were located. That part of the Cherokee Outlet west of the 98th meridian, the Panhandle, and much of old Greer County has few Indian residents. None of these areas were used as reservations or settlement areas for Indians. Caddo, Cherokee, and Adair counties each have between 4,000 and 4,500 Indian citizens. Caddo County was the center of the most densely settled area by the Plains tribes, especially the Wichita, Caddo, Kiowa, Comanche, and Apache groups (Map 48). Cherokee and Adair counties along with Delaware County formed the most densely populated part of the Cherokee Nation. Most of the Indians belonging to the Five Nations still reside in their respective areas, Osage County is dominated by members of the Osage tribe, and the Cheyenne-Arapaho Indians form the principal groups in Blaine and Custer counties.

There are no Indian reservations in Oklahoma, and there have been none since statehood. Many Indians have moved to the larger urban centers where there are better chances for employment or better opportunities to develop business or professional careers. Oklahoma City and Tulsa have a larger total Indian population than the other urban centers of the state. Such towns as Anadarko, Clinton, Durant, Atoka, Tahlequah, and Pawhuska, however, have a larger percentage of citizens with some Indian blood than do the metropolitan centers.

The number of Indians from the major tribal groups living in Oklahoma are:

Five Nations	Population
Creek	20,909
Cherokee	11,257
Seminole	7,372
Choctaw	6,550
Chickasaw	5,703
Remains of Small Groups in Northeast (Ottawa County)	
Quapaw, Miami, Peoria,	
Delaware, Seneca, Cayuga,	
Wyandotte, Ottawa, Shawnee	12,140
Plains Tribes	
Osage	8,960
Cheyenne-Arapaho	6,674
Kiowa	6,250
Comanche	6,250
Pawnee	2,110
Sac and Fox	1,980
Ponca	1,910
Caddo	1,760
Oto-Missouri	1,410
Kickapoo	1,100
Kiowa-Apache	1,000
Wichita	580
Iowa	276

The Bureau of Indian Affairs also states that one group, known as the Citizen Pottawatomie group, numbers 10,968. Many tribes of lesser number are to be found in the eastern and west-central parts of Oklahoma.

76. POPULATION: DISTRIBUTION OF INDIANS, 1970

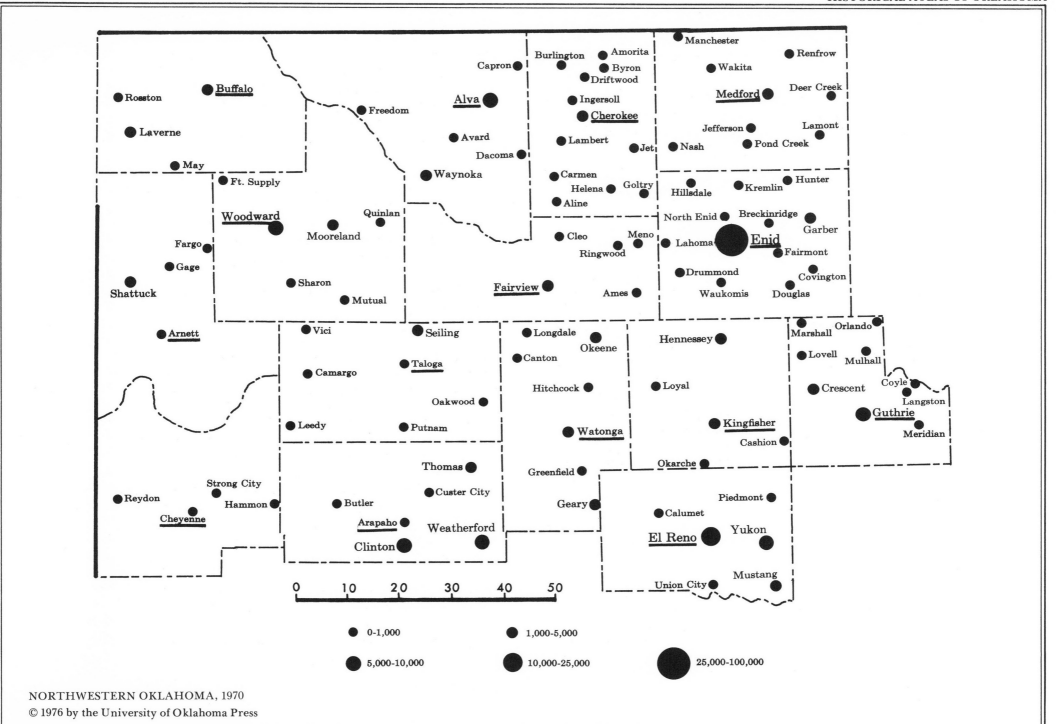

Manchester
Renfrow
Burlington
Amorita
Byron
Wakita
Capron
Driftwood
Alva
Medford
Deer Creek
Ingersoll
Cherokee
Avard
Lamont
Jefferson
Rosston
Buffalo
Dacoma
Lambert
Jet
Nash
Pond Creek
Laverne
Freedom
Carmen
Hunter
May
Helena
Goltry
Hillsdale
Kremlin
Ft. Supply
Aline
North Enid
Breckinridge
Woodward
Quinlan
Cleo
Meno
Garber
Mooreland
Ringwood
Lahoma
Enid
Fairmont
Fargo
Gage
Drummond
Covington
Shattuck
Sharon
Waukomis
Douglas
Mutual
Fairview
Ames
Arnett
Vici
Seiling
Longdale
Marshall
Orlando
Okeene
Hennessey
Lovell
Camargo
Taloga
Canton
Mulhall
Coyle
Hitchcock
Loyal
Crescent
Langston
Leedy
Oakwood
Putnam
Watonga
Kingfisher
Guthrie
Cashion
Meridian
Thomas
Greenfield
Okarche
Strong City
Custer City
Piedmont
Reydon
Hammon
Geary
Calumet
Cheyenne
Butler
El Reno
Yukon
Arapaho
Weatherford
Clinton
Mustang
Union City

0   10   20   30   40   50

● 0-1,000   ● 1,000-5,000

● 5,000-10,000   ● 10,000-25,000   ● 25,000-100,000

NORTHWESTERN OKLAHOMA, 1970

© 1976 by the University of Oklahoma Press

77. NORTHWESTERN OKLAHOMA, 1970

Northwestern Oklahoma is characterized by small towns in which the most prominent features are elevators and stock pens because this part of the state is noted for large wheat farms and even larger ranches. Both farm size and ranch size increase toward the west as the amount of dependable yearly rainfall decreases. Most land in the area is classified as plains, but there are variations, such as the Glass Mountains and the Antelope Hills. In the vicinity of Fort Supply and Arnett is found the transition zone from the Central Lowlands to the Great Plains.

Enid, the largest city in the northwestern part of Oklahoma, is the sixth-largest in the state in population. This city is known especially for its large elevators and is the third-largest wheat-storage center in the United States, being exceeded only by Minneapolis and Kansas City. Also an industrial center, Enid has an oil refinery and several small manufacturing activities. The city is an important commercial and educational center.

Many communities in the area are known for specific attributes. Weatherford and Alva are sites of state universities. Clinton and El Reno are important railroad transfer points, and each has industrial activities of statewide importance. State parks are located near Cherokee, Watonga, Freedom, and Waynoka. Guthrie is of historical significance as the first capital of the state.

The Cherokee Outlet and the Cheyenne and Arapaho Reservation occupied much of this part of the state. Large parts of each were leased to cattlemen and served as pasturelands for many thousand head of cattle. The Cherokee Outlet was the largest area opened for settlement at one time. Few Indians live in the Outlet area, but many descendants of the Cheyennes and Arapahoes live near the towns and cities that have developed on their former reservation.

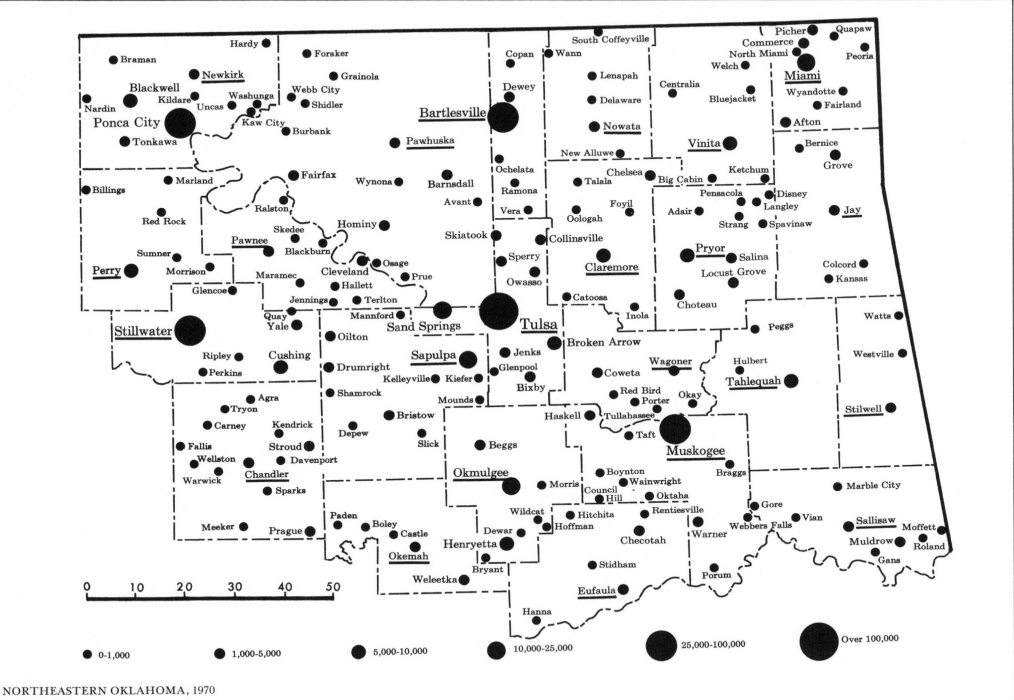

Picher
Quapaw
Commerce
North Miami
Welch
Wyandotte
Miami
Peoria
Fairland
Afton
Bernice
Grove

South Coffeyville
Copan
Wann
Lenapah
Centralia
Bluejacket
Delaware
Nowata
Vinita
Ketchum

Braman
Hardy
Foraker
Newkirk
Grainola
Blackwell
Webb City
Washunga
Shidler
Kildare
Uncas
Nardin
Kaw City
Ponca City
Burbank
Tonkawa

Dewey
Bartlesville

New Alluwe
Ochelata
Chelsea
Big Cabin
Pensacola
Disney
Talala
Adair
Langley
Jay
Ramona
Foyil
Strang
Spavinaw

Marland
Fairfax
Wynona
Barnsdall
Avant
Vera
Oologah
Billings
Ralston
Red Rock
Skedee
Hominy
Skiatook
Collinsville
Pryor
Salina
Pawnee
Blackburn
Sperry
Claremore
Locust Grove
Colcord
Sumner
Maramec
Osage
Prue
Owasso
Kansas
Perry
Morrison
Cleveland
Hallett
Glencoe
Jennings
Terlton
Catoosa
Choteau
Quay
Mannford
Inola
Peggs
Watts
Stillwater
Yale
Sand Springs
Tulsa
Oilton
Broken Arrow
Westville
Ripley
Cushing
Sapulpa
Jenks
Wagoner
Hulbert
Perkins
Drumright
Glenpool
Tahlequah
Kelleyville
Kiefer
Bixby
Shamrock
Mounds
Red Bird
Okay
Stilwell
Agra
Bristow
Coweta
Porter
Tryon
Depew
Haskell
Tullahassee
Carney
Kendrick
Slick
Taft
Fallis
Stroud
Beggs
Muskogee
Wellston
Davenport
Boynton
Braggs
Warwick
Chandler
Okmulgee
Morris
Wainwright
Marble City
Sparks
Council Hill
Oktaha
Paden
Wildcat
Rentiesville
Gore
Vian
Sallisaw
Meeker
Boley
Hitchita
Webbers Falls
Moffett
Prague
Castle
Dewar
Hoffman
Warner
Muldrow
Roland
Henryetta
Checotah
Gans
Okemah
Bryant
Stidham
Porum
Weleetka
Eufaula
Hanna

0 10 20 30 40 50

● 0-1,000   ● 1,000-5,000   ● 5,000-10,000   ● 10,000-25,000   ● 25,000-100,000   ● Over 100,000

NORTHEASTERN OKLAHOMA, 1970

© 1976 by the University of Oklahoma Press

78. NORTHEASTERN OKLAHOMA, 1970

Much of the history of Oklahoma has been enacted on the Ozark Plateau, in the Osage Hills, and on the plains of the northeastern quarter of the state. In this area De Soto may have explored along the Grand River, Wilkinson followed the Arkansas River, Washington Irving made part of his famous tour of the prairies, the Chouteaus established trading posts, the Cherokees founded their nation, and several battles of the Civil War were fought. During more recent decades the "boom and bust" of mineral development has had a great influence on the area. Lead and zinc mining have been of prime importance in the Picher area; coal has been mined near Henryetta, Claremore, and other communities; petroleum has been pumped from large oil fields such as Three Sands, Burbank, Glen Pool, Barnsdall, and Slick, as well as many other fields of less importance. Because of these and other activities, the northeast quarter of the state has a moderate population density, and it is in this part of Oklahoma that the greatest number of Indians live.

Tulsa, the second city in population in Oklahoma, is the urban center serving much of this part of the state. Although Tulsa is nationally known as an oil center, it has a number of large manufacturing enterprises, is an important aviation center, and is known for the Philbrook Art Center, the Gilcrease Museum, and other cultural facilities. Tulsa is also an important transportation center, having access to the great manufacturing centers of the nation by water via the Arkansas River Navigation Channel from the Port of Catoosa, as well as by rail, highway, and air.

The cities of northeastern Oklahoma are centers of varied activities. Muskogee has large glass manufacturers. Bartlesville is noted for its research work with minerals. Ponca City is the home of a large oil refinery. Oklahoma State University is located in Stillwater. Claremore is the heart of the Will Rogers country. Tahlequah is famous for its Cherokee history, and Pawhuska is the Osage center.

Many large man-made lakes and reservoirs are scattered along the principal rivers of the area. Several state parks have been established, and many private recreational facilities are now in operation. The natural beauty of the Ozarks, as well as the development of well-operated playgrounds, is helping this part of Oklahoma become a national tourist attraction.

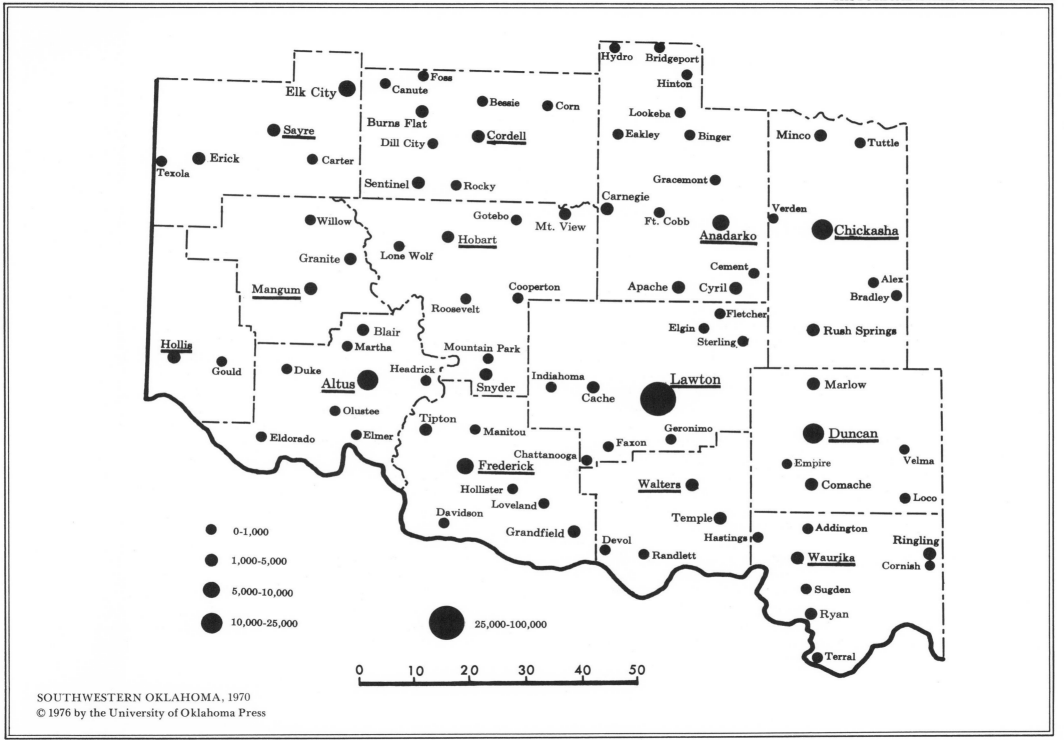

Hydro · Bridgeport
Foss · Hinton
Elk City · Canute
Bessie · Corn · Lookeba
Burns Flat · Eakley · Binger
Sayre · Cordell · Minco · Tuttle
Dill City
Erick · Carter · Gracemont
Texola · Sentinel · Rocky · Carnegie · Verden
Gotebo · Mt. View · Ft. Cobb · Chickasha
Willow · Anadarko
Hobart · Cement · Alex
Granite · Lone Wolf · Apache · Cyril · Bradley
Mangum · Cooperton · Fletcher · Rush Springs
Roosevelt · Elgin
Blair · Sterling
Martha · Mountain Park · Marlow
Hollis · Headrick · Indiahoma · Lawton
Gould · Duke · Altus · Snyder · Cache · Duncan
Olustee · Geronimo · Velma
Tipton · Empire
Eldorado · Elmer · Manitou · Faxon · Comache
Chattanooga · Loco
Frederick · Walters
Hollister · Temple · Addington
Loveland · Ringling
Davidson · Hastings · Waurika · Cornish
Grandfield · Devol · Randlett · Sugden
Ryan
Terral

● 0-1,000

● 1,000-5,000

● 5,000-10,000

● 10,000-25,000

● 25,000-100,000

0   10   20   30   40   50

SOUTHWESTERN OKLAHOMA, 1970
© 1976 by the University of Oklahoma Press

79. SOUTHWESTERN OKLAHOMA, 1970

Except for the granite outcrops of the Wichita Mountains, rolling plains dominate most of the landscape of southwestern Oklahoma. Ranches and wheat farms are common, but they are not as large as those in the northwestern or Panhandle areas of the state. Irrigation agriculture is common throughout the region. Water from Lake Altus is used to irrigate cotton, wheat, and other crops on the flatlands south of Altus. Near Hollis water is pumped from deep wells to irrigate large fields of cotton. In other places water is taken directly from the rivers and streams to irrigate fields of peanuts, alfalfa, or grain crops.

Most of the incorporated communities of southwestern Oklahoma are small. Many have elevators, but the cotton gin is also a common landmark. Many smaller cities and towns are noted for special features. Anadarko is famous as a center of activity for the Plains Indians, Rush Springs is known for its watermelons, Mangum is remembered as the "capital" of old Greer County, Hinton is the location of Red Rock Canyon State Park, Corn is known for its progressive agricultural activities, and Cyril is the home of a large refinery.

Southwestern Oklahoma is in many respects the military part of the state. Lawton, the third largest city in Oklahoma, is adjacent to Fort Sill, one of the principal artillery posts in the nation. Altus is a center for extensive Air Force activities.

Historically this area has contributed much to the state. Kiowa, Comanche, Apache, Wichita, and other Plains tribes were settled there. Old Greer County, that area between the 100th meridian and the North Fork of Red River, was added to Oklahoma by a Supreme Court decision. The Chisholm Trail is still marked by a line of communities extending northward from Terral to Tuttle. The last of the land openings was the Big Pasture area in southern Comanche and Cotton counties.

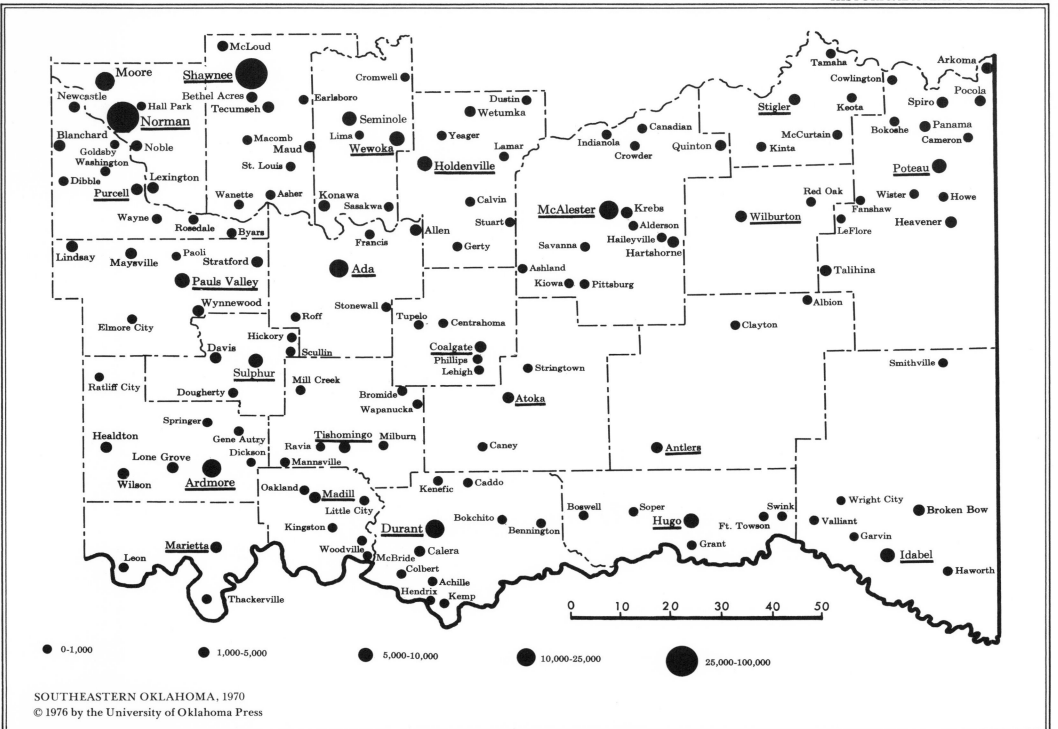

SOUTHEASTERN OKLAHOMA, 1970

© 1976 by the University of Oklahoma Press

80. SOUTHEASTERN OKLAHOMA, 1970

Southeastern Oklahoma has a greater variety of landscapes than any other part of the state, and this variety helps explain the distribution of villages, towns, and cities. The Ouachita Mountains contain few incorporated communities, as indicated by the blank spaces in Atoka, Pushmataha, McCurtain, Pittsburg, Latimer, and LeFlore counties. In contrast, the fertile Coastal Plain, extending from Marietta to Haworth, has many incorporated towns and villages, chiefly because of agricultural activity. Coal mining is widespread southwest and east of McAlester, the Greater Seminole Oil Field occupies the triangle from Shawnee to Holdenville to Ada, and in the Arbuckle Mountains much glass sand, clay, limestone, sand, and gravel is quarried.

Norman, in Cleveland County, is the fourth city in total population in the state and is the largest city in area in southeastern Oklahoma. It is near Oklahoma City, which extends into the northern part of Cleveland County. The University of Oklahoma and Central State Hospital are the principal interests in Norman, but the city also serves as the trade center for a well-populated area.

Each of the larger incorporated communities is notable for one or more activities. Shawnee, Ada, and Ardmore are industrial centers. Seminole is noted for its oil interests. State universities are located in Ada and Durant. Wewoka was the capital of the Seminole Nation, and Tishomingo served as the capital of the Chickasaw Nation. Pauls Valley and Lindsay are important agricultural centers. McAlester is the chief city in the Oklahoma coal fields. Wright City is the home of a large lumber mill, and a large paper mill is located in Valliant. Many of the smaller communities like Sulphur and Antlers have large ranches located nearby.

This part of Oklahoma included all of the Choctaw Nation and much of the Chickasaw Nation. The Texas Road, the Butterfield Stage Route, and a part of the California Trail once crossed this area. Many academies and missions were established before and shortly after the Civil War. The Choctaws and Chickasaws were slaveholders and joined with the Confederate States. Many Indians still live in this part of Oklahoma.

80.   SOUTHEASTERN OKLAHOMA, 1970

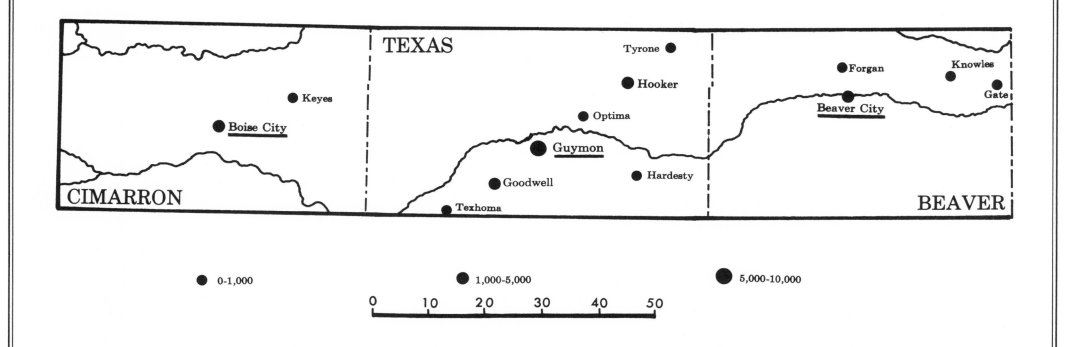

TEXAS

Tyrone ●

● Forgan   Knowles
                  ●

Keyes ●   ● Hooker   Gate
                                  ●
● Boise City   ● Optima   Beaver City

                ● Guymon

CIMARRON   ● Goodwell   ● Hardesty   BEAVER

                ● Texhoma

● 0-1,000   ● 1,000-5,000   ● 5,000-10,000

0   10   20   30   40   50

OKLAHOMA PANHANDLE, 1970
© 1976 by the University of Oklahoma Press

81. OKLAHOMA PANHANDLE, 1970

The Panhandle is the most sparsely populated part of Oklahoma. Though its three counties total 5,672 square miles in area, only 26,779 persons live in them—a population density of only 4.7 persons per square mile. Cimarron County has a smaller total population than any other county in the state.

Most incorporated places in the Panhandle have populations under 1,000. In practically all instances these small communities are service centers for their local area only. Most villages have one or two general stores, a service station, a post office, a school, and one or more elevators. The busiest time of the year is the harvest season, when wheat is being shipped either to market or to storage centers. During such periods elevators work to capacity.

The Hugoton Gas Field, the largest in the United States, extends across western Texas and eastern Cimarron County into Kansas. Within this area the income of most villages is increased by workers in the gas field, but the services rendered by the community are little different from those of other Panhandle towns. Keyes is the home of one of the largest helium plants in the nation.

In all three counties the town having the greatest population is the county seat. Guymon is the largest city in the Panhandle, but its population is less than 10,000. Goodwell, the home of Oklahoma Panhandle State University, has a fine museum concerned largely with Panhandle history. Beaver City was the former county seat of all of the Panhandle when the area was attached to Oklahoma Territory.

The Oklahoma Panhandle was under the flags of Spain, Mexico, and Texas before becoming a part of the United States. At one time the people of the area formed the Cimarron Territory, selected Beaver City as their capital, elected senators and a representative, and asked for admission as a state.

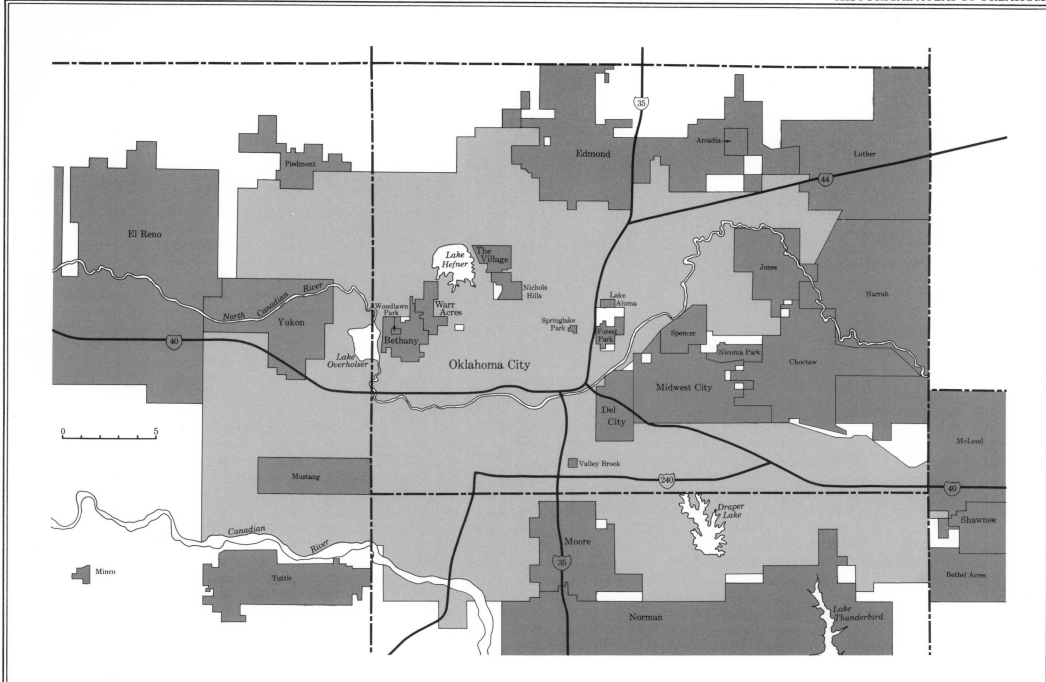

OKLAHOMA CITY METROPOLITAN AREA, 1974

© 1976 by the University of Oklahoma Press

Oklahoma City, the largest city in population in the state, is one of the largest cities in area in the United States. As shown on Map 82, it includes more than 600 square miles. Areas of land in McClain, Cleveland, Canadian, and Pottawatomie counties, as well as in Oklahoma County, are within the incorporated limits of the city. Oklahoma City is adjacent to Norman and Midwest City, with populations of 52,117 and 48,114 respectively, and borders or surrounds twenty-three other incorporated municipalities.

Oklahoma City is located near the center of the state in the Red Beds region. Its site was selected by the Santa Fe Railroad in 1886, when that company was extending its trackage through Oklahoma Territory. At first the place served only as a stop where the engines could get fuel and water; only the agent lived there. At noon on April 22, 1889, the opening "run" into Oklahoma Territory took place. By nightfall a tent city of about 10,000 persons had formed on the site. Soon after the opening date many people moved to other places in the new territory, hoping to find better locations. Later, many sold their holdings and returned to their home states. Thus, when the first census was taken in 1890, Oklahoma City had a population of only 4,151. Since that date the population of the city has increased greatly during each ten-year period. In 1970, after more than eighty years, Oklahoma City recorded a population of 359,671.

Oklahoma City and its neighboring communities form the commercial and industrial heart of the state. Meat packing, electrical industries, publishing and printing, and various other industries have large payrolls. Midwest City is the home of the Tinker Field aviation complex, the University of Oklahoma is located in Norman, Edmond is the home of Central State University, and Nichols Hills is known for its large and beautiful homes. Del City, Warr Acres, The Village, Moore, and other communities are largely "bedroom" communities for persons employed in Oklahoma City and Midwest City. Most of the smaller places in Oklahoma County were incorporated during the 1950–60 decade.

Growth of Principal Metropolitan Area Cities

City	1910	1920	1930	1940	1950	1960	1970
Bethany	......	485	2,032	2,590	5,705	12,342	21,785
Del City	......	......	....	....	2,504	12,934	27,133
Edmond	2,090	2,452	3,576	4,002	6,068	8,577	16,333
El Reno	7,872	7,737	9,384	10,078	10,991	11,015	14,510
Midwest City	......	......	....	....	10,166	36,058	48,114
Moore	225	254	538	499	942	1,783	18,761
Nichols Hills	......	......	....	942	2,606	4,897	4,478
Norman	3,724	5,004	9,603	11,429	27,006	33,412	52,117
Oklahoma City	64,205	91,295	185,389	204,424	243,504	324,253	359,671
The Village	......	......	....	....	....	12,118	13,695
Warr Acres	......	......	....	....	2,378	7,153	9,887
Yukon	1,018	1,016	1,455	1,660	1,990	3,076	8,411

Note: Bethany, Del City, Midwest City, Nichols Hills, The Village, and Warr Acres were not incorporated until the decade before the first census shown.

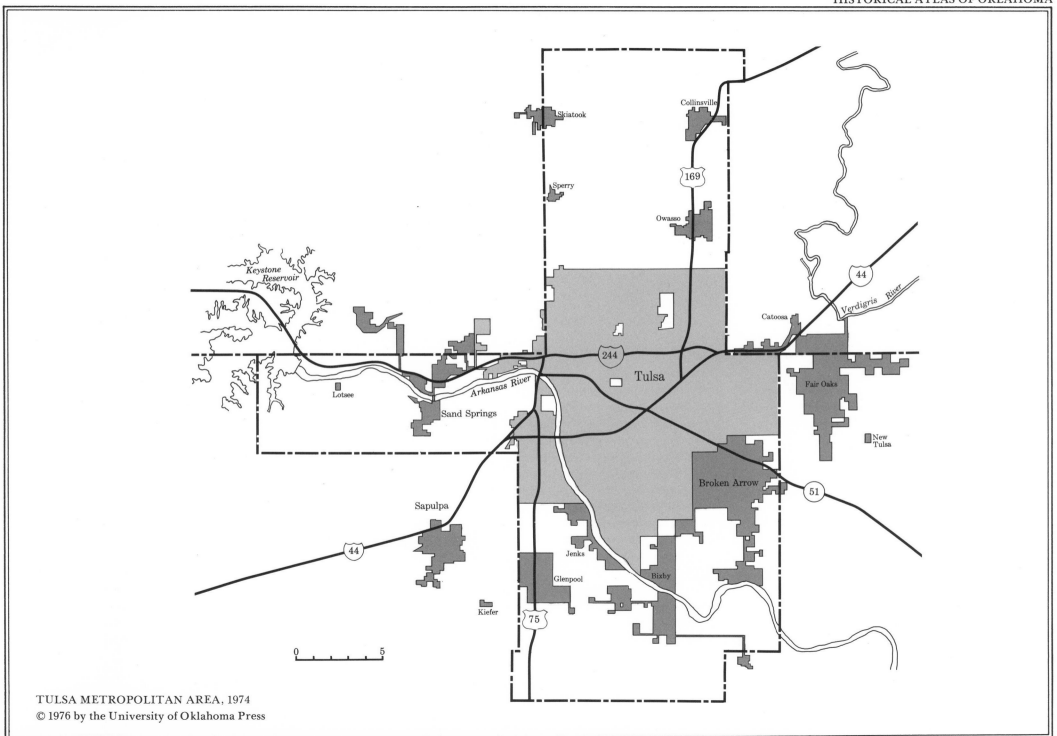

Skiatook

Collinsville

169

Sperry

Owasso

Keystone
Reservoir

244

Catoosa

Verdigris River

44

Tulsa

Arkansas River

Fair Oaks

Lotsee

Sand Springs

New
Tulsa

Broken Arrow

51

Sapulpa

44

Jenks

Bixby

Glenpool

Kiefer

75

0   5

TULSA METROPOLITAN AREA, 1974
© 1976 by the University of Oklahoma Press

83. TULSA METROPOLITAN AREA, 1974

Tulsa was founded as a Creek Indian village before the Civil War. The first post office was established in 1879. In 1882 the Atlantic and Pacific Railroad built into the Cherokee Nation, but when the builders learned that Cherokee laws prohibited trading except by native, intermarried, or adopted Cherokee citizens, the rails were extended into the Creek Nation where whites were permitted to trade by posting bond. There, on the site of the present Tulsa business section, the railroad established a terminal with a roundhouse and loading pens. From this point large herds of cattle were then shipped to stockyards in Kansas City, St. Louis, and Chicago.

Tulsa is located in the transition zone between the Sandstone Hills and the Prairie Plains regions. The major part of the city is on low, rolling hills and on the flat between these hills and the east, or left, bank of the Arkansas River. During its growth the city has also added territory west and south across the river and now includes such early settlements as Red Fork, West Tulsa, and Garden City. Tulsa, now the second largest city in Oklahoma, has a population of 328,491 and covers approximately 175 square miles of territory. During recent years Tulsa has also extended its boundaries to the north and east.

Tulsa is the oil center for Oklahoma and a large part of the great Mid-Continent Oil Area. When oil was first discovered in the vicinity of Tulsa, the city built a bridge across the Arkansas River and invited the oil companies to make Tulsa their headquarters; it also built a modern hotel. When Tulsa was once established as a principal oil center it continued to grow. Many oil companies have located their home offices in Tulsa. Manufacturers and distributors of all kinds of oil-field supplies are based there. It soon became an oil-refining center, and is still the largest refining center in Oklahoma. Banks and other financial institutions that understood the problems of petroleum financing also moved to Tulsa.

Since the "oil boom" period a variety of industrial and commercial activities have developed in the metropolitan area, especially those connected with aviation. In 1971 the Arkansas River Navigation Channel was opened with the port of Catoosa as its terminal. This gives the Tulsa area direct water connections with industrial centers of the Mississippi-Ohio valley as well as ocean-going vessels at New Orleans. The Tulsa metropolitan area has long been recognized as a cultural and tourist center. The University of Tulsa and Oral Roberts University are nationally known educational centers. Gilcrease Museum, Philbrook Art Museum, and the nearby Woolaroc Museum as well as several state parks that have been developed adjacent to nearby lakes, attract thousands of visitors to the city each year.

Growth of Principal Metropolitan Area Cities

City	1910	1920	1930	1940	1950	1960	1970
Broken Arrow	1,576	2,086	1,964	2,074	3,262	5,928	11,787
Sand Springs	......	4,076	6,674	6,137	6,994	7,754	11,519
Sapulpa	8,282	11,634	10,533	12,249	13,031	14,282	15,159
Tulsa	18,182	72,075	141,258	142,157	182,740	261,685	328,471

REFERENCES

References are listed for individual maps. Publication information for books (place, publisher, and date) is given in the first listing of each book and is not repeated in subsequent references.

Map 1. Location Within the United States

Bollinger, C. J., *The Geography of Oklahoma* (Chicago, Rand McNally, 1930), 6.

Espenshade, Edward B., Jr. (ed.), *Goode's World Atlas*, Fourteenth Edition (Chicago, Rand McNally, 1974), 102–103.

Gould, Charles N., *Geography of Oklahoma* (Ardmore, Okla., Bunn Brothers, 1909), 1–2.

Morris, John W., *Oklahoma Geography* (Oklahoma City, Harlow, 1961), 2–4.

National Geographic Atlas of the Fifty United States (Washington, National Geographic Society, 1960), 6–9.

Snider, L. C., *Geography of Oklahoma* (Norman, Oklahoma Geological Survey, 1917), 23.

Map 2. Longitude and Latitude of Oklahoma

Bollinger, *The Geography of Oklahoma*, 6.

Clark, Joseph Stanley, "The Eastern Boundary of Oklahoma," *Chronicles of Oklahoma*, Vol. XI, No. 4 (December, 1933), 1084–1110.

——, "The Northern Boundary of Oklahoma," *Chronicles of Oklahoma*, Vol. X, No. 3 (September, 1932), 271–90.

Espenshade, *Goode's World Atlas*, 116–17.

Gould, *Geography of Oklahoma*, 2–3.

——, *Travels Through Oklahoma* (Oklahoma City, Harlow, 1928), 1–43.

Morris, *Oklahoma Geography*, 3–5.

National Geographic Atlas of the Fifty United States, 18–19.

Snider, *Geography of Oklahoma*, 23–24.

Map 3. Geographic Regions of Oklahoma

Fenneman, Nevin M., *Physiography of Western United States* (New York, McGraw Hill, 1930), 1–30.

Loomis, Frederick B., *Physiography of the United States* (Garden City, Doubleday Doran, 1937), 5, 184–87.

Morris, *Oklahoma Geography*, 21–34.

——, *The Southwestern United States* (New York, Van Nostrand, 1970), 5–10.

Smith, J. Russell, *Oklahoma: People, Resources, and Industries* (Philadelphia, John C. Winston, 1935), 7–9.

Map 4. Contour Map of Oklahoma

Gould, Charles N., "Dedication of the Monument on Black Mesa," *Chronicles of Oklahoma*, Vol. VII, No. 1 (March, 1929), 34–54.

Johnson, Kenneth S., Carl C. Branson, and Others, *Geology and Earth Resources of Oklahoma* (Norman, Oklahoma Geological Survey, 1972), 2.

Map 5. Landforms of Oklahoma

Bollinger, C. J., "A General Relief Map of Oklahoma," *Proceedings of the Oklahoma Academy of Science*, IX, 83–84.

——, *The Geography of Oklahoma*, 16–31.

Espenshade, *Goode's World Atlas*, 78–79.

Gould, *Geography of Oklahoma*, 5–23.

————, *Travels Through Oklahoma*, 44–64.

Harper, Horace J., "Studies on the Origin of the Sandy Land Along Cimarron River in Oklahoma," *Proceedings of the Oklahoma Academy of Science*, XIII, 24–27.

Harris, Charles W., "Salt Plains of Oklahoma," *Proceedings of the Oklahoma Academy of Science*, XXXV, 162–63.

Morris, *Oklahoma Geography,* 7–13, 21–34.

Ruth, Kent, and the Staff of the University of Oklahoma Press (eds.), *Oklahoma: A Guide to the Sooner State* (Norman, University of Oklahoma Press, 1957), 9–13.

Snider, *Geography of Oklahoma*, 24–26, 60–92.

Map 6. Rivers and Lakes of Oklahoma

Bollinger, *The Geography of Oklahoma*, 7–9.

Clinton, Fred S., "Tulsa's Water Resources—Springs and Spavinaw," *Chronicles of Oklahoma*, Vol. XXIII, No. 1 (Spring, 1945), 59–70.

Dott, Robert H., "Water Supplies for Industry in Oklahoma," *Proceedings of the Oklahoma Academy of Science*, XXIV, 73–74.

Evans, O. F., "Some Reasons for the Parallel Courses of Streams in Oklahoma," *Proceedings of the Oklahoma Academy of Science*, VII, 152–54.

Gould, Charles N., "Dams, Reservoirs and Water Supplies in Oklahoma," *Proceedings of the Oklahoma Academy of Science*, XXI, 117–18.

Johnson, *Geology and Earth Resources of Oklahoma*, 8.

Keso, Edward E., "Our Diminishing Water Supply," *Proceedings of the Oklahoma Academy of Science*, XXXIV, 226–30.

Morris, *Oklahoma Geography*, 13–19.

————, *The Southwestern United States*, 12–18.

Olson, Ralph E., "Water for Practically Everybody," *Proceedings of the Oklahoma Academy of Science*, XXXVI, 19–29.

Snider, *Geography of Oklahoma*, 26–34.

Wright, Muriel H., "Early Navigation and Commerce Along the Arkansas and Red Rivers in Oklahoma," *Chronicles of Oklahoma*, Vol. VIII, No. 1 (March, 1930), 65–80.

Maps 7 and 8. Temperature and Rainfall Maps of Oklahoma Frost Dates and Growing-Season Maps of Oklahoma

Bollinger, *The Geography of Oklahoma*, 10–11.

————, "A Preliminary Division of Oklahoma into Major and Minor Provinces on the Basis of Rainfall Adequacy," *Proceedings of the Oklahoma Academy of Sciences*, V, 119–23.

Castelli, Joseph R., "An Analysis of Oklahoma Precipitation" (Master's thesis, University of Oklahoma, 1960).

Climate and Man (Washington, U.S. Department of Agriculture, 1941), 1065–1074.

Climatic Summary of the United States, Section 42, Western Oklahoma (Washington, U.S. Department of Agriculture, Weather Bureau, 1934).

Climatic Summary of the United States, Section 43, Eastern Oklahoma (Washington, U.S. Department of Agriculture, Weather Bureau, 1934).

Gould, *Geography of Oklahoma*, 70–72.

Morris, *Oklahoma Geography*, 41–44.

————, *The Southwestern United States*, 10–12.

Ruth, *Oklahoma: A Guide to the Sooner State*, 13–15.

Smith, J. Warren, "Rainfall of the Great Plains in Relation to Cultivation," *Annals of the Association of American Geographers*, X, 69–74.

Snider, *Geography of Oklahoma*, 37–39.

Visher, Stephen S., *Climatic Atlas of the United States* (Cambridge, Harvard University Press, 1954).

Map 9. Generalized Natural–Vegetation Map of Oklahoma

Duck, L. G., and Jack B. Fletcher, *A Game Type Map of Oklahoma* (Oklahoma City, State of Oklahoma Game and Fish Department, 1943).

Espenshade, *Goode's World Atlas*, 82–83.

Gibson, Arrell M., *Oklahoma: A History of Five Centuries* (Norman, Harlow, 1965), 10–12.

Gould, *Travels Through Oklahoma*, 76–81.

Gray, Fenton, and H. M. Galloway, *Soils of Oklahoma* (Stillwater, Oklahoma State University Experiment Station, 1959), 13–15.

Morris, *Oklahoma Geography*, 81–89.

———, *The Southwestern United States*, 18–20.

Map 10. Spanish Claims in the United States

Adams, James Truslow (ed.), *Atlas of American History* (New York, Charles Scribner's Sons, 1943), 4–7.

Bolton, H. E., and T. M. Marshall, *The Colonization of North America, 1492–1783* (New York, Macmillan, 1922), 32–34, 40–46.

Gibson, *Oklahoma: A History of Five Centuries*, 25–27.

Kagan, Hilde Heun (ed.), *The American Heritage Pictorial Atlas of United States History* (New York, American Heritage, 1966), 28–35.

Lewis, Anna, "Oklahoma as a Part of the Old Spanish Dominion," *Chronicles of Oklahoma*, Vol. III, No. 1 (April, 1924), 45–58.

Perkins, Dexter, and Glyndon G. Van Deusen, *The United States of America*, 2 vols. (New York, Macmillan, 1962), I, 8–11.

Map 11. Spanish Explorers in Oklahoma

Bolton, H. E. (ed.), *Spanish Explorations in the Southwest, 1542–1706* (New York, Scribner's, 1916), 205–11, 250–66; map, 212.

Gibson, *Oklahoma: A History of Five Centuries*, 26–31.

Hammond, George P., and Agapito Rey (eds. and trans.), *Don Juan de Oñate, Colonizer of New Mexico*, 2 vols. (Albuquerque, University of New Mexico Press, 1953), I, 5–31; II, 746–60, 836–77.

McReynolds, Edwin C., *Oklahoma: A History of the Sooner State* (Norman, University of Oklahoma Press, 1954), 6–13.

Morris, *The Southwestern United States*, 21–25.

Thomas, A. B., "Spanish Exploration of Oklahoma, 1599–1792," *Chronicles of Oklahoma*, Vol. III, No. 1 (April, 1924), 45–58.

Winship, George Parker (ed.), "The Coronado Expedition, 1540–1542," Bureau of American Ethnology *Fourteenth Annual Report*, Part I (Washington, D.C., 1892–93), 341–593.

Map 12. French Claims in the United States

Davidson, Marshall B., *Life in America*, 2 vols. (Boston, Houghton Mifflin, 1954), I, 24–34.

French, Benjamin F. (ed.), *Historical Collections of Louisiana*, 5 vols. (New York, Wiley and Putnam, 1846–53), I, 25ff.

Gibson, *Oklahoma: A History of Five Centuries*, 32–33.

McReynolds, *Oklahoma: A History of the Sooner State*, 17–20.

Margry, Pierre, *Découvertes et établissements des Français dans l'ouest et dans le sud de l'Amerique Septentrionale (1614–1754)*, 6 vols. (Paris, Maison neuve et cie., 1879–88), VI, 245–306.

Morison, Samuel Eliot, *The Oxford History of the American People*, 3 vols. (New York, Oxford University Press, 1972), I, 75–78.

Map 13. French Explorers in Oklahoma

Bolton, H. E. (ed.), *Athanase de Mézières and the Louisiana-Texas Frontier, 1768–1780*, 2 vols. (Cleveland, Arthur H. Clark, 1914), Preface; I, 46–48, 52–54.

Gibson, *Oklahoma: A History of Five Centuries*, 32–39.

Harper, Elizabeth Ann, "The Taovayas Indians in Frontier Trade and Diplomacy," *Chronicles of Oklahoma*, Vol. XXXI, No. 3 (Autumn, 1953), 268–89.

McReynolds, *Oklahoma: A History of the Sooner State*, 17–20.

Wright, Muriel H., "Pioneer Historian and Archeologist of the State of Oklahoma," *Chronicles of Oklahoma*, Vol. XXIV, No. 4 (Winter, 1946–47), 396–414.

Map 14. Spanish and British Claims after 1763

Adams, *Atlas of American History*, 49.

Kagan, *The American Heritage Pictorial Atlas of United States History*, 52–53, 62.

McReynolds, *Oklahoma: A History of the Sooner State*, 21–30.

Mussey, David S., *The United States of America*, 2 vols. (Boston, Ginn, 1933–37), I, 60, 113; map, I, 114.

Map 15. Louisiana Purchase and Adams–Onís Treaty

Adams, *Atlas of American History*, 94–95.

Gibson, *Oklahoma: A History of Five Centuries*, 45–47.

Kagan, *The American Heritage Pictorial Atlas of United States History*, 128–29.

MacDonald, William (ed.), *Selected Documents Illustrative of the History of the United States, 1776–1861* (New York, Macmillan, 1901), 160–65 (No. 24).

McReynolds, *Oklahoma: A History of the Sooner State*, 36–50.

Morris, *The Southwestern United States*, 26–27.

Map 16. American Explorers, 1806–1821

Fessler, W. Julian, "Jacob Fowler's Journal (Oklahoma Section)," *Chronicles of Oklahoma*, Vol. VIII, No. 2 (June, 1930), 181–88.

Foreman, Grant, "Early Trails Through Oklahoma," *Chronicles of Oklahoma*, Vol. III, No. 2 (June, 1925), 99–119.

Gibson, *Oklahoma: A History of Five Centuries*, 63–66.

James, Edwin, *The Stephen H. Long Expedition* (vols. XIV–XVII of *Early Western Travels, 1748–1846*, ed. R. G. Thwaites, 32 vols. [Cleveland, Arthur H. Clark, 1904–1907]), XIV, map.

James, General Thomas, *Three Years Among the Indians and Mexicans*, ed. Milo M. Quaife (Chicago, R. R. Donnelley,

1953).

Thomas Nuttall's Journal of Travels into the Arkansas Territory (vol. XIII of Thwaites' *Early Western Travels*).

Map 17. American Explorers, 1832–1853

American State Papers, 38 vols. (Washington, D.C., 1832–61), *Military Affairs*, V, 373–82.

Fessler, W. Julian, "Captain Nathan Boone's Journal," *Chronicles of Oklahoma*, Vol. VII, No. 1 (March, 1929), 59–105.

Gregg, Josiah, *Diary and Letters*, ed. Maurice Garland Fulton, 2 vols. (Norman, University of Oklahoma Press, 1941, 1944), I, 9, 43ff.

Irving, Washington, *A Tour on the Prairies* (vol. XVI of Thwaites' *Early Western Travels*), 170–91.

McReynolds, *Oklahoma: A History of the Sooner State*, 72–74.

Morrison, W. B., *Military Posts and Camps in Oklahoma* (Oklahoma City, Harlow, 1936), 9, 32, 73, 78, 79, 93–99.

Thomas, Carolyn, "Nathan Boone," *Chronicles of Oklahoma*, Vol. XIX, No. 4 (December, 1941), 322–47.

Map 18. Homelands of Oklahoma Indians

Hodge, F. W. (ed.), *Handbook of American Indians North of Mexico*, Bureau of American Ethnology *Bulletin No. 30*, 2 vols. (Washington, D.C., 1907–1910).

Kagan, *The American Heritage Pictorial Atlas of United States History*, 22–27.

Underhill, Ruth, *Red Man's America* (Chicago, University of Chicago Press, 1953).

Wissler, Clark, *Indians of the United States* (Garden City, Doubleday, 1966).

Wright, Muriel H., *A Guide to the Indian Tribes of Oklahoma* (Norman, University of Oklahoma Press, 1951).

Map 19. Indian Territory, 1803–1830

A Compilation of all the Treaties Between the United States and the Indian Tribes (Washington, D.C., 1873), 575–76 (lines 25,730 to 25, 771).

Foreman, Grant, *Indians and Pioneers* (Norman, University of Oklahoma Press, 1937), 41, 131n.

Harlow, Victor E., *Oklahoma History* (Oklahoma City, Harlow, 1961), 101–104.

Mathews, John Joseph, *The Osages: Children of the Middle Waters* (Norman, University of Oklahoma Press, 1961), 409, 414ff., 466, 588.

Map 20. Removal of the Five Tribes

Debo, Angie, *The Road to Disappearance* (Norman, University of Oklahoma Press, 1941), 72–107.

———, *The Rise and Fall of the Choctaw Republic* (Norman, University of Oklahoma Press, 1934), 1–79.

Foreman, Grant, *Indian Removal* (Norman, University of Oklahoma Press, 1953).

Gibson, *Oklahoma: A History of Five Centuries*, 91–120.

———, *The Chickasaws* (Norman, University of Oklahoma Press, 1971), 163–83.

McReynolds, *Oklahoma: A History of the Sooner State*, 109–66.

———, *The Seminoles* (Norman, University of Oklahoma Press, 1957), 88–242.

Spalding, Arminta Scott, "From the Natchez Trace to Oklahoma: Development of Christian Civilization Among the

Choctaws, 1800–1860," *Chronicles of Oklahoma*, Vol. XLV, No. 1 (Spring, 1967), 2–24.

Starkey, Marion L., *The Cherokee Nation* (New York, Knopf, 1946), 1–102.

Wardell, Morris L., *A Political History of the Cherokee Nation, 1838–1907* (Norman, University of Oklahoma Press, 1938), 3–19.

Map 21. Choctaw–Arkansas Boundaries

Clark, Joseph Stanley, "The Boundaries of Oklahoma" (Master's thesis, University of Oklahoma, 1932), 25–65.

Harlow, *Oklahoma History*, 105–109.

Kappler, Charles J., *Indian Affairs: Laws and Treaties*, 2 vols. (Washington, D.C., 1902), II, 211–14.

Strickland, Rex W., "Establishment of Old Miller County, Arkansas Territory," *Chronicles of Oklahoma*, Vol. XVIII, No. 2 (June, 1940), 154–70.

Map 22. Cherokee Lands in the West

Gittinger, Roy, *The Formation of the State of Oklahoma* (Norman, University of Oklahoma Press, 1939), 98n.

Kappler, *Indian Affairs*, II, 140–44, 288–92, 439–49, 942–50.

Socolofsky, Homer E., and Huber Self, *Historical Atlas of Kansas* (Norman, University of Oklahoma Press, 1972), map 13.

Map 23. Indian Territory, 1830–1855

Dale, Edward Everett, and Morris L. Wardell, *History of Oklahoma* (New York, Prentice Hall, 1948), 136–42.

Foreman, *Indian Removal*, 29–37, 69, 104.

Kappler, *Indian Affairs*, II, 264–68, 310–19, 341–43, 388–91, 394–95, 486–88.

Map 24. Important Routes and Trails

Dott, Robert H., "Lieutenant Simpson's California Road Through Oklahoma," *Chronicles of Oklahoma*, Vol. XXXVIII, No. 2 (Summer, 1960), 154–79.

Foreman, Grant, *History of Oklahoma* (Norman, University of Oklahoma Press, 1942), 6, 9, 68, 71, 73, 129, 146, 152, 352.

Gibson, *Oklahoma: A History of Five Centuries*, 179, 180, 182, 261, 267.

Gunning, I. C., *The Butterfield Overland Mail Through Eastern Oklahoma* (Wilburton, Okla., Eastern Oklahoma Historical Society, 1971).

Hafen, LeRoy R., *The Overland Mail, 1849–69* (Cleveland, Arthur H. Clark, 1926), map, 343.

McReynolds, *Oklahoma: A History of the Sooner State*, 130–31, 178, 198, 253.

Wright, Muriel H., "The Butterfield Overland Mail One Hundred Years Ago," *Chronicles of Oklahoma*, Vol. XXXV, No. 1 (Spring, 1957), 55–71.

Map 25. Missions in Oklahoma

Campbell, O. B., *Mission to the Cherokees* (Oklahoma City, Metro Press, 1973).

Dale and Wardell, *History of Oklahoma*, 142–46.

Debo, *The Road to Disappearance*, 208, 209.

Hinds, Roland, "Early Creek Missions," *Chronicles of Oklahoma*, Vol. XVII, No. 1 (March, 1939), 48–61.

Lauderdale, Virginia E., "Tullahassee Mission," *Chronicles of Oklahoma,* Vol. XXVI, No. 3 (Autumn, 1948), 285–300.

McReynolds, *Oklahoma: A History of the Sooner State,* 74–76.

Wardell, *A Political History of the Cherokee Nation,* 120.

Map 26. Indian Territory, 1855–1866

Dale and Wardell, *History of Oklahoma,* 160–78.

Gibson, *Oklahoma, A History of Five Centuries,* 121–40.

Kappler, *Indian Affairs,* II, 706–14, 756–63.

McReynolds, *Oklahoma: A History of the Sooner State,* 208–23.

Monaghan, Jay, *Civil War on the Western Border, 1854–1865* (Boston, Little Brown and Company, 1955).

Wardell, Morris L., "A History of No Man's Land, or Old Beaver County," *Chronicles of Oklahoma,* Vol. XXXV, No. 1 (Spring, 1957), 11–33.

Map 27. Forts, Camps, and Military Roads, 1817–1876

Culberson, James, "The Fort Towson Road," *Chronicles of Oklahoma,* Vol. V, No. 4 (December, 1927), 414–21.

Foreman, *A History of Oklahoma,* 68–70, 96–99, 100–14, 157–60.

Gibson, *Oklahoma: A History of Five Centuries,* 98–100, 186–87, 250–58.

Lackey, Vinson, *The Forts of Oklahoma* (Tulsa, Tulsa Printing Company, 1963).

Lewis, Anna, "Camp Napoleon," *Chronicles of Oklahoma,* Vol. IX, No. 4 (December, 1931), 359–64.

Morrison, *Military Posts and Camps in Oklahoma.*

Van Zandt, Howard F., "The History of Camp Holmes and Choteau's Trading Post," *Chronicles of Oklahoma,* Vol. XIII, No. 3 (September, 1935), 316–37.

Map 28. Civil War Battle Sites

Connelley, William E. *Quantrill and the Border Wars* (New York, Pageant Book Company, 1956), 198.

Debo, *The Road to Disappearance,* 163.

John Ross Manuscripts, Phillips Collection, University of Oklahoma Library.

Monaghan, *Civil War on the Western Border.*

Shoemaker, Arthur, "The Battle of Chustenahlah," *Chronicles of Oklahoma,* Vol. XXXVIII, No. 2 (Summer, 1960), 180–84.

U.S. Commissioner of Indian Affairs, *Annual Report,* 1861.

U.S. War Department, *The War of the Rebellion: A Compilation of the Official Records of the Union and Confederate Armies,* four series, 128 vols. (Washington, D.C., 1880–1901), Series I, Vol. VIII, 23, 24; Vol. XIII, 325, 326, 754; Vol. XXII, Part I, 378–82, 447–62; Vol. LIII, Supplement, 1034–35.

Wardell, *A Political History of the Cherokee Nation,* 216.

Maps 29 and 30. First Battle of Cabin Creek
Battle of Honey Springs

Cubage, Annie Rosser, "Engagement at Cabin Creek, Indian Territory, July 1 and 2, 1863," *Chronicles of Oklahoma,* Vol. X, No. 1 (March, 1932), 44–51.

Fischer, LeRoy H., "Honey Springs Battlefield Park," *Chronicles of Oklahoma,* Vol. XLVII, No. 1 (Spring, 1969), 515–30.

Foreman, *A History of Oklahoma,* 121–22.

Freeman, Charles R., "The Battle of Honey Springs," *Chronicles of Oklahoma,* Vol. XIII, No. 2 (June, 1935), 154–68.

Gibson, *Oklahoma: A History of Five Centuries,* 206, 209.

McReynolds, *Oklahoma: A History of the Sooner State,* 178, 216–17, 220.

Monaghan, *Civil War on the Western Border, 1854–1865*, 279, 290, 308–10.

Map 31. Battle Sites Other Than the Civil War

Eaton, Rachel C., "The Legend of the Battle of Claremore Mound," *Chronicles of Oklahoma*, Vol. VIII, No. 4 (December, 1930), 369–77.

Gibson, *Oklahoma: A History of Five Centuries*, 96, 224.

Nye, Captain W. S., "The Battle of Wichita Village," *Chronicles of Oklahoma*, Vol. XV, No. 2 (June, 1937), 226–28.

Rister, Carl Coke, *No Man's Land* (Norman, University of Oklahoma Press, 1948), 128ff.

Map 32. Battle of the Washita

Foreman, *A History of Oklahoma*, 157–60.

Hornbeck, Lewis N., "The Battle of the Washita," *Sturms Oklahoma Magazine*, Vol. V, No. 5 (January, 1908), 30–34.

Nesbitt, Paul, "Battle of the Washita," *Chronicles of Oklahoma*, Vol. III, No. 1 (April, 1924), 3–32.

Tahan, "The Battle of the Washita," *Chronicles of Oklahoma*, Vol. VIII, No. 3 (September, 1930), 272–81.

Vestal, Stanley, *Warpath and Council Fire* (New York, Random House, 1948), 143–63.

Map 33. Indian Territory, 1866–1889

A Compilation of All the Treaties Between the United States and the Indian Tribes, 85–97, 114–22, 285–303, 810–18.

Gittinger, *The Formation of the State of Oklahoma, 1803–1906*, 88–98.

Kappler, *Indian Affairs*, II, 910–15, 918–37, 942–50.

Map 34. Tribal Locations in Oklahoma

Gibson, *Oklahoma: A History of Five Centuries*, 235–58.

Gittinger, *The Formation of the State of Oklahoma, 1803–1906*, 17, 18, 106, 107, 112.

McReynolds, *Oklahoma: A History of the Sooner State*, 235–44.

Wright, *A Guide to the Indian Tribes of Oklahoma*.

Maps 35 and 36. Cherokee Nation: Political Divisions Cherokee Nation: Important Places

Campbell, O. B., *Vinita, I. T.: The Story of a Frontier Town of the Cherokee Nation, 1871–1907* (Oklahoma City, Metro Press, 1972).

Cunningham, Hugh T., "A History of the Cherokee Indians," *Chronicles of Oklahoma*, Vol. VIII, No. 3 (September, 1930), 291–314; No. 4 (December, 1930), 407–40.

Foreman, *A History of Oklahoma*, 148, 149, 150, 151, 245, 251.

Gibson, *Oklahoma: A History of Five Centuries*, 121, 131, 145, 154, 217, 220, 226, 241, 282, 285.

Hewes, Leslie, "Cherokee Occupance in the Oklahoma Ozarks and the Prairie Plains," *Chronicles of Oklahoma*, Vol. XXII, No. 3 (Autumn, 1944), 324–37.

Litton, Gaston L., "The Principal Chiefs of the Cherokee Nation," *Chronicles of Oklahoma*, Vol. XV, No. 3 (September, 1937), 255–70.

McReynolds, *Oklahoma: A History of the Sooner State*, 58, 63, 71, 80, 161, 189, 209, 210, 216, 409.

Wardell, *A Political History of the Cherokee Nation*, 33–46, 206–207, 344n.

Map 37. Three Forks Area

Debo, *The Road to Disappearance*, 253–57.

Foreman, Grant, *Muskogee: The Biography of an Oklahoma Town* (Norman, University of Oklahoma Press, 1943), 3, 4, 6, 7, 8, 136, 154, Map 20.

Harris, Phil, *This Is Three Forks Country* (Muskogee, Hoffman Printing Company, 1965).

Ruth, *Oklahoma: A Guide to the Sooner State*, 170–71, 299, 301ff.

Maps 38 and 39. Choctaw Nation: Political Divisions
Choctaw Nation: Important Places

Debo, *The Rise and Fall of the Choctaw Republic*, 49, 59, 74–76, 81, 83, 85, 91, 104, 129, 151–59.

Foreman, *A History of Oklahoma*, 34, 35, 39, 151, 277, 278.

Gibson, *Oklahoma: A History of Five Centuries*, 24, 31, 50, 91, 98, 103, 104, 121–29, 164, 175, 232, 240, 454.

Gunning, *The Butterfield Overland Mail Through Eastern Oklahoma*.

——, I. C., *The Edwards Store or Old Red Oak* (Wilburton, Eastern Oklahoma Historical Society, 1972).

Wright, *A Guide to the Indian Tribes of Oklahoma*, 14, 105–18.

Wright, Muriel H., "Additional Notes on Perryville, Choctaw Nation," *Chronicles of Oklahoma*, Vol. VIII, No. 2 (June, 1930), 146–48.

——, "Brief Outline of the Choctaw and Chickasaw Nations in the Indian Territory, 1820 to 1860," *Chronicles of Oklahoma*, Vol. VII, No. 4 (December, 1929), 388–418.

——, "Organization of Counties in the Choctaw and Chicka-

saw Nations," *Chronicles of Oklahoma*, Vol. VIII, No. 3 (September, 1930), 315–34.

Maps 40 and 41. Creek Nation: Political Divisions
Creek Nation: Important Places

Debo, *The Road to Disappearance*, 113, 120, 122, 124ff., 138, 174, 180–82, 310, 332, 352.

Gibson, *Oklahoma: A History of Five Centuries*, 24, 50, 74, 85, 87, 90–92, 105–107, 121–22, 133–35, 155–58, 217, 220, 292, 327.

Grayson, G. W., "Okmulgee Constitution," *Chronicles of Oklahoma*, Vol. III, No. 3 (September, 1925), 216–28.

Morton, Ohland, "Early History of the Creek Indians," *Chronicles of Oklahoma*, Vol. IX, No. 1 (March, 1931), 17–26.

——, "The Government of the Creek Indians," *Chronicles of Oklahoma*, Vol. VIII, No. 1 (March, 1930), 42–64; No. 2 (June, 1930), 189–225.

Wright, *A Guide to the Indian Tribes of Oklahoma*, 138, 139.

Maps 42 and 43. Chickasaw Nation: Political Divisions
Chickasaw Nation: Important Places

Cassal, Reverend Hillary, "Missionary Tour in the Chickasaw Nation," *Chronicles of Oklahoma*, Vol. XXXIV, No. 4 (Winter, 1956–57), 397–416.

Foreman, *A History of Oklahoma*, 37, 74.

Gibson, *The Chickasaws*.

Johnson, Neil R., *The Chickasaw Rancher* (Stillwater, Redlands Press, 1961).

McReynolds, *Oklahoma: A History of the Sooner State*, 74, 75, 76, 181, 182, 270–73.

Morrison, W. B., "Colbert Ferry on Red River, Chickasaw Nation, I.T.," *Chronicles of Oklahoma*, Vol. XVI, No. 3 (September, 1938), 302–14.

Oklahoma Red Book, 2 vols. (Oklahoma City, Chamber of Commerce of the State of Oklahoma, 1912), I, 228.

Wright, *A Guide to the Indian Tribes of Oklahoma*, 84–97, 167, 259.

Wright, Muriel H., "Brief Outline of the Choctaw and Chickasaw Nations in the Indian Territory, 1820 to 1860," *Chronicles of Oklahoma*, Vol. VII, No. 4 (December, 1929), 388–418.

———, "Organization of Counties in the Choctaw and Chickasaw Nations," *Chronicles of Oklahoma*, Vol. VIII, No. 3 (September, 1930), 315–34.

Map 44. Seminole Nation, 1889

Gibson, *Oklahoma: A History of Five Centuries*, 24, 86, 90, 107, 118–21, 135, 159, 171, 184, 197, 217, 229, 243, 282, 292.

McReynolds, *The Seminoles*.

Spoehr, Alexander, "Oklahoma Seminole Towns," *Chronicles of Oklahoma*, Vol. XIX, No. 4 (December, 1941), 377–80.

Wright, *A Guide to the Indian Tribes of Oklahoma*, 228–37.

Wright, Muriel H., "Seal of the Seminole Nation," *Chronicles of Oklahoma*, Vol. XXXIV, No. 3 (Autumn, 1956), 262–71.

Map 45. Small Indian Groups in Northeast Oklahoma

Gibson, *Oklahoma: A History of Five Centuries*, 24, 51, 73, 74, 81, 94, 95, 96, 121, 140, 215, 241, 248, 250.

Gittinger, *The Formation of the State of Oklahoma*, 7, 17, 18, 106–12, 263–67.

Martin, Lucille J., "A History of the Modoc Indians," *Chronicles of Oklahoma*, Vol. XLVII, No. 4 (Winter, 1969–70), 398–446.

Wright, *A Guide to the Indian Tribes of Oklahoma*, 182, 184, 185, 238–40, 263–64.

Map 46. Cattle Trails

Chrisman, Harry E., *Lost Trails of the Cimarron* (Denver, Sage Books, 1961), 34–61.

Foreman, *A History of Oklahoma*, 223–25, map 226.

Gard, Wayne, *The Chisholm Trail* (Norman, University of Oklahoma Press, 1954).

Gibson, *Oklahoma: A History of Five Centuries*, 179, 261, 267.

McReynolds, *Oklahoma: A History of the Sooner State*, 250–66.

Tennant, H. S., "The History of the Chisholm Trail," *Chronicles of Oklahoma*, Vol. XIV, No. 1 (March, 1936), 108–22.

Map 47. Leases of the Cherokee Outlet

Chapman, Berlin B., "How the Cherokees Acquired and Disposed of the Outlet," *Chronicles of Oklahoma*, Vol. XV, No. 2 (June, 1937), 205–25.

Dale, Edward Everett, "The Cherokee Strip Livestock Association," *Chronicles of Oklahoma*, Vol. V, No. 1 (March, 1927), 58–78.

Foreman, *A History of Oklahoma*, 226, 237.

Gittinger, *The Formation of the State of Oklahoma*, 144–46, 198–200.

McReynolds, *Oklahoma: A History of the Sooner State*, 262–66.

Milam, Joe B., "The Opening of the Cherokee Outlet," *Chronicles of Oklahoma*, Vol. IX, No. 3 (September, 1931), 268–86; Vol. X, No. 1 (March, 1932), 115–37.

Map 48. Land Openings

Cooper, Charles M., "The Big Pasture," *Chronicles of Oklahoma*, Vol. XXXV, No. 2 (Summer, 1957), 138–46.

Foreman, *A History of Oklahoma*, 238–60.

Gibson, *Oklahoma: A History of Five Centuries*, 294–302.

Gittinger, *The Formation of the State of Oklahoma*, 184–210.

Hastings, James K., "The Opening of Oklahoma," *Chronicles of Oklahoma*, Vol. XXVII, No. 1 (Spring, 1949), 70–75.

Kennan, Clara B., "Neighbors in the Cherokee Strip," *Chronicles of Oklahoma*, Vol. XXVII, No. 1 (Spring, 1949), 76–88.

McReynolds, *Oklahoma: A History of the Sooner State*, 278–307.

White, Carl Robe, "Experiences at the Opening of Oklahoma," *Chronicles of Oklahoma*, Vol. XXVII, No. 1 (Spring, 1949), 56–69.

Map 49. Unassigned Lands, 1889

Asplin, Ray, "A History of Council Grove in Oklahoma," *Chronicles of Oklahoma*, Vol. XLV, No. 4 (Winter, 1967–68), 433–50.

Foreman, *A History of Oklahoma*, 204, 214, 221.

Gibson, *Oklahoma: A History of Five Centuries*, 289, 292, 293, 295.

Gittinger, *The Formation of the State of Oklahoma*, 98, 179–82.

Guthrey, E. Bee, "Early Days in Payne County," *Chronicles of Oklahoma*, Vol. III, No. 1 (April, 1925), 74–80.

McReynolds, *Oklahoma: A History of the Sooner State*, 260, 275, 286, 288.

Map 50. Iowa, Sac and Fox, Kickapoo, Pottawatomie Lands

Chapman, Berlin B., "Establishment of the Iowa Reservation," *Chronicles of Oklahoma*, Vol. XXI, No. 4 (December, 1943), 366–77.

Gibson, *Oklahoma: A History of Five Centuries*, 24, 51, 74, 127, 215, 242, 243.

Gittinger, *The Formation of the State of Oklahoma*, 205, 207 n.61.

McReynolds, *Oklahoma: A History of the Sooner State*, 298 n.40, 300, 301.

————, *The Seminoles*, 336–42.

Ragland, Hobert D., "Some Firsts in Lincoln County," *Chronicles of Oklahoma*, Vol. XXIX, No. 4 (Winter, 1951–52), 419–28.

Map 51. Leases and Allotments:
Cheyenne and Arapaho Reservation

Dale, Edward Everett, "Ranching on the Cheyenne-Arapaho Reservation," *Chronicles of Oklahoma*, Vol. VI, No. 1 (March, 1928), 35–59.

Foreman, *A History of Oklahoma*, 223–28.

Gibson, *Oklahoma: A History of Five Centuries*, 282–83.

McReynolds, *Oklahoma: A History of the Sooner State*, 259–61.

Records, Ralph H., "Recollections of April 19, 1892," *Chronicles of Oklahoma*, Vol. XXI, No. 1 (March, 1943), 16–27.

Map 52. Indian Territory, 1889

Debo, *The Rise and Fall of the Choctaw Republic*, 58–79.

————, *The Road to Disappearance*, 124, 188ff.

Gibson, *The Chickasaws*, 247–67.

"Laws of the Seminole Nation," Indian Archives (Oklahoma Historical Society), chapters L, LII, and LVII.

McReynolds, *The Seminoles*, 358–60.

Wardell, *A Political History of the Cherokee Nation*, 33, 43, 206, 207.

Map 53. Osage Nation, 1900–1906

Burwell, Kate Pearson, "The Richest People in the World." *Sturm's Statehood Magazine*, Vol. II, No. 4 (June, 1905), 88–96.

Forbes, Gerald, "History of the Osage Blanket Lease," *Chronicles of Oklahoma*, Vol. XIX, No. 1 (March, 1941), 70–81.

McGuire, Paul, *Osage County* (Pawhuska, Okla., Adrin, 1969).

Mathews, John Joseph, *The Osages* (Norman, University of Oklahoma Press, 1961).

———, *Wah'kon-tah* (Norman, University of Oklahoma Press, 1932).

Wright, *A Guide to the Indian Tribes of Oklahoma*, 160–64, 189–98.

Map 54. Oklahoma Territory, 1890–1899

Gibson, *Oklahoma: A History of Five Centuries*, 287–98.

Gittinger, *The Formation of the State of Oklahoma*, 110, 210, 255, 263.

Harlow, *Oklahoma History*, 328–32.

McReynolds, *Oklahoma: A History of the Sooner State*, 240–300.

Map 55. Oklahoma Territory–Indian Territory, 1900

Cunningham, Robert E. (ed.), *Indian Territory: A Frontier Photographic Record by W. S. Prettyman* (Norman, University of Oklahoma Press, 1957).

Gibson, *Oklahoma: A History of Five Centuries*, 298–316.

Harlow, *Oklahoma History*, 333–41.

Richards, O. H., "Early Days in Day County," *Chronicles of Oklahoma*, Vol. XXVI, No. 3 (Autumn, 1948), 313–24.

Map 56. Proposed State of Sequoyah

Debo, Angie, *And Still the Waters Run* (Princeton, Princeton University Press, 1940).

Foreman, *A History of Oklahoma*, 311–13.

Gibson, *Oklahoma: A History of Five Centuries*, 328.

McReynolds, *Oklahoma: A History of the Sooner State*, 313–14.

Maxwell, Amos, *The Sequoyah Constitutional Convention* (Boston, Meador Press, 1953).

———, "The Sequoyah Convention," *Chronicles of Oklahoma*, Vol. XXVIII, No. 2 (Summer, 1950), 161–92; No. 3 (Autumn, 1950), 299–340.

Map 57. Counties of Oklahoma Territory and Registration Districts of Indian Territory, 1906

Dale and Wardell, *History of Oklahoma*, 301–303, 315–18.

Doyle, Thomas H., "Single Versus Double Statehood," *Chronicles of Oklahoma*, Vol. V, No. 2 (June, 1927), 117–48; No. 3 (September, 1927), 266–86.

Gibson, *Oklahoma: A History of Five Centuries*, 338.

Gittinger, *The Formation of the State of Oklahoma*, 305–13.
Harlow, *Oklahoma History*, 382–89, 401, 403.

Map 58. Convention Delegate Districts

Clark, Blue, "Delegates to the Constitutional Convention," *Chronicles of Oklahoma*, Vol. XLVIII, No. 4 (Winter, 1970–1971), 400–15.
Ellis, A. H., *History of the Oklahoma Constitutional Convention* (Muskogee, Okla., Economy Printing Company, 1923), 14–37, 49–52, 115–19.
Gibson, *Oklahoma: A History of Five Centuries*, 329.
Gittinger, *The Formation of the State of Oklahoma*, 257 n.45.

Map 59. Oklahoma Counties, 1907

Constitution of the State of Oklahoma, Article XVII—Counties; paragraph 8—Counties and County Seats.
Fitzpatrick, H. L. (ed.), *The Oklahoma Almanac* (Norman, Oklahoma Almanac, 1960), 133–44.

Map 60. Oklahoma Counties, 1970

Fitzpatrick. *The Oklahoma Almanac*, 196–250.
Foreman, *A History of Oklahoma*, 259.
Gibson, *Oklahoma: A History of Five Centuries*, 349.

Map 61. Fort Smith Boundary

Clark, "Boundaries of Oklahoma," 25–65.
Kappler, *Indian Affairs*, II, 211–14.

Map 62. Areas Involved in Question of Title

Foreman, *A History of Oklahoma*, 259–60.
McReynolds, *Oklahoma: A History of the Sooner State*, 257, 301–302.
Moore, Webb Leonidus, *The Greer County Question* (San Marcos, Texas, The Press of San Marcos, 1939).
Rister, *No Man's Land*.
Strickland, "Establishment of Old Miller County, Arkansas Territory," 154–70.

Map 63. Townships and Ranges

Gibson, *Oklahoma: A History of Five Centuries*, 5.
Parker, Mary Ann, "The Eluvice Meridian," *Chronicles of Oklahoma*, Vol. LI, No. 2 (Summer, 1973), 150–58.
Rucker, Alvin, "Initial Point in Oklahoma," *Chronicles of Oklahoma*, Vol. V, No. 3 (September, 1927), 328–32.

Map 64. Railroads in Oklahoma, 1870–1975

Gardner, Charles, "Railroad Abandonment in Oklahoma," (Master's thesis, University of Oklahoma, 1958).
George, Preston, and Sylvan R. Wood, "The Railroads of Oklahoma," Railway and Locomotive Society, *Bulletin No. 60* (January, 1943).
Gibson, *Oklahoma: A History of Five Centuries*, 261–66.
Hofsommer, Donovan L., "Kaw and the Railroad," *Chronicles of Oklahoma*, Vol. L, No. 3 (Autumn, 1973), 297–306.
Johnson, Walter A., "Brief History of the Missouri-Kansas-

Texas Railroad Lines," *Chronicles of Oklahoma*, Vol. XIV, No. 3 (Autumn, 1946), 340–58.

McReynolds, *Oklahoma: A History of the Sooner State*, 270–77.

Self, Nancy Hope, "The Building of the Railroads in the Cherokee Nation," *Chronicles of Oklahoma*, Vol. XLIV, No. 2 (Summer, 1971), 180–205.

Map 65. Oklahoma Academies

Baird, W. David, "Spencer Academy, Choctaw Nation, 1842–1900," *Chronicles of Oklahoma*, Vol. XLV, No. 1 (Spring, 1967), 25–43.

Carr, Susan, "Bloomfield Academy and Its Founder," *Chronicles of Oklahoma*, Vol. II, No. 4 (December, 1924), 366–79.

Coppock, Mary Blue, "Stella Friends Academy," *Chronicles of Oklahoma*, Vol. XXXVII, No. 2 (Summer, 1959), 175–81.

Foreman, Carolyn Thomas, "Chickasaw Manual Labor Academy," *Chronicles of Oklahoma*, Vol. XXIII, No. 4 (Winter, 1945–46), 338–57.

———, "St. Agnes Academy for the Choctaws," *Chronicles of Oklahoma*, Vol. XLVIII, No. 3 (Autumn, 1970), 323–30.

Laracy, John, O. S. B., "Sacred Heart Mission and Academy," *Chronicles of Oklahoma*, Vol. V, No. 2 (June, 1927), 234–50.

Miller, Lorna Eaton, "Wheelock Mission," *Chronicles of Oklahoma*, Vol. XXIX, No. 3 (Autumn, 1951), 314–23.

Mitchell, Irene B., "Bloomfield Academy," *Chronicles of Oklahoma*, Vol. XLIV, No. 4 (Winter, 1971–1972), 412–26.

Moffitt, James A., "Early History of Armstrong Academy," *Chronicles of Oklahoma*, Vol. XXI, No. 1 (March, 1943), 88–91.

Perry, Dan W., "The Indians' Friend, John H. Seger," *Chronicles of Oklahoma*, Vol. X, No. 3 (September, 1932), 348–68.

Trevathan, Robert E., "School Days at Emahaka Academy," *Chronicles of Oklahoma*, Vol. XXXVIII, No. 3 (Autumn, 1960), 265–73.

Wardell, Morris L., "Protestant Missions Among the Osages," *Chronicles of Oklahoma*, Vol. II, No. 3 (September, 1924), 285–97.

Map 66. Oklahoma Colleges and Universities: Inactive

Balyeat, Frank A., "Oklahoma University at Guthrie," *Chronicles of Oklahoma*, Vol. XXXVII, No. 3 (Autumn, 1959), 288–93.

Dale and Wardell, *History of Oklahoma*, 478–91.

Kinchen, Oscar A., "Oklahoma's First College, Old High Gate at Norman," *Chronicles of Oklahoma*, Vol. XIV, No. 3 (Autumn, 1946), 312–23.

McReynolds, *Oklahoma: A History of the Sooner State,* 320.

A System of Higher Education for Oklahoma (Oklahoma City, Oklahoma State Regents for Higher Education, 1942), 57, 62–64, 68, 72.

Maps 67 and 68. Oklahoma Junior Colleges: Active Oklahoma Senior Colleges and Universities: Active

Dale and Wardell, *History of Oklahoma*, 478–91.

Gibson, *Oklahoma: A History of Five Centuries,* 436–38.

Hastings, James K., "Oklahoma Agricultural and Mechanical College and Old Central," *Chronicles of Oklahoma*, Vol. XI, No. 4 (December, 1933), 1084–1110.

Hume, Carleton Ross, "Some Early History of Oklahoma University," *Chronicles of Oklahoma*, Vol. XX, No. 4 (December, 1942), 397–98.

McReynolds, *Oklahoma: A History of the Sooner State*, 296, 320, 324, 337, 417–19.

Oklahoma Educational Directory, Bulletin No. 119-W (Oklahoma City, State Department of Education, 1973), 19–23.

A System of Higher Education for Oklahoma, 53–131.

Map 69. Agricultural Regions of Oklahoma

Dale and Wardell, *History of Oklahoma*, 375–401.

Fite, Robert C., "Climatic Factor in Wheat Farming on the Southern Great Plains," *Proceedings of the Oklahoma Academy of Science*, Vol. XXIX, 97–98.

Gibson, *Oklahoma: A History of Five Centuries*, 444–48.

McReynolds, *Oklahoma: A History of the Sooner State*, 397–402.

Meredith, N. L., "The Middle Way: The Farmers' Alliance in Indian Territory, 1889–1896," *Chronicles of Oklahoma*, Vol. XLVII, No. 4 (Winter, 1969–70), 377–87.

Morris, *Oklahoma Geography*, 57–80.

Ruth, *Oklahoma: A Guide to the Sooner State*, 67–71.

Steward, Roy P., "Henry C. Hitch and His Times," *Chronicles of Oklahoma*, Vol. L, No. 1 (Spring, 1972), 41–64.

1969 Census of Agriculture, Vol. I, Part 36, Section 2, County Data, Oklahoma (Washington, D.C., U.S. Department of Commerce, Bureau of the Census, 1972).

Map 70. Petroleum and Natural Gas

Crumley, Russell W., *Roughneck: The Way of Life in the Oil Fields* (Evanston, Ill., Row Peterson, 1941).

Dale and Wardell, *History of Oklahoma*, 421–26.

Foreman, *A History of Oklahoma*, 327–34.

Gibson, *Oklahoma: A History of Five Centuries*, 449–53.

Johnson, *Geology and Earth Resources of Oklahoma*, map 7.

Keeler, W. W., "Indians and the Petroleum Industry—Oklahoma Friends," *Cimarron Valley Historical Society, 1973 Journal*, 183–91.

McReynolds, *Oklahoma: A History of the Sooner State*, 402–405.

Morris, *Oklahoma Geography*, 90–94.

Ruth, *Oklahoma: A Guide to the Sooner State*, 46–47.

Map 71. Mineral Resources Other Than Petroleum and Natural Gas

Dale and Wardell, *History of Oklahoma*, 406–21.

Gibson, A. M., "Early Mining Camps in Northeastern Oklahoma," *Chronicles of Oklahoma*, Vol. XXXIV, No. 2 (Summer, 1956), 193–202.

———, *Oklahoma: A History of Five Centuries*, 454–55.

Johnson, *Geology and Earth Resources of Oklahoma*, map 6.

Kalisch, Philip A., "Ordeal of the Oklahoma Coal Miners," *Chronicles of Oklahoma*, Vol. XLVIII, No. 3 (Autumn, 1970), 331–40.

McReynolds, *Oklahoma: A History of the Sooner State*, 266–70, 405–407.

Morris, *Oklahoma Geography*, 94–102.
Nieberding, Velma, "Old Peoria: A Mother of Mining Camps," *Chronicles of Oklahoma*, Vol. L, No. 2 (Summer, 1972), 142–55.
Ruth, *Oklahoma: A Guide to the Sooner State*, 47–50.

Map 72. Sub-State Planning Districts

Senate Bill No. 290, An Act Relating to State Officers and Employees and to the Oklahoma Resources Development Act of 1965; Providing for Duties of Oklahoma Industrial Development and Park Commission in Establishing Boundaries for Planning Regions; . . . . . .
Sub-State Planning Districts in Oklahoma (Oklahoma City, State Planning Coordination Office, 1972).

Map 73. Congressional Districts, 1970

Directory and Manual, State of Oklahoma (1957 [map p. 125], 1961, 1963, 1971).
Gibson, *Oklahoma: A History of Five Centuries*, 438.

Map 74. Supreme Court Judicial Districts

Directory and Manual, State of Oklahoma (1957, 1961, 1963).

Map 75. Population: Gain/Loss, 1940–1970

Doerr, Arthur H., "Relationship Between Mineral Production and Population in the Oklahoma Portion of the Tri-State Lead and Zinc District," *Proceedings of the Oklahoma Academy of Science*, Vol. XXXV, 161–62.
Morris, *Oklahoma Geography*, 167–68.
———, *The Southwestern United States*, 35–57, 107–10.

1970 Census of Population (Washington, D.C., U.S. Department of Commerce, Bureau of the Census, 1972), Vol. I, Part A, Section 2, 38–10, 38–13, 38–16, 38–17.

Map 76. Population: Distribution of Indians, 1970

American Indians (Washington, D.C., U.S. Department of Commerce, Bureau of the Census, 1972), Part 36, Section 2, Oklahoma.
Morris, John W., "Distribution of Indians in Oklahoma," *Proceedings of the Oklahoma Academy of Science*, Vol. XLI, 193–95.
———, *The Southwestern United States*, 35–46.

Map 77. Northwestern Oklahoma, 1970

Alley, John, *City Beginnings in Oklahoma Territory* (Norman, University of Oklahoma Press, 1939), 13–27, 46–72.
Chapman, Berlin B., "The Founding of El Reno," *Chronicles of Oklahoma*, Vol. XXXIV, No. 1 (Spring, 1956), 79–108.
Clark, Blue, "Buffalo, A County Seat," *Chronicles of Oklahoma*, Vol. LI, No. 1 (Spring, 1973), 2–20.
Morris, *Oklahoma Geography*, 142.
Ruth, *Oklahoma: A Guide to the Sooner State*, 147–53.

Map 78. Northeastern Oklahoma, 1970

Alley, *City Beginnings in Oklahoma Territory*, 88–95.
Barnes, Seymour, "The Founding of Ponca City," *Chronicles of Oklahoma*, Vol. XXXV, No. 2 (Summer, 1957), 154–62.
Bennett, Joanne Rainey, *A Pictorial History of Bartlesville* (Bartlesville, Okla., Washington County Historical Society, 1972).

Cunningham, Robert E., *Perry: Pride of the Prairie* (Stillwater, Okla., Frontier Printers, 1973).
———, *Stillwater: Where Oklahoma Began* (Stillwater, Okla., Arts and Humanities Council, 1969).
Foreman, Carolyn Thomas, "Early History of Webbers Falls," *Chronicles of Oklahoma*, Vol. XXIX, No. 4 (Winter, 1951–52), 444–83.
Foreman, *Muskogee: The Biography of an Oklahoma Town.*
Morris, *Oklahoma Geography*, 137–38, 139–40.
Ruth, *Oklahoma: A Guide to the Sooner State*, 142–47, 163–71, 193–204, 209–14.
Vinson, Lackey, *The Choteaus and the Founding of Salina: Oklahoma's First White Settlement* (Tulsa, Claude F. Neerman, n.d.).
Wilson, L. W., "A History of Wagoner," *Chronicles of Oklahoma*, Vol. L, No. 4 (Winter, 1972–73), 486–96.

Map 79. Southwestern Oklahoma, 1970
Conover, G. W., *Sixty Years in Southwest Oklahoma* (Anadarko, Okla., N. T. Plummer, 1927).
Morris, *Oklahoma Geography*, 138–39.
Sager, Meta C., "Early Grady County History," *Chronicles of Oklahoma*, Vol. XVII, No. 2 (June, 1939), 184–88.
Ruth, *Oklahoma: A Guide to the Sooner State*, 153–62.

Map 80. Southeastern Oklahoma, 1970
Alley, *City Beginnings in Oklahoma Territory*, 73–87.
Biles, J. Hugh, *The Early History of Ada* (Ada, Okla., Oklahoma State Bank of Ada, 1954).

MacCreary, Henry, *Queen of Three Valleys: A Story of Durant* (Durant, Okla., The Democrat Printing Company, 1946).
Medlock, Julius Lester, *When Swallows Fly Home: Tales of Old Center* (Oklahoma City, Northwest Publishing Company, 1962).
Morris, *Oklahoma Geography*, 140.
Ruth, *Oklahoma: A Guide to the Sooner State*, 137–42, 171–78, 204–208.

Map 81. Oklahoma Panhandle, 1970
Estep, Raymond, "The First Panhandle Land Grant," *Chronicles of Oklahoma*, Vol. XXXVI, No. 4 (Winter, 1958–59), 358–70.
Kinchen, Oscar A., "The Squatters in No Man's Land," *Chronicles of Oklahoma*, Vol. XXVI, No. 4 (Winter, 1948–49), 385–98.
Morris, *Oklahoma Geography*, 141–42.
Rister, *No Man's Land.*
Wardell, Morris L., "History of No Man's Land," *Chronicles of Oklahoma*, Vol. XXXV, No. 1 (Spring, 1957), 11–33.

Map 82. Oklahoma City Metropolitan Area, 1974
Alley, *City Beginnings in Oklahoma Territory*, 28–45.
Eastman, James N., "Founding of Tinker Air Force Base," *Chronicles of Oklahoma*, Vol. L, No. 3 (Autumn, 1973), 326–46.
Morris, *Oklahoma Geography*, 129–34.
———, *The Southwestern United States*, 86, 92, 112, 115, 120.
Ruth, *Oklahoma: A Guide to the Sooner State*, 179–92.

Scott, Angelo C., *The Story of Oklahoma City* (Oklahoma City, Times-Journal Publishing Company, 1939).

Map 83. Tulsa Metropolitan Area, 1974

Debo, Angie, *Tulsa: From Creek Town to Oil Capital* (Norman, University of Oklahoma Press, 1943).

Morris, *Oklahoma Geography*, 134–37.

———, *The Southwestern United States*, 17, 67, 92, 120.

Ruth, *Oklahoma: A Guide to the Sooner State*, 214–29.

INDEX